Survivors of Steel City

Chatto & Windus LONDON

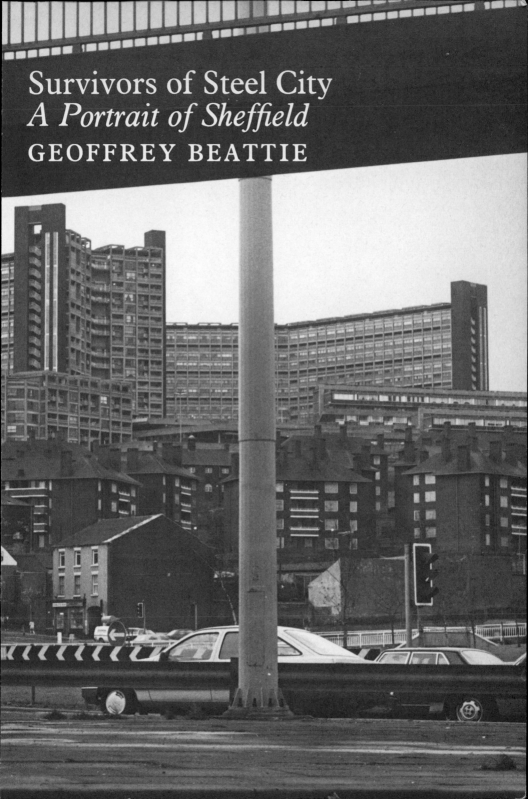

Survivors of Steel City
A Portrait of Sheffield
GEOFFREY BEATTIE

Title page illustration: Hyde Park Flats: civic pride – right in the centre of Sheffield

Published in 1986 by
Chatto & Windus Ltd
40 William IV Street
London WC2N 4DF

British Library Cataloguing in Publication Data
Beattie, Geoffrey
    Survivors of steel city
    1. Sheffield (South Yorkshire) – Social
    conditions
    I. Title
    942.8′210858   HN398.S5

    ISBN 0-7011-3031-8

Photoset by Rowland Phototypesetting Ltd
Bury St Edmunds, Suffolk
Printed in Great Britain by
Redwood Burn Ltd
Trowbridge, Wiltshire

Contents

Acknowledgements

This book started life as a single article for the *Guardian*. The article was conceived out of curiosity. There I was in a nightclub in Sheffield on a Monday night – or rather a Tuesday morning – at 2 am. There was snow on the ground outside and fog everywhere else. Driving conditions were treacherous, and the taxi drivers had given up and gone home. But the club wasn't just ticking over, it was positively buzzing. What was going on? Who were these people? What did they do for a living? (And how were they going to get up for work in the morning?) Where did their money come from? I spent four years trying to answer just some of these questions. In the process I learned a bit about life in the steel mills and the mines and a lot about life on the dole. I also came to realise that some of the people from the nightclub didn't have to get up in the morning anyway – even to sign on. This was one of my more interesting discoveries.

I wrote many of the observations reported in this book for the *Guardian* and I owe an immense debt of gratitude to John Course, the Northern Features Editor of that paper, for his constant encouragement. A couple of articles were also written for *New Society* and I would like to extend my thanks to Paul Barker, the editor of *New Society*. At the beginning of my research there were many enquiries whether I was writing articles for the *Worksop Guardian*. By the end, the *Guardian* and *New Society* were required reading in certain sections of Sheffield society. Indeed, I suspect that some of the best-read bouncers in the country are to be found in Sheffield. I am extremely grateful to all of my informants for their invaluable assistance and seemingly unlimited patience. But some I bothered again and again, and a special thank you must go to Dave Allen, Rod Johnson, Dave Growns and Patrick Maloney, who put up with me to the end (or at least this temporary staging post).

The Summing Up by W. Somerset Maugham quoted by kind permission of the Executors of the Estate of W. Somerset Maugham (and William Heinemann Ltd). Extract from 'Bring On The Night' reproduced by kind permission of Virgin Music (Publishers) Ltd.

Illustrations

All photographs are by the author.

The grey streets of Sheffield

1 · Introduction

> **We poison our lives with fear of burglary and shipwreck and ask anyone, the house is never burgled and the ship never goes down.**
> Jean Anouilh, *The Rehearsal*, 1950

Prospects

Working Men!

To you I dedicate a work, in which I have tried to lay before my . . . countrymen a faithful picture of your condition, of your sufferings and struggles, of your hopes and prospects. I have lived long enough amidst you to know something about your circumstances; I have studied the various official and non-official documents as far as I was able to get hold of them. I have not been satisfied with this, I wanted more than a mere *abstract* knowledge of my subject, I wanted to see you in your own homes, to observe you in your condition and grievances, to witness your struggle against the social and political power of your oppressors. I have done so: I forsook the company and the dinner-parties, the port-wine and champagne of the middle classes, and devoted my leisure hours almost exclusively to the intercourse with plain Working Men; I am both glad and proud of having done so.

So began Friedrich Engels' preface to the original German edition of *The Condition of the Working Class in England* in 1845. Life has changed a bit since Engels spent his months in Manchester in the 1840s; what exactly would a sketch of life in England look like now? The Poor Law has gone, the workhouses have gone, and cholera has disappeared, to be replaced by Social Security, streets rife with unemployment, and heart disease. That much is obvious, but what about the sufferings and struggles, the hopes and prospects of the working people? In this book I will try to shed some light on these and other matters.

I, too, was not content with an abstract knowledge of the subject. I wanted to see ordinary people in their homes, and not just in their homes but in their offices and factories and in their pubs, nightclubs and casinos. Life indeed has changed. I may have forsaken the company and the dinner parties of the middle classes but it certainly wasn't necessary to forsake the champagne. Dom Pérignon, Lanson, even old Asti Spumante oiled the wheels of some of the new industrial workers on their nights off. The old 'shampoo', as many a wide boy liked to call it, cleansed the soul for another day of grind in post-industrial Britain.

As a social psychologist, I have tried to draw sketches that are based around people. I have attempted to describe parts of some individuals' lives and to consider how they themselves view their social world. It took psychologists a long time to realise that they are not alone in trying to understand behaviour – most people get an apprenticeship of three score years and ten in this field. When you talk to individuals about how they spend their days you don't just get abstract physical descriptions, but descriptions intermingled with interpretation, explanation and, at times, justification. I have tried to give some hint of how people interpret and explain their own lives to others, and to themselves.

All our yesterdays

Engels wrote his classic description of the condition of the working class in England at the time of the Industrial Revolution. Life in England was revolutionised by the invention of the steam engine and of machines for spinning and weaving cotton, in the second half of the eighteenth century. Engels based his account of the condition of the workers on a comparatively short (21-month) visit to Manchester, beginning in November 1842. By then the Industrial Revolution had resculptured the face of England. The condition of the workers was grim. Here are some descriptions of the working-class districts of Manchester:

One particular cellar which lay below the level of the river was continually flooded with water which gushed in through a hole, which had been stuffed full of clay. The handloom weaver who lived there had to clean out his cellar every day and empty the water out into the street. (Engels, 1845; 1958 edition, p. 73.)

or

. . . in Parliament Street there was only one privy for three hundred and eighty people and in Parliament Passage there was only one privy for thirty houses packed with human beings. (Loc. cit., p. 74.)

Conditions were no better outside the great industrial towns:

In the Alston Moor lead-mining district one comes across the same sort of lodging-houses . . . Mitchell states that he was in one of these bedrooms which was 18 feet long by 15 feet wide. The room accommodated 56 persons (42 men and 14 boys) in 14 beds. These were arranged in bunks as on board a ship, so that half the occupants of the room slept above the other half. There was no ventilation to get rid of the foul air . . . What must this room have been like on a hot summer's night if it was filled to capacity, with 56 sleeping lodgers? And this is the abode of 'free-born Britons', not between decks on an American slaver. (Loc. cit., p. 277.)

Today houses may be damp, they may be short of amenities, they may even be crowded, but never like this.

The state of the workers' houses was one yardstick Engels used to measure their general standard of living, but he considered others as well. Here is Engels' description of the state (and style) of dress of English workers in the 1840s:

The vast majority of the workers are clad in rags. The material from which the workers' clothes are made is by no means ideal for its purpose. Linen and wool have practically disappeared from the wardrobes of both men and women, and have been replaced by cotton . . . All workers in England wear hats and they are of the most varied shapes – round, cone-shaped, cylindrical, broad-brimmed, narrow-brimmed, or without a brim. Only the younger men in the factory towns wear caps. Anyone who does not possess a hat makes himself a low, four-cornered cap out of paper . . . Their heavy cotton clothes, though thicker, stiffer and heavier than woollen cloth, do not keep out the cold and wet to anything like the same extent as woollens. (Loc. cit., pp. 78–79.)

Engels also describes how he saw workers, particularly women and children, going about barefoot (a growing habit among the English which he attributes to the influence of the Irish immigrants). Workers are no longer clad in rags and they no longer go about barefoot. Fashions have indeed changed – hats for men have gone out, Korean trainers have come in. Cotton remains just as popular.

Factory work in the Industrial Revolution was harsh. Workers had to keep pace with the new machines for long hours in terrible conditions – in 'low crowded, dusty, or damp rooms; impure air, heated atmospheres, constant perspiration' (Barry, 1840, p. 72). Nine-year-olds worked a six-and-a-half-hour day, thirteen-year-olds a twelve-hour day. The new machines were not diurnal and night work was introduced with some not entirely foreseeable consequences.

One factory owner stated that during the two years when his establishment was on night work the number of illegitimate children born was doubled. The morale of the factory became so deplorably low that night work had to be discontinued. (Loc. cit., p. 170.)

Engels was adamant – 'No worse fate can befall a man than to have to work every day from morning to night against his will at a job that he abhors.' (Loc. cit., p. 133.) Industrial work was seen by Engels as the greatest social evil (rather as unemployment is seen by some today). The devil itself, no less, tempting the unfortunate into sin and debauchery.

Engels was also concerned about the plight of the unemployed – the 'surplus population' of England who somehow had to eke out an existence in the days before the Social Security counter. He comments:

It is remarkable what tasks the 'surplus population' will perform . . . On all the main roads leading into big towns, there is a great deal of wheeled traffic, and a large number of people are to be seen with little carts in which they collect freshly-dropped horse dung for sale. At the risk of their lives these people dart on to the street between fast moving carriages and omnibuses. Frequently they have to pay a few shillings a week for the privilege of collecting the dung. (Loc. cit., p. 98.)

The kind of bobbing and weaving which goes on today is very different, as we shall see later. The alternative then was the Poor Law, introduced in 1834.

It forbade all outdoor relief in money or food. The only relief offered to the poor was admission to the new workhouses which were promptly erected all over the country . . . The food is worse than that enjoyed by the poorest labourer in employment. In return the pauper is forced to work harder than he would in a normal job . . . Their diet generally consists of potatoes, very bad bread, gruel, and little or no beer . . . The pauper who fails to do the work allocated to him has to go without food. The pauper who wants to go outside must ask the workhouse master for permission . . . The men are engaged in stone-breaking . . . Women, children and old folk pick oakum . . . Pauper families are separated in the workhouse so as to stop the 'superfluous' population from breeding and to save the children from the 'demoralizing' influence of their parents. Fathers, mothers and children are housed in different wings of the workhouse and are allowed to see each other only at fixed, rare intervals and then only if – in the opinion of the workhouse officials – their conduct has been exemplary. (Loc. cit., pp. 324–25.)

Discipline in the workhouses was at times inordinately cruel. Engels cites a report in the *Northern Star* of 6 April 1844 about a little girl locked up in the mortuary for three nights because she wet her bed. In another case:

Four [young] tramps . . . were locked in a 'black hole' under some stairs where they were left for between eight and ten days. It was in the depth of winter and yet the tramps had no clothes. (Loc. cit., p. 326.)

The workhouses have gone and the unemployed need no longer work to survive. Families can stay together in unemployment in principle – even if the friction and the tension associated with unemployment cause many to break up, in practice. Physical suffering has been replaced by something more abstract, more psychological. We shall see examples of this later. And we shall also see how this psychological suffering can at times lead to physical symptoms (for example, asthma), in some cases just as real and just as severe as those that the workhouses might have produced.

As always the workers sought solace wherever they could find it:

The worker comes home tired and exhausted from his labours. He finds that his comfortless and unattractive dwelling is both damp and dirty. He urgently needs some stimulant; he must have something to recompense him for his labours during the day and enable him to face the prospect of the next day's dreary toil. He is out of sorts; his nerves are on edge and he feels thoroughly depressed . . . Moreover, his need for company can be satisfied only in the public house, for there is nowhere else where he can meet his friends.

In these circumstances the worker is obviously subject to the strongest temptation to drink to excess, and it is hardly surprising that he often succumbs. Given these conditions, it is in fact inevitable that a large number of workers should have neither the moral nor the physical stamina to resist the temptation. (Loc. cit., p. 116.)

Alison (1840) reported that by 1840 there was one public house to every ten dwelling houses in Glasgow. Gaskell (1833) estimated a similar ratio for Manchester. Engels was appalled by the 'bestiality' of drunkenness and the sight of 'drunkards staggering in the road or lying helpless in the gutter' (p. 143).

The workers (and the unemployed) still seek solace in stimulants today, and drunkards unfortunately do still stagger. But it seems a pity that Engels didn't try to make more sense of what went on inside public houses. Instead he played the role of distant (and morally outraged) observer, noting the raw material going in – the workers who 'stream from the slums' – and the finished product – the workers helpless in the gutter – as if he was detailing the input/output workings of yet another factory. As if there was nothing of interest going on in between. Drinking, meeting friends and socialising, with all they entail, can be active, skilled and even creative accomplishments and not just more bumps on the rocky road to ruin. In this book we will spend some considerable time in drinking establishments, trying to ascertain what really goes on in such places and trying to work out the real significance of some of this activity.

The long hours of work in poor conditions in the Industrial Revolution, punctuated with excessive drinking and appalling housing, had not surprisingly a deleterious effect on health. The Poor Law Commissioners' report on the sanitary condition of the labouring population shows that the average age of death of the 'gentry and professional persons' was thirty-five years, of 'tradesmen and their families' twenty-two years and of 'labourers, mechanics and servants' fifteen years (Chadwick, 1842). Chadwick reports that in Manchester nearly 54 per cent of the workers' children died before their fifth birthday. This compared with 20 per cent of the children of the middle classes. The health care provided by charitable institutions was inadequate. The Manchester Infirmary dealt with 22,000 patients a year but, as Engels points out, 'what does that amount to in a city in which . . . three quarters of the inhabitants need medical attention every year?' (Loc. cit., p. 117.) At the time, Manchester had 400,000 inhabitants (loc. cit., p. 54). The workers could not afford doctors' fees so they turned to others offering cheaper remedies. Nearly 25,000 boxes of Parr's Life Pills, for example, taken to relieve fever, constipation *and* diarrhoea, were sold each week. Another common medicine was Godfrey's Cordial – a mixture of tincture of opium (laudanum) and treacle. Engels notes:

Women who work at home and have to look after their own and other people's children dose them with this medicine, not only to keep them quiet, but because of a widely prevalent notion that it strengthens the child. Many women give the children this medicine while they are new-born infants, and go on dosing them without realizing the harmful consequences of this method of 'strengthening the heart' until the children die. When the child's system develops a greater resistance to the effects of opium, the dose is gradually increased. When Godfrey's Cordial is no longer effective it is replaced by pure laudanum and doses of from fifteen to twenty drops at a time are given. In evidence before a Parliamentary enquiry the Nottingham coroner stated that one druggist had admitted using 13 cwt of treacle in a year in the manufacture of Godfrey's Cordial. (Loc. cit., p. 118.)

Health has improved dramatically since the 1840s (see Townsend and Davidson, 1983, p. 65). The death rate (per 1000) has fallen from about 22 to 6, although inequalities in health have been maintained. Even today men and women in unskilled jobs have a two and a half times greater chance of dying before reaching retirement age than their professional counterparts (see Townsend and Davidson, 1983, p. 51). Parr's Life Pills and Godfrey's Cordial have gone out of fashion. Valium has come in.

Britain's new profile

The face of industrial England has changed considerably since Victorian times. The new technology has passed over its rugged surface and shaved it close; the microchip has shaved it closer still. A lot of 'excess' labour has been removed in the process. And then the mad dog of recession staggered in and bit off large lumps of 'surplus' matter. Fever set in. Mrs Thatcher complained about 'the new bouts of inflation' and she looked in desperation for '*healthy* trends in certain aspects of economic policy'. She chided 'those people who talk about unemployment but say nothing, in practical terms, about how to *cure* it'. She told us to take comfort from the fact that the mad dog had been to other places as well: 'There's been a world recession; not our fault – Germany and France are *suffering* as well.'

There have been many casualties – Engels' surplus population has grown and grown. In the summer of 1985 there were over 3 million out of work – 13.4 per cent of the working population. Nearly 1.5 million people had been unemployed for more than a year. The rate of unemployment had doubled since 1980. In some regions, the picture was even bleaker. In Greater London, for example, unemployment was running at 10.5 per cent; in South Yorkshire (covering Barnsley, Doncaster, Rotherham and Sheffield) it was 17.3 per cent. Certain sections of the population suffer worse than others (the young, the old, the disabled, blacks). There were 1,233,000 people under twenty-five unemployed in the UK.

Work today is easier, but more uncertain. In the factories and mines, the workers have shorter hours in better conditions for higher pay. In 1983 in the coal industry, for example, men worked an average of 45.3 hours per week. The average pay was £148. In the metal manufacturing industry the average number of hours was 42.2 for average earnings of £176. No more sixteen-hour day by fourteen-year-old workers in mines who found that in the end they owed the company money. Coal miners today still 'gobble coal dust' (as one put it); workers in steel mills still sweat buckets. But practices like the following, described by Engels, have disappeared.

Coal is sold by weight but the miners' wages are generally calculated by the tub . . . If the tub contains more than a fixed quantity of slack . . . the miner is not only paid nothing for that tub, but he is fined as well. The system of fines is so highly developed in the coal mines that it is actually possible for a poor devil to work for a whole week and then when he goes to the foreman for his wages . . . he learns not only that no wages are due to him but that he owes the company something in fines. (Engels, 1958, pp. 285–86.)

W. P. Roberts, the Victorian social reformer, drew up a new contract for miners in 1844 demanding payment by weight of coal cut, with the weights to be checked by inspectors, and the abolition of this hated system of fines. He also demanded an obligation by the mine owners to find at least four days' work a week for miners whom they regularly employed.

We now live in the Utopia dreamed of by Roberts and others. As far as Utopias go, it's a pretty limited one, based on a few fair principles. But life in this Utopia is not all it might be – the mad dog of recession has little respect for the boundaries of this Utopia, or any other, and it has been scratching at the fence to get in. Some politicians even seem to have held up the wire for it. Life in this Utopia is dominated by anxiety and apprehension – this apprehension led to the one-year-long miners' strike. There were 22.3 million working days 'lost' in this dispute; 22.3 million days lost in despair about pit closures and redundancies. But why the anxiety? What's so bad about unemployment these days? After all, don't the unemployed live in conditions not even dreamed of by social reformers in Victorian times? A comfortable existence, an easy life. No need to get up in the morning, no need to get your hands dirty; TV, video nasties (at a pound a night). So what's wrong with all this? The answer seems to be – quite a lot. The obvious physical harm of the first industrial revolution has been replaced by the more insidious harm of the second (the microchip revolution). Two psychologists from Sheffield University, Paul Jackson and Peter Warr (1983), studied in some detail a large sample of unemployed men. They found that a fifth of the sample experienced psychological deterioration since losing their job. (A few individuals' psychological health, however, improved with unemployment.) The deterioration included anxiety, depression, insomnia, irritability, lack of confidence, inability to concentrate and general nervousness.

Michael Banks and Paul Jackson in 1982 investigated the association between unemployment and risk of psychiatric morbidity in two groups of teenagers. These young people were interviewed at times of up to two and a half years after leaving school at sixteen. Banks and Jackson found that generally there were more psychiatric problems among the unemployed, and because of the particular nature of their research they were able to conclude that the experience of unemployment was more likely to increase than to decrease psychiatric symptoms. Such research confirms work carried out in the 1930s. P. Eisenberg and P. F. Lazarsfeld, for example, had in 1938 catalogued no less than twenty-eight indices of psychological deterioration in unemployment, including 'a shattered sense of proportion, "inferiority", lowered self-confidence, vacillating morale, expectation of failure, hopelessness, depression, distrust and apathy'. But why? Peter Warr suggested in 1983 that there are nine features of the unemployed person's role which may bring about reduced psychological wellbeing. First, and most obvious, is the reduced income. Warr reports that two-thirds of his sample of unemployed working-class men had an income half or less of their income when employed. This is a bitter blow to a generation reared on materialism and brought up on a diet of glossy adverts and constant incitements to buy, change, keep ahead. The second potentially damaging feature of unemployment is that with work gone and income reduced, the variety in a person's life becomes restricted. There is more inactivity, sleeping during the day, sitting around watching TV or the video. Work also provides goals. In unemployment there are fewer goals and a smaller scope for important decision-making (there is more scope for trivial decision-making like what time to get up in the morning). Many jobs, even apparently mundane ones, allow the practice of certain skills; unemployment allows the practice of few skills. With unemployment there is an increase in what Warr calls 'psychologically threatening activities', such as making applications in the knowledge that they will probably end in rejection. There is also a good deal of insecurity about the future in the unemployed and reduced contact with other people. Work got you out of the house, and you may not have liked your workmates but you were at least afforded some degree of human contact with them. Unemployment can and does isolate people. And finally there is the individual's self-concept, in our society often tightly bound up with his or her position in paid employment. With the position gone, the self-concept deflates – a bit like a balloon, but more rapidly. As Colin Thunhurst said in the *Sheffield Star*:

On Monday June 24th a 19 year old Derbyshire youth threw himself from the top of High Tor. He had on him a note simply saying 'Put it down to unemployment'. The reasons why people kill themselves are never simple. Everybody, at some time or other, asks him or herself what life is about and whether it's worth continuing. For most of us this comes at an occasional time of crisis. For the unemployed, particularly the increasing number of long term unemployed, crises are no longer occasional.

The general psychological impact of unemployment is clearly deleterious but it is not equally so for every person. As always, some suffer more than others. Research has shown that those with the highest 'employment commitment', i.e. those who really do want a job, suffer the most distress

(Warr, 1983, p. 307). Middle-aged unemployed men also experience greater distress than those who are younger or older (Hepworth, 1980) – partly because of the greater financial strain on this group. And for those workers between twenty and fifty-nine years old, the longer the period of unemployment, the greater the distress. The association between increased duration of unemployment and greater psychological ill-health does not seem to hold for teenagers or for those approaching retirement, however (Jackson and Warr, 1983). Working-class unemployed people also seem to suffer more than their middle-class counterparts because, it is suggested, they have more financial problems and greater difficulty filling the time (Warr, 1983, p. 305).

Warr also found that some individuals were particularly likely to undergo very severe physical deterioration with unemployment. These were individuals who had a chronic health impairment to begin with – such as arthritis, bronchitis, a heart complaint or a slipped disc. The longer they were unemployed, the worse this became. For people without a chronic health problem there was no association between duration of unemployment and reported physical deterioration (Jackson and Warr, 1983). The weak get weaker (significantly so), the strong get by. Warr's study of the effects of personal vulnerability on health has so far been confined to physical health. But he says ominously, 'It seems likely that a similar pattern might be found for psychological vulnerability, and we clearly shall be looking out for that.' (1983, p. 305.)

Unemployment harms some people more than others. The middle-aged working-class man with a strong commitment to work and some physical complaint to begin with, who has been unemployed for a long time, sinks into a deep psychological and physical quagmire. Sheffield and other industrial towns in the north of England are full of such people – stagnant and buried up to their necks in debt and apathy, their physical condition worsening.

Steel City blues

In this book, I will provide a glimpse of life in Britain in industrial decline by focusing on one city – Sheffield. Why Sheffield? Sheffield was at the centre of the first industrial revolution and now it seems to be in the front line of the devastation caused by Britain's sharp decline. Sheffield was famous for steel, and metal goods and textiles were the two most important products of

British industry in the first industrial revolution. But Sheffield steel is now too expensive, it is said. Others can make it cheaper. The foreign competition was too severe – a microcosm of Britain's industrial fate. The steel industry has indeed been particularly hard hit by the recession, and coal mining (following the 1984–1985 miners' strike) looks next to suffer (between the start of this strike and the summer of 1985, 34 pits were closed nationally). Unemployment nationally was 13.4 per cent in 1985; in South Yorkshire, it was 17.3 per cent.

The region may be typical in terms of its rapid rise and even more rapid decline in industrial Britain, but it is unique in some ways.

It stands out in one respect, again and again taking the national lead and setting the tone for national movements. This was its independence of spirit, its rebelliousness. In Politics, the tradition runs from the Society for Constitutional Information, in its day the largest in the country, opposing the early ideals of the French Revolution to the corrupt tyranny which then misgoverned Britain; it continues with the particular flavour of Sheffield Reform Politics, and with the bitter opposition to the New Poor Law and with Chartism, to the radical MPs of the nineteenth century, to almost unique support for Anarchism at the end of the century and to the Labour strongholds of today. In Religion, it runs from the strong early Puritanism and Non-conformity to the leadership of Radical Methodism breaking away again and again from the Conservative trend of the Wesleyans. In trade union history the trend is possibly strongest of all. Here we have a remarkably early burgeoning of craft unionism, self-confident even in the face of legal prohibition. (Pollard, 1976, p. 5.)

This trend has continued to the present day – it is still a Labour stronghold in politics; in religion, the Charismatic movement has mushroomed in Sheffield. In trade-union affairs the most notable single action in the region was Arthur Scargill's moving the NUM headquarters to Sheffield – for, one suspects, ideological as well as practical reasons – and orchestrating the miners' strike from there.

Sheffield is two hours and twenty minutes by train from London but they often seem worlds apart. It is the very centre of South Yorkshire. As Sidney Pollard puts it, 'South Yorkshire, let us face it, has always been land-locked, inward-looking and provincial. It has therefore always been somewhere near the very heart of England.' (Pollard, 1976, p. 3.) The industrial heartland of Britain now feels its pulse faltering. Its role was always critical in Britain's industrial past and has been recognised as such.

No true understanding of British history is possible without a deep understanding of what went on in the regions such as South Yorkshire and why. It is in the internal economic and social development of these regions, their geographical and temporal juxtaposition, that the key to British history as a whole must be found. That is what made Britain in the past and will continue to make her in the future. (Pollard, 1976, p. 4.)

Sheffield is a town whose name is synonymous with steel, a name once carved on a million household products from Bangor to Bombay. As Engels himself notes, 'Metal goods are, next to textiles, the most important products of British industry' (loc. cit., p. 224). Sheffield steel formed one of the commercial bases for the first industrial revolution with all the attendant consequences. Edwin Chadwick, in his report on the sanitary conditions of the labouring population of Great Britain, wrote:

Sheffield is one of the dirtiest and most smokey towns I ever saw . . . one cannot be long in the town without experiencing the necessary inhalation of soot, which accumulates in the lungs, and its harmful effects are experienced by all who are not accustomed to it. There are however numbers of persons in Sheffield who think the smoke healthy. (1842.)

Dirty and unequal. In 1895 it was said that there was 'no other manufacturing town where the contrast between the dwelling places of the rich and poor are so strongly marked, or the separation between them so complete.' (Royal Commission on Secondary Education, 1895, p. 165.)

Engels also described the working conditions in Sheffield:

The most unhealthy type of work is the grinding of knife-blades and forks which, especially where a dry stone is used, always leads to the death of the operative at an early age. The unhealthy nature of this work is caused partly by the fact that the grinder works in a bent position. His breast and stomach suffer from the pressure put upon them. But the main danger of this trade comes from breathing in particles of sharp metallic dust thrown up into the air during the grinding process. The average expectation of life of a dry grinder is barely 35 years, while that of a wet grinder is rarely more than 45. (1958, pp. 229–30.)

Attempts to protect the grinders by covering the grinding wheels and by drawing off the dust by suction had limited success. The grinders often destroyed the safety apparatus themselves because, as Engels notes, 'they feel that if their trade becomes safer, it will attract more workers and so lead to a fall in wages. They believe in "a short life and a merry one".' (Loc. cit., p. 231.)

And a short life it was. The major causes of death between 1837 and 1842, as recorded by Dr G. C. Holland, physician to the Sheffield General Infirmary (see Thunhurst, 1985), were 'consumption', 'convulsions', 'inflammation of lungs', 'decay of nature', 'accidents' and 'scarlet fever', in that order. Inflammation of lungs alone produced more deaths than 'decay of nature' (i.e. a natural death). Old age was rarely given a chance to creep up on you.

But a merry one it might have been. Engels notes gravely:

Immorality among the young people of Sheffield appears to be worse than anywhere else . . . In Sheffield, on Sundays young people hang about the streets all day gambling by tossing coins or by organising dog fights. They frequent gin shops assiduously, where they sit with their girlfriends until late in the evening, when it is time for the couples to take their solitary walks. In one low beer shop visited by the Commissioner (J. C. Symons) forty to fifty young people of both sexes were sitting. Nearly all of them were under seventeen years of age and every youth had his girlfriend with him . . . Known prostitutes were among the company. (Loc. cit., pp. 231–32.)

Things have changed, in some ways. The Public Health Act of 1848 included directions to build houses with drains, pave streets and cleanse water. The smoke went much later. The rate of mortality has decreased dramatically. (The rate of cardiovascular disease, however, increased by 6.5 per cent between 1848 and 1972 in Britain generally. Cancer has shown a 5.2 per cent increase; see Thunhurst, 1985, p. 16. These two categories cover three in every four deaths that occur in Sheffield today.) But the death rate in Sheffield is still above the national average by about 10 per cent; 4 per cent if you take into account the age of the population. (Thunhurst, 1985, p. 32.) Life expectancy in Sheffield is on average 68.4 years for men, 74.9 for women. But it is still unequally distributed – the range of life expectancy in men is over 8.5 years from electoral ward to ward, and for women it is almost 6 years. All five wards of Sheffield Central show consistently elevated mortality rates both for men and women; in contrast, Sheffield Hallam has much lower than average rates. Stocksbridge shows an exceptionally high rate of heart disease; Castle, Manor, Netherthorpe, Norton and Southey Green have particularly high rates of cancer. Life is healthier generally in Sheffield today but still very unequal – the unhealthy districts are all working-class. Colin Thunhurst (1985) found that 'variations in mortality rate correlate most strongly, at a ward level, with indicators of social class, indicators of unemployment, the proportion of single parent households and the proportion of households without a car' (p. 116). The situation today is still reminiscent of that described in the report of T. Griffiths, the first medical officer of health for the borough of Sheffield (1873): 'The beautiful residences of the suburbs surround localities of undoubted danger.'

In the midst of such physical danger and psychological threat, young people in Sheffield today still frequent pubs 'assiduously where they sit with their girlfriends until late in the evening', but when they leave it is more likely to be for a crowded disco than for a 'solitary walk'. The solitary walk comes much later. There is safety in numbers, or at least it feels as if there is. Moreover, as Engels said about the worker, the 'need for company can be satisfied only in the public house for there is nowhere else where he can meet his friends'. And there's nowhere else that young people can go to escape the tension at home (heightened by unemployment because the whole family are there – all of the time) and nowhere they can act the way they feel like acting – free from the scornful eye of their parents, and free from the constraining context of the parental home. The crowded pubs and packed nightclubs should not too readily be seen as evidence of gross moral turpitude, even to the Victorian observer who hasn't been quite able to leave his finely tuned moral ear at the door of the noisy establishments. Pubs and nightclubs fulfil important functions in providing appropriate contexts for the presentation of social front and in the construction of the individual's ultimate social reality. We shall see much more of this later.

In this book I attempt to provide a series of sketches of what life is like in Steel City in the 1980s. I will not be following Engels' lead – he focused mainly on the physical conditions of the workers, and the 'surplus population', who inhabited a world in which the conditions at home and at work were indeed appalling. The physical landscapes today may still, on occasion, be bad but never as bad as they were. It is the psychological landscapes that are perhaps the most frightening today – the mountains of acute anxiety and apprehension separated by valleys of deep despair, all covered by the debris of dashed expectations and hope, volcanic mounds of greed where record levels of material acquisitiveness (pumped up as never before by the new 'scientific' advertising) are held down, just, by Social Security payments, and where the desire to work has been trampled by the swaggering recession.

I could try to paint a picture of life in Sheffield by documenting the damp and crowded conditions of the workers, still often with few amenities, but I won't. Instead, I'll attempt to give a glimpse of lives by describing what people do there today, how they talk about it, and how, on occasion, they explain their predicament or comparative good fortune. I am interested not so much in how many people sleep to a room as in what the individuals do when they are in the room, how they get to the room in the first place, and what they do to fill their day when not in the room. I am interested in how they use the few resources available to make a bit of money, and how they use the same resources to present themselves in a way that allows their ego to remain intact – to still *be* something. I am interested in how the social performance of people in a town in decline is organised. Pubs, nightclubs and casinos are probably important to this end and I will quite unashamedly spend some considerable time in them. Cheers.

The remainder of the book is organised in seven chapters. 'The survival of the fittest' focuses on the workers, the unemployed and the homeless, with a brief aside to a management consultant whose job it is to 'save' industry. The unemployed are partly his casualties. In 'Bring on the night' I try to get a feeling for the significance of night-time activities in nightclubs and casinos, where things are often not what they seem. Then on to individuals who are engaged in 'just a bit of bobbing and weaving' – not collecting dung any more but working as con men, minders, bouncers, pimps and masseuses to make ends meet. Then on to 'The professionals at work' – burglars, nurses, store detectives, car salesmen, dancers and clairvoyants. Then to individuals on 'The road to Mandalay' – on their way somewhere – anywhere: Charismatic Christians, students doing finals, poseurs waiting to be discovered, and drug users. In 'Playing the part' I attempt to analyse some of the social performances I witnessed, to understand how some of the multifarious roles people play are constructed. The Postscript shows that Steel City is indeed in a state of flux – I follow up some of the individuals to see what has happened to them by the end of 1985.

2 · The survival of the fittest

> . . . work has a greater effect than any other technique of living in the direction of binding the individual more closely to reality; in his work he is at least securely attached to a part of reality, the human community.

Sigmund Freud, *Civilization and its Discontents*, 1930

A street in Crookes

Summer had to come to 'Brick Street' some time and the mist eventually did lift from the Rivelin Valley so that you could see the grey slab flats of Stannington (they turned out to be brown and white, but they had looked grey all year). Swallows appeared overhead, dipping for flies. Boys with fishing nets set forth. Funny, I thought that sticklebacks had gone for ever, but they obviously knew different. Old familiar smells – hot tarmac, rain on warm pavements – returned to haunt the memory and tease the imagination. Steel City was heating up after a year of wind and rain. Cold Steel City to chill the bone and dampen the spirit, but now the chill had gone.

But Brick Street was different this summer. The noises were different. The feeling was different. People were getting up later. There was no bustle. It was now a street of people who didn't work. Some were retired, some hadn't got a job yet; but most had been made redundant. Work was never really discussed. People were bitter. Casual enquiries about work or job prospects could hurl you into an endless spiral of accusation and complaint. 'Thatcher.' 'Foreign steel.' 'Bloody recession.' Most people only fall down this well once. Some things are better left unsaid; everybody knows that everybody else knows who's to blame and that's all that matters. And anyway, there were more important things to talk about – the decorating, the price of houses, the weather. This summer, especially the weather.

The women seemed to rise first. Two old retired dears brought their milk in first. They lived side by side and hated each other. Both were in their seventies, both were widows and both natives of Sheffield. One had a son, one hadn't got anyone. Mrs Hill's son came to visit her once a week in his S-registration Polo. He would sit for an hour in her house on a Sunday, then leave. If it was a good day they would drive for an hour. But one Sunday he had his two corgis with him. He was supposed to be taking his mother to Chatsworth for the day but, Mrs Hill says, 'There was no room with the dogs in the back. I don't mind. It would have been too cramped. It's a good day for just sitting out anyway,' and then she went off to the bingo. Her luck was in – she won a tenner. 'It pays me to go,' she said.

Mrs Hill's neighbour, whom she always referred to as Mrs What's-her-name (despite the fact that she had an excellent memory), was new to the street. She had bought the terraced house after her husband died – it was a step down for her from lower-middle to upper-working. She had lived in Sheffield all her life, but not in this street. Mrs Hill didn't like her – she didn't like strangers. Mrs Hill left her living-room curtains undrawn well into the night and watched the comings and goings. Mrs Hill patrolled up and down her living room pretending to tidy it but really she was just watching the street. Her black and white television was always on. (Errol Flynn in the afternoon, Magnum at night.) Mrs What's-her-name also watched the street, but from behind drawn living-room curtains and after she had gone to bed she liked to watch from behind the bedroom curtains (Mrs What's-her-name was from a higher social class). You didn't have to page the oracle in our street; you just asked Mrs Hill. She knew who was moving and why; she was good on the price of houses, she was tops on adultery and divorce. She told Mrs What's-her-name the spicier bits, but they were both a bit deaf, so they shouted. It was strange to hear yourself talked about in this way, but of course they thought they were whispering – it would have been too embarrassing to tell them. Mrs Hill went to the shops at 10 am and 3 pm. Mrs What's-her-name went at 11 am and 4.30 pm. Mrs What's-her-name also went somewhere at 7 pm, although no one knew where. Mrs Hill had tried to wheedle it out of her but Mrs What's-her-name's lips were sealed. Mrs Hill suspected that she took a drink.

Mr Smith and Mr Forrest were another unlikely pair. Both were steel-workers, both redundant for two years. Both bitter. Mr Smith was in his forties. His wife was a clerk, his daughter had just left school but hadn't got a job yet. Fred Smith had been decorating his home all year. Now he had reached the outside, he was replacing the window frames and varnishing the door. He started at about 9 am and took breaks every few hours out in the sun. He didn't sit out in the sun before he started, but only after he had worked for a couple of hours and at the end of the day. At the end of the day, he didn't wash immediately, he liked to leave the dirt on for a bit, he liked to feel he had been grafting. He could then sit and enjoy the sun for a bit – he'd

earned it. He liked this stage of the decorating, its hard work, plenty of graft; all the poncey bits done. He didn't know what he'd do when the decorating was finished, though.

Mr Forrest, the other former steelworker, was fifty-seven, and lived at the bottom of the street. In a street overlooking the Bole Hills and the Rivelin Valley – a street which was really exposed – Mr Forrest had the most exposed house of all. The wind tore at his house, he was constantly replacing his tiles and his guttering. He had been made redundant just over two years earlier. He didn't mind much at the time – his wife was very ill with kidney failure. This summer she wasted and died. He always referred to her as Mrs Forrest. 'Mrs Forrest is in a better place now,' he said. But he didn't let her death get him down. He was constantly on the move, constantly busy. He ran everywhere with his dog Suki. 'I could be out dancing every night,' he said, 'if I'd got the brass.' He was always up ladders replacing people's guttering, unblocking their drains, digging their gardens – he needed any money people could afford to give him. He'd work for a day for a couple of quid. He got business by worrying people. 'The next time we have a good storm that drainpipe is going to come right off.' 'Oh,' said Mrs What's-her-name. 'I could do it for you tomorrow.' 'Oh, all right then.' And off he went, whistling his happy tune. He talked in the same kind of shout as the old people because he was deaf from the years in the noisy steel mill. The whole street shouted their private messages at each other. There was little privacy here.

It was a funny, old-fashioned street. There was no graffiti, little vandalism. There were too many people watching what was going on for these to occur. Everybody knew everybody else's business. And yet the houses themselves with their neat little gardens were very private. No posh houses, mind. They were just stone terraced houses or fifty-year-old unfashionable red-brick terraced houses. Privately owned houses for the working class with the discipline and the thrift, once a way station for the economically mobile steelworkers reared in council houses. And houses for the retired folk when they found themselves with a bit of money.

But now things were different. Instead of standing on the parapets and planning their advance into new unconquered territories, these people were in a state of siege. Constantly reworking their decorations, their fortifications, constantly mending their guttering, varnishing their doors, constantly polishing their J-registration cars. These people wouldn't be leaving their castles and they knew it. They also wouldn't have to retreat, thanks to redundancy payments.

So this summer, the sun was shining and the temperature rose but they were not tempted out. These were the working class, reared on discipline and hard work; sitting in the sun was redolent of idleness and waste. Sitting in the sun was skiving. And these were the people who didn't skive, who had timetables fixed and immutably etched on their brains, the people who thrived on overtime. But now the overtime had gone, as had the work. So they were poorer and a bit disillusioned. Some of them had lost all their aspirations and yet the little foremen in their heads still made them feel guilty for enjoying the hot summer sun.

And the sun was shining and the grey slab flats of Stannington across the valley seemed even closer. And the three-bedroom semis of middle-class Sheffield seemed a million miles away.

Unemployed steelworker

Fred Smith was a Sheffield man, born and bred. Sheffield is famous for its steel and for twenty-two years Fred had worked for Hadfield's, the private steel firm in Sheffield. But not any longer. He had been made redundant in 1981 when the Leeds Road plant closed. For two years, Fred had had time to sit and think about what might have been, to sit and brood. Two years is a long time. Not surprisingly, Fred was bitter about the industry which had paid him off and about the country which had allowed it to happen. 'I wouldn't go back now if you paid me,' said Fred, not noticing the irony of what he has just said.

Fred started in the firm of Brown–Bayley in Sheffield in 1959. (It was taken over by Hadfield's in 1974). He was twenty-one and had just completed his national service in the RAF. He was born and brought up in Darnall in the east end of Sheffield. This is where the big steel mills and factories were situated. Once they operated twenty-four hours a day, the furnaces in constant use, manned by three eight-hour shifts. The air thick with smoke. Now the mills were silent and the furnaces had been extinguished. Cold, dead hulks. When Fred started in 1959, Hadfield's employed about 10,000 workers – now there were fewer than 800. The Leeds Road plant was closed completely, leaving just the Vulcan Road plant in operation. In a town which owes its worldwide reputation to steel, these figures clank ominously.

The steel industry was, and is, a tough manly business. Fred didn't have any misty-eyed view of his former work. 'Hell' was the way he described it.

'Up to your ankles in dust from the insulation tiles. Swept out once a week by a special gang on overtime but a few days later you were up to your ankles in it again.' There were three eight-hour shifts; one from 6 am to 2 pm, one from 2 pm to 10 pm and one from 10 pm to 6 am. Fred laughed as he remembered the shifts. 'In them days, the pubs closed at 10 pm. The afternoon shift used to start really at 1 pm and finish at 9 pm so you could have a pint on the way home. By mutual consent with the other shifts, of course. In the melting shop they had to send out for their beer. It wasn't just a practice, it was a custom. It was the only way of stopping the men going outside for a pint. They brought the beer in in half-gallon cans and allowed a ten-minute break. The heat in the melting shop was fierce. You needed a pint.' It may have been hell but there was companionship – what Fred missed most about his work. 'When the afternoon shift finished, the gang would go to the Greyhound pub or the Attercliffe Liberal Club for an hour's drinking,' said Fred.

Working in a steel mill was a hot, dusty and dangerous job. Three of Fred's friends had been killed during his time at Hadfield's, the last one not long before Fred was made redundant. 'A load fell off a fork-lift truck on top of him,' said Fred, 'and I was sitting playing dominoes with him in the canteen ten minutes before it happened.' Despite the obvious changes, safety equipment seems to have been minimal before about 1967. Before then, Fred said that they would make their own protective clothing out of any sacking they could find lying about to cover their trousers in a giant apron. Clogs they bought themselves. 'Shoes didn't last a day,' he said. 'Steel helmets only arrived in '67 and even then, many people did without. It wouldn't have done a lot for my friend anyway, would it?' There were also no showers. 'You travelled back to Attercliffe or Darnall dirty.'

It may indeed have been a hell but it was a hell with a career structure. Fred started as a pit labourer at just over £8 per week in 1959 – 'the lowest of the low – the general dogsbody'. He was part of a four-man gang consisting of a header man who made the feeder heads for the moulds, a second pit man who raked the dirt out of the mould before casting with a vacuum, and the first pit man – the gaffer in charge of the gang. His promotion was rapid – 'it was in them days – there was a big turnover as men headed for cleaner jobs in the cutlery industry and elsewhere.' Fred became 'header man' within a year, then he did charge-wheeling in the blast furnace, then became trainee foreman, then shift supervisor, all within another year. As shift supervisor he had to accept a drop in salary at first but it was a cleaner job. 'Anything was better than working on pit side,' he said, 'it was really dirty, really scruffy.' In 1962 he earned £14 per week as shift supervisor. By 1981 it was £8500 per annum – good money by anybody's standards. But then came the crash. He heard in May 1981 that the Leeds Road plant was to close. It came as a shock. 'We always thought it would be the Vulcan Road plant – its equipment was older – nearly thirty years old. The equipment in the Leeds Road plant was only five or six years old. It didn't make sense. Me and all my mates were sick. We thought we were all there for life. All my mates who I'd been to primary school with were all made redundant at the same time. We went to London to lobby our MP but it did no good.' Fred still quibbles about the productivity indices which suggested that British steelmaking was comparatively poor in performance compared with other EEC countries. He could argue his case well – 'but,' he said, 'no one listened.'

When the news of the closing sank in, the local technical colleges were invited to send guest lecturers to the firm to tell the men about what retraining courses were available. Fred opted for a course in electronic servicing – and while he was on the course he got full pay for fifty-two weeks but he failed to get a job afterwards. 'All the firms want experienced men and here am I at forty-five with paper qualifications but no experience. What use is that? I wish I'd done something else like getting an HGV licence, it would have been more useful.'

Money had recently started to get tight for the first time. With his £5000 redundancy payment he had paid off his mortgage on his terraced house in Crookes – another working-class district of Sheffield, but upmarket from Darnall. He had bought a neat little house which now had red tulips overflowing in a small, well cared-for garden with a plaque outside which read 'Mr and Mrs Smith live here'. Since being made redundant, Fred had worked his way through the house, decorating every room in turn. It was in good taste – no flying ducks or swarthy beauties on the wall. But since his retraining course finished, he was down to his dole money and his wife's salary (his wife was a clerk). 'It's down to essentials now,' he said.

But money wasn't the only problem. His wife was now the breadwinner. She went out to work every day. She brought back the bacon. He stayed at home and got their sixteen-year-old daughter ready for school. 'She's doing O levels at the moment. She's applied for forty jobs but only had one interview.' He made the dinner and did the cleaning and the shopping. 'I don't mind cooking,' he said. 'I did a bit when I was at work because of the shifts. I don't like cleaning, though. My wife says I don't do it right. She's always telling me off about cleaning. I only do the surface stuff really. She does the deep-down cleaning at weekends. I do like shopping, though – I like to see what the prices are and to make sure that I'm not being fiddled. I'd never done any cleaning or shopping before but I do nearly it all now. I've no timetable. I just do what I feel like, except of course for the tea which I have to get ready for half five. Most of my old mates don't do anything about the house. Especially the older ones in their fifties and sixties. They're just not used to it. They just sit about the house. In the old days the man of the family would be served first in Sheffield. But luckily in our family it wasn't like this. Just as well. I'm just one of the family now, not head of the family.'

But wasn't he glad to be out of that hot, dusty and dangerous place – to be sitting in the spring sunshine in his garden full of tulips? 'Not really,' he said. 'I miss the lads at work. I've no male company any longer. I still see my mates from work. The problem is they live all over Sheffield. We meet for a drink about once a month and I meet another friend who was made redundant at the same time who's now a bus conductor once a week, but it's not the same. Up in Crookes when I go into Shoppers Paradise supermarket, it's full of young mums or grannies. There's only about three other redundant steel workers in all of Crookes and I didn't really know them before. Darnall's not the same. Most of it's been knocked down and the last time I went to the Greyhound pub it was in new hands – it wasn't doing any business since the steel mill closed down. There's not much happening in Sheffield any more. It's a dead town. But I've just got an allotment. I like to see things growing.'

Making the day last

Brian had always looked forward to going to town. Always. When he was a boy he loved going to the stamp counter of Woolies with his father – just once a week. It was the highlight of his fairly routine schedule. And then on to Lipton's with the smell of cheddar cheese which hung over the whole shop and the sausages on sticks out to taste. It was all such a treat. And when he was working, he had the whole weekend to look forward to. The pub on Friday and Saturday – not that exciting in itself, but wonderful when you didn't have to get up the next day. And Saturday afternoon shopping sandwiched in between. Time to get the overalls off, get really clean and go round the shops with the wife. If he ever had to go to town during the week, it was always a quick dash in his overalls, but on Saturdays, he had the whole morning to sit about, dress and get ready. And here he was in town, midweek, nice and clean, no overalls, no dirt down his fingernails, plenty of time, and it wasn't even raining. Yet it was all so depressing.

The problem was time, he thought. The days were so long and a trip to town wasn't a break from anything, now he was redundant. He went to town to pass time and when you're trying to pass time you see things differently, you notice things that the rich and famous, the busy, even the employed never see. It's as if you pick out all the bad bits and then that's all you end up able to see. He could remember his father used to say that you could tell when a storm was coming by the way the wind whipped the litter along the pavement. He really noticed the wind today – and the litter. The wind was so low and it led the chip papers and the Wimpy boxes and the Coke cartons all in a merry little dance. The red and white cartons flashed along the grey pavement like so many grubby tropical fish. And yet there was no storm in the making – nothing to break the monotony or the mood. Shows what my bloody father knew, he thought. And he was sure there hadn't been that much litter in the good old days. He felt like picking some of it up and putting it in the litter bins but he was afraid people might think he was some nutter out on day release from Middlewood.

He went into the Wimpy bar and ordered a Coke. It came in a carton. He kept thinking about what his wife's cousin had told them. She worked in a building society, the one that gives a little Xtra help and the cashiers tilt their heads while they're smiling. She had been telling them about customers these days making deposits of 25p or even 15p. It never happened before, and it wasn't for a joke. They were quite serious, and they all could justify it by saying they were just evening up their accounts. It meant they came in four or five times a week for a bit of a chat, even a formal and ritualised one, centering on the exchange of a few coppers. Perhaps it'll be like that in a couple of months for me, he thought. Perhaps I'll start ringing Directory Enquiries for an intimate conversation. He wanted to down his Coke in one, but he knew he had to make it last.

So this was life on the dole, he thought to himself. Making a trip down Fargate – all 200 yards of it – last an hour. Funny, in the good old days of Saturday shopping, it did last an hour – but then he used to be weaving in and out of shops, instead of weaving between the chip wrappers. And there were mates to chat to. Now he didn't like meeting old friends – it was too embarrassing. Most of them were still working, and those that weren't all felt sorry for themselves. So now he did the Fargate run every day except Saturday. Better to be out when your mates were locked away behind the factory doors, he thought.

Brian was forty-six and had been unemployed for only two months but it felt like years; before that he worked for a big engineering firm in Sheffield for twenty-five years. He was an electrician. He always knew the firm would run into problems. It was large, too large; he used to boast that because of its size it could carry a lot of dead weight, including himself. And he had always been amazed how little anyone had to do. He worked on a test bed on the production line. Things were always slack at the start of the week and he and his mates would sit around reading, and then go in at weekends on time and a half and double time to get the work done. On nights it was even worse. The night shift was from 9 pm to 7 am, but they'd be able to get the work done in three hours by stretching some of the safety rules a bit. ('Well, rules were made to be broken,' they would all say.) After that it was time for a kip. Brian chose the dark room. The only disadvantage was that it was a bit cold in there so he'd lay some corrugated cardboard down on the floor. The night foreman just didn't bother. But every so often there would be a bit of commotion at the top and all the foremen would be given strict instructions to stop people getting their heads down. This purge would last for a couple of weeks – then it was back to normality. The management, Brian thought, was a joke. They ruled without any authority. Brian had always feared the worst. He knew that the survival of such a factory in a recession was going to be difficult anyway, and with a workforce accustomed to sleeping on the job, and a management without the power to stop it, it was going to be impossible. And the worst came to pass. In November 1983, they were told that the factory would close in six months. Three-quarters of the workforce were paid off in March 1984. Brian was one of the 'lucky' ones – he got to stay until the end.

Those were the days of hope and prayer, and considerable recrimination. Hope and prayer that the factory could somehow survive, and recrimination as to why it had to happen in the first place. Management blamed workers and vice versa. Local MPs took an interest in the cause and hopes rose. Sheffield Corporation considered the reintroduction of trolley buses to provide some work for the factory, and hopes rose still further. But the economics just didn't make sense in the end. The trolley-bus order would have guaranteed jobs for about ten. Hopes shot through the roof and plummeted to earth. It was like pissing in the wind, thought Brian.

Brian stayed on till August 1984 in a deserted factory, trying to finish off an order for the Ministry of Defence. Production lasted until June 1984. During the last eight months, representatives from the Department of Employment and a team of redundancy 'counsellors' came in to give a series of lectures in an effort to ease this particular rite of passage. Brian found the lady from the Department of Employment somewhat disconcerting when she suggested that the rules and regulations about unemployment benefit were so complicated that nobody really knew what anybody was entitled to. The redundancy counsellors gave a lecture on finding a job. All that Brian remembered of it was that they suggested dog-walking, pet-sitting and fish-feeding for neighbours on holiday as real possibilities. They also gave lectures on interview technique, but it all seemed so obvious. Dress reasonably and don't squirm or fidget. Brian didn't squirm or fidget anyway. So, equipped with his knowledge (and £6500 redundancy money) Brian joined the army of the unemployed, with strict orders to sign on and search for jobs and trudge the streets for the long, long, empty hours.

So he sat in a Wimpy bar with no one really to blame. He would have liked somebody to blame – anybody would have done, the Japs, Thatcher, the multinationals – but he couldn't stop thinking about the dark room and the corrugated cardboard. It made it all that much worse. And he thought about his mates from the night shift who worked in the machine shop and who weren't able to slip off for a kip, and he thought how depressed they must feel. They grafted while others slept and here they were all in the same boat – all up the creek without a paddle, and just a lifeline dangled by the Department of Employment for minimal assurance. He tried cheering himself up – he wasn't as badly off as some. At least he had some interests outside work. He was a keen marathon runner. When he was still employed he would sometimes do 20 miles during the day (and sleep off the running fatigue during work hours). So when the axe threatened, he thought that it wouldn't be that bad. It would leave him time for extra training. He might even be able to break the three-hour marathon barrier.

But things didn't turn out like that. On his very first day on the dole he went out for a run with his wife. She had just taken up running and he was going to be her mentor. He says he was quite relaxed and quite happy about redundancy, but that day, that critical day when it finally materialised, he found that he just couldn't keep up with her. He tried going out with his old running club and the same thing happened – they left him behind. He had never had asthma in his life but suddenly here he was puffing and panting and gasping for breath. The other runners couldn't understand it. It got so bad that he couldn't even walk home from the Job Centre without continually stopping. He read somewhere that nerves could bring on asthmatic symptoms but he refused to believe that was what was happening with him. He thought perhaps it was his house-cleaning, which he did while his wife went to work, or the fact that there was a lot of dust in the factory for the last few weeks before the closure. He was looking for some physical cause, something that he could put his finger on and say, 'That's it', something tangible. He didn't want to believe that it was something psychological, that it was all in the mind.

He had never liked work, he had often told people. He had a lot of outside interests and unemployment would just mean he could spend more time doing them, he kept saying. Between gasps, that is.

He could see the bitter irony in the whole thing. If it goes on like this, he thought, it'll soon take me an hour just to walk down Fargate. I'll not even have to drag my feet. And he left the Wimpy bar and positioned the Coke carton with meticulous precision right in the middle of the litter bin. The whole careful movement took nearly a minute and a half. Just as well nobody's watching, he thought.

Masher Metham's change of heart

Gentle sounds filtered through the suburbs – birds singing, children laughing in the distance, and Keith, the painter, whistling as he painted the outside of the semi. You could envy him his job on a day like this – up there in the warm air, whistling away with not a care in the world, or so it seemed. Spring, the season for nature's steady regrowth and man's hasty repainting, had arrived (if a trifle late) and here he was, as natural as a daffodil, as happy as a lark. The workers on their way to the afternoon shift in the factories, or what remained of them, cast envious glances his way. Theirs was a world of heat and dust and noise, and here he was soaking up the first sun of the year. His daffodil-yellow Datsun had a sign fixed to the side proclaiming his status – 'Keith Metham, Interior Decorator, Estimates free'. He was his own boss and they were envious all right.

And Keith came down off his ladder. 'Mind you, I know what life in the steel mills is like, I worked in them for nineteen years. I left school at fifteen back in the early sixties and served my time as a fitter – in Doncaster's. My dad got me a job there. He said, "Get on down there, son, they've all got cars, them that work there." He didn't tell me, though, that they were working seven days a week for them. Doncaster's weren't bad, mind, it was an easy-going firm. The money weren't right fantastic but there was plenty of overtime. It's gone downhill a bit since then – when I started there were thirty-odd fitters and thirty-odd fitters' mates, now there are about five

fitters left. They got rid of the fitters' mates years ago. It weren't bad being a fitter in Doncaster's – if you wanted to be at it eight hours a day you could, but you didn't have to. It was up to you. You got a lot of freedom, most of the work was maintenance but you weren't tied to any particular machine. You could have a walk around the factory and nobody would say, "What are you doing here?" You could really go where you pleased. You could have as many tea breaks as you wanted. My nickname used to be "Masher Metham" because I'd have a brew-up every couple of hours. But I left Doncaster's in 1976 because overtime was getting a bit scarce. There had been quite a few strikes. So I moved to a small strip mill in Sheffield, Effingham Steel, but I just stayed there for about twelve months. I left because there were one or two rumours about them closing. Accurate, as it turned out. I moved on to an iron foundry – William Cook's – my father-in-law got me the job there, but after a few months I moved on again to a better-paid job at Niagara Forge. I got that job through one of the gaffers I'd known from Doncaster's. So you see I've been through quite a few steel mills and most of the jobs I've had were through friends or relatives. That seems to be how you get on in life, you know.

'Niagara Forge were great, very steady, if you know what I mean, very cushy actually. If the machines weren't breaking down, there wasn't a lot to do. As a fitter you could always find something to do, but most didn't bother. There was no supervision. At Doncaster's there had been a foreman on every shift but at Niagara all the gaffers just worked nine while five. After five there was no one in charge. I used to work on the afternoon shift from two while ten. The production workers had a quota to meet, and when they reached their target, they'd go home, usually about nine o'clock. That would just leave me and the lads in the saw shop in the factory. I lived locally and sometimes I'd nip home at night and get some supper and then go back to work to clock out. Well, there weren't a lot to do, and no gaffers about. If anyone spotted me I'd just say I'd nipped out for a packet of cigarettes. There was no real harm in it, but sometimes we used to take it in turns to clock each other out. This was very common in the steel mills. This one night one of the lads from the saw shop was clocking four cards, one of which was mine, but a couple of gaffers nipped back and caught him. We all got the sack. We were really surprised because everybody did it and none of us had been in any trouble before. I just reckoned they were looking to make a few redundancies and they saw the opportunity to get rid of another four. It was bloody sickening actually, especially when I found I couldn't get another job. I'd get the interviews all right but then they'd ask why I left my last employment. When I told them I was sacked for a clocking offence, that were it.

'I got desperate. I was unemployed for a few years in all – quite a long time to think about things. I'd got two young lads and I felt bloody stupid. I should have used my loaf and not been caught like that. But there were no gaffers on at Niagara and perhaps the firm should have kept a closer eye on things. We'd all got into a rut there; when you had to do a hard day's work you really felt put out. We'd all got into this rut and just couldn't get back out of it. It were too easy to skive. So here I was – sacked and without any chance of a job. Who was going to employ me?

'During the time I was unemployed I did a hell of a lot of redecorating of my own house. It was the flashiest house in the neighbourhood. I had to keep active. I could see others, who were just happy to plod along, deteriorating badly. I was getting desperate for a job – at one point I thought about buying an ice-cream van. What I was really interested in, though, was painting and decorating. I've always done quite a bit myself and people always said I had a flair for it. My brother's a decorator and even he reckoned I were all right. So when I heard about this particular scheme from the Manpower Services I thought I'd give it a go. It's a scheme to finance new businesses – they pay you forty quid a week for the first year to see you over the worst period. The only qualification is that you should have been out of work for three months, and I qualified for that easily. One problem was that you need a thousand quid of your own money. After four years on the dole I hadn't got that kind of money. So what I did was put an advert in the local Sheffield free paper and got 600 quid's worth of business lined up. I then took the orders to my bank manager who agreed on a loan. I was away.

'I'm my own boss now. I have to make it work. I've nothing else to turn to. I got my name put on the side of my car for forty quid. It makes you feel a little bit above the other blokes going to work for somebody else. And I've got a chequebook with a business account number. It makes you feel as if you've gone up a little bit in the world. My rates are very reasonable – thirty quid a day in summer, twenty-five in winter. Mind you, they have to be – there's all these blokes on the fiddle in Sheffield who can charge less. It's a cut-throat business. I've got work fixed up for the next four weeks. There's no guaranteed work in this business. If anyone cancels at the last minute and I have to stay at home, I get right irritable – I'm in a right mood. I know it's all up to me. If I sit on my ass I don't get paid. There's no long tea breaks now, it's just a quick wet and half a cig, then back to the job. I've always really been conscientious, it's just that in the steel mills you didn't have to do the work. If you made work for yourself, people would say, "Who's this clown trying to impress?"

'The only thing that really bothers me is that I've always believed in every man to his own trade. I served my time as a fitter, not as a painter. I bumped into an old friend recently and he said, "What do you know about decorating?" And I said I must know something about it, because I'm being paid good money for doing it. But he had a point, I suppose. I don't know all the technical jargon for the job, but I know I do good work. Ask any of my customers.' (I did, and he does.) 'I'd always done a fair bit of decorating and I picked up a bit at a course at college.

'As far as the future's concerned, I believe the steel industry in Sheffield has gone down the Swanee. The Japs can do everything more cheaply than we can, and we just can't be like them. It's not that the British are workshy or anything, it's just the incentives aren't there. I've two lads, one thirteen and one eleven, and I hope that one day they'll come in with me. Not as painters or decorators, mind, I'd really like one to go into the building side of things and one into the joinery side. Then I could finish up with a little building firm, we could do house extensions and owt like that. But that's all a long time in the future.'

Keith glanced nervously at his watch. Time was clearly money, now, and he mounted his ladder again. 'Well, it's back to the grind, I suppose, but I love it really. No matter how hard I've got to work, I still enjoy it. I'd work through the night if I had to, to finish a job. I know my future depends on what I do today. I suppose I didn't so much take the plunge into self-employment, more a case of being pushed. But the gaffers who gave me the sack did me a favour really. I've discovered some joy and some real satisfaction in work at long last. And not before bleedin' time.'

The striking miner

Bobby was a 25-year-old South Yorkshire miner. He had been on strike for the full thirty-four weeks – 'Thirty-five actually, we came out a week before everybody else.' His allegiances were clear. 'Arthur Scargill's the best leader the miners ever had. Joe Gormley sold us down the bloody river, when he retired they sent him forty pieces of silver. As for Margaret Thatcher, it's simple – I hate her.' What about the Nottinghamshire miners? 'They make me bloody sick. If it had been the other way round, Yorkshire would have supported them. They're just out for themselves. I'm one hundred per cent behind the strike. I didn't think it would go on this long, mind. I thought it would last a few weeks at the most and I really thought the government would back down, but after this length of time it's like fighting a battle. We've lost so much there's no point in turning back. It's us or them now.'

Bobby had been attracted to mining for the money, pure and simple. There was no romanticism attached to mining in his mind. He started when he was seventeen after a brief spell in an engineering firm. 'I doubled my wages right away. I started with two mates – one stuck it for a day, the other for six months – he's selling Ferraris for a living now.' Bobby trained as a fitter in the pit and spent eighteen months working on the surface before going underground. 'It's no bloody joke down there, gobbling coal dust all the time. Down the mine it's always either too hot or too cold, but there is unity among the men. You get the odd back-stabbers, mind, but most of the men are great. You've got to stick together.' Bobby was earning a flat rate of £130 plus up to £75 a week in bonuses. He drove a Triumph Stag. 'I always liked flash cars,' he said. 'I had to be ready to go down the pit at 6.30 and I lived ten miles away from the pit. Mind you, we'd finish at a quarter to two and I'd go home and have a good kip. Before I started courting I used to go out every night until about 3 am. I was always knackered at work, but it was good money.'

Before the strike began, Bobby had been managing to put a little money away. 'Well, my girlfriend's always talking about marriage,' he said, almost apologetically. 'Then the government dropped a bollock,' said Bobby. 'They forced us into it – bringing in MacGregor and forcing a confrontation in the spring, when coal stocks were high. They wanted a fight – they wanted to get even for what we did to Heath in '74. Scargill may be a bit pig-headed, but he's a good leader.'

So how did Bobby survive? He was luckier than most – he didn't have a family to support and he lived with his parents, although his father was unemployed. 'The best I can,' he said. 'I got £12 for the first week on strike because we were picketed out and £65 in food tokens from the Sheffield Labour Council – I gave those to my mum. But that's not enough to survive on. Oh yes, and I had two food parcels from the local Miners' Club. The lady who dished them out said the food was from Russia and Poland but –' he laughed – 'they were all local brands – two tins of Heinz beans, a tin of skimmed milk, a packet of tea bags and a tin of stewed meat. You can get food parcels every fortnight if you like, but it's a long way to go for a few tins of beans.

'The first things to go when the strike began were my savings and then my car. I knew from the start I couldn't afford to run the Stag. I sold it and bought a Mini but my savings clearly weren't going to last too long, so I had to have a look round for other jobs. The first job I got was store-detecting – this was two weeks after the strike began. I just worked Saturdays – six hours a day in one of the big stores in Sheffield. £1.50 an hour, cash in hand.'

'But what would have happened if you'd seen one of the hard-up striking miners nicking something?' I enquired.

Bobby just smiled at the irony of the situation. 'On the first day I did see somebody nicking something. I don't know whether he was a miner or not, but he got away anyway,' Bobby said with relief.

After that Bobby got a job on the door of a nightclub for a few months – £12 a night. Here he heard some strong views expressed about the miners. 'I couldn't believe it – these women who worked in the club were worse off than me and yet they supported Thatcher and suggested Scargill should be shot.' During the day he was doing a spot of window-fitting and installing double glazing. 'I also do up cars for people I know, I'm quite good with engines.' Over the summer months he did some labouring on building sites. 'A friend got me the job,' he said. On Saturdays he now worked in a trendy shop selling expensive and fashionable clothes. 'It's a friend of mine who runs the shop.' His full week, however, with all these little jobs lined up end to end and all yielding cash in hand, didn't get him more than £25 a week. 'Enough to get by on though,' he said. He was not alone in working during the strike. One of his mates from the pit was steel-erecting in London. Another was working for the family garage business. Another was doing property repairs. Yet another was a bouncer.

But what did the miners who do picket duty every day think of Bobby's commercial ventures? 'They just laugh,' he said, 'and ask how I'm fixed for a drink. They thought it was hilarious, me acting as a bouncer. Some of them are right big blokes, and I'm not that big. In fact when I was working at the nightclub, the other bouncers had to keep an eye on me to make sure I didn't get into any trouble. I've seen some miners in the shop and they don't mind me working. When I went down to Orgreave to do some picketing I told all my mates about my jobs.

'Orgreave,' he said, 'was an experience.' He told me that most miners phoned their union representative to find out where to go picketing, but he said he just heard about the 7000 pickets at Orgreave on the radio, so off he went. He didn't go dressed for trouble. 'I was dressed as if I was going up town with some nice clothes on and these fashionable slip-on shoes on. When I got there all the miners were laid in these fields. It was a beautiful sunny day. There were these riot police with shields but they all went for a break. Then these guys started going round telling everyone to get up. They wanted the riot police to sweat, out in the heat. So some of the pickets rolled a tyre at the police line and some started throwing stones. The police backed off. The next minute the riot police were back all banging their shields and chanting, like something out of bloody *Zulu*. Then came the horses. It was a pitched battle. We all ran off chased by these bloody horses. One of my shoes came off and I had to pick it up and run back to my Mini. It was an eye-opener to see those police with their shields and batons, all chanting. You hear all this bollocks about pickets getting £15 a day, but anyone I've talked to only gets £1 a day plus their petrol.'

Bobby was extremely pragmatic in his approach. 'My view is that if the miners win this one we'll have a good run before anything else happens. I just want to earn a little bit of money like everybody else. I want a bit of security. I don't want to end up on the bloody scrap heap. People say the strike's political, sure it is, because we're opposing the government. I support Scargill because he's our leader. I know he's supposed to be a communist, but to be honest I don't know a hell of a lot about it. I only know about the political parties in this country.

'But sometimes,' he added, 'I think anything has to be better than Thatcher.'

Unemployed graduates

A while ago Norman Tebbit produced an apothegm which will undoubtedly cling to him for the rest of his parliamentary career, like stubborn dog muck to the sole of one's shoes. 'Get on your bike.' But for many the advice was unnecessary. Large numbers of people have always migrated in search of jobs, not least the flocks of school leavers bound for university in different parts of the country, and later jobs, often elsewhere still. And getting to these places wasn't merely a matter of fast pedalling but seven years' hard slog at school, and a minimum of three years' hard slog at university, with a number of strategically placed hurdles to cross in between – O levels, A levels, finals. And for working-class children it was arguably a hard slog against the odds – alone in your bedroom, reciting 'amo, amas, amat' while your friends were saying something similar in a live tongue to some interested party. For working-class kids it meant being different and determined. But it was worth it. Education was the long slippery rope dangled into the arena of the working class, enabling the most able and the most determined to haul themselves out – 'to make something of themselves', 'to better themselves'. And the rope may have been slippery and it may have been long, but at least it was there. But what about today? With the cold winds of the recession biting deep, what's happened now? What, for example, has happened to those halfway up the rope?

The statistics furnished by the Universities' Statistical Record tell us that 11 per cent of 1982 university graduates in this country were unemployed six months after graduation. Not bad, especially compared to school leavers, but this statistic is only part of the picture. A number of graduates take temporary jobs after graduating – to gain work experience or experience relevant to the career they wish to pursue – but what happens to them subsequently? We don't really know. What proportion of graduates take permanent jobs for which they are grossly overqualified in the first place? I recently saw an application by a student for a job in a John Lewis shop. In the section headed 'education: school/college', 'school' and 'college' had been crossed out and 'university' typed in. A sure sign of the times.

Furthermore, although the overall unemployment figure for graduates is 11 per cent, there is a lot of variation between different disciplines and even between the sexes. Thus, nearly 30 per cent of 1982 male philosophy graduates were unemployed six months after graduation, and 25 per cent of female philosophy graduates; 19 per cent of 1982 male graduates in biochemistry were unemployed six months after graduation, and 9 per cent of female graduates in this subject; whereas only 4 per cent of 1982 male graduates in law were unemployed six months after graduation, and 3 per cent of female graduates. It does seem that women are slightly more likely than men to get jobs after graduation (11 per cent unemployment for men and 10 per cent for women in the case of 1982 graduates). Why this is so is not clear – do women have to be more determined to get to university in the first place and does this determination help them to get jobs? Do they have more realistic job aspirations? In fields like biochemistry, for example, are women more likely than men to take jobs as laboratory technicians? Are they better at interviews? Are they better at presenting themselves generally?

At least we know that sex affects job prospects, especially in some subjects, even if we are not sure why. But what about social class? In times of recession, the number of well-qualified candidates may be too large and so employers focus on other, 'more peripheral' things – presentability, self-confidence, appropriateness of dress, perhaps even accent. In these, the well-schooled middle-class student may have a distinct advantage. But what happens to the working-class student who has climbed so far up that slippery rope of education, but whose further progress, whose transition from working to middle class, is blocked? I talked to a number of such individuals.

John was twenty-seven, he came from Clay Cross – his father had been a miner there. He left school with good A levels and was offered a place at university, but opted instead for a place at North Staffordshire Polytechnic on a business studies course, because he thought that the applied degree would be more useful for finding a job afterwards. He graduated with a lower second-class degree in 1979 and got on an MA course in accounting and finance at Lancaster University. He said his father was ill during the latter part of the course when a dissertation was required. He didn't complete the course in 1980, but resubmitted his dissertation in 1981 and then received his MA. But despite an MA and a hundred job applications, John couldn't find a job. He was unemployed for a year. He hated being on the dole – 'it was a bit like being in a coma,' he said. He was back in Clay Cross now – his uncle had got him a job in his iron foundry. He threaded nuts onto bolts for a take-home pay of about £90 per week.

How does he feel about this job? 'It's a job,' he said. 'Some of the graduates I've met couldn't do it, so I'm proud that I can. I have to work shifts, of course, one shift starts at 5.30 am but I don't mind. The men at work don't take the piss, they know what state the country is in. The production manager's son is an unemployed teacher, so he understands as well. They don't treat me any special, mind. Well, at one point I was offered a different job in the same factory. An office job came up when I'd been there for eight weeks – a clerk's job – the girl who had the job beforehand left to have a baby. You need four O levels for the job and here was I with an MA. I turned it down because it paid £40 a week less. They were trying to help but it was half the money for a job which didn't involve getting your hands dirty. Money means a lot to me these days. I can really understand the mentality of people when they go out on strike over pay. In a job like this, your whole life is geared to what's outside and for that you need money. A threat to your money is a threat to your life. Since working in the foundry for a year, I've saved £2300, but I'd better be careful in case I'm made redundant – you can only have so much savings.'

John was a quietly spoken lad, a bit reserved, a bit shy. He probably didn't shine in interviews despite being solid, quietly articulate, conscientious and thrifty. University had given him a training without shaping his appearance or style and without providing a useful veneer. 'University was a bit of a shock,' he said. 'It was a good laugh in sociology tutorials – one lad said all the shop stewards should be lined up against a wall and shot.' He laughed when he thought about it. This was clearly a view he'd never heard expressed in Clay Cross, not even applied to the bosses instead. He thought his prospects looked bleak.

Andrew's story was different. He was twenty-six and came from a family of self-improvers. His father's father had been a bus driver; his mother's father a telephone engineer; his father an executive officer in the Civil Service (he died when Andrew was thirteen); his mother a supervisor in a telephone exchange. He grew up on a working-class estate in Blackpool and attended the local primary school. But three As at A level got him a place at Worcester College, Oxford, when he was seventeen. He graduated in 1978 with a first in German and Latin. Now he was unemployed. He did a postgraduate certificate of education after graduating and then landed a teaching job in Halifax, but he packed it in to return to Oxford to do an M.Litt. This turned out to be a serious mistake because he didn't enjoy research. Postgraduate research can be a lonely and disheartening business. In earlier times – in kinder times – this probably wouldn't have been a fatal mistake because the world smiled sweetly on bright young things with firsts from Oxford. But today's climate is different. Andrew was clearly worried – he'd been unemployed for six months and the prospects for his immediate future didn't look so good. As he put it, 'Oxford degrees stand you in good stead for the job I don't want or wouldn't be socially equipped to deal with – the City, the senior Civil Service, merchant banks and so on. I'm looking for a job in teaching again because it's one of the more classless of the professions.'

I asked Andrew what class he thought he belonged to and he gave a wry smile. He remembered that when he used to go back home from Oxford at vacations, he'd tell his friends he'd just got back from college – Worcester – he never mentioned that he was attending Oxford University. It sounded too snobbish. In terms of class, he said he was definitely 'not working-class any longer, although it's the only community I ever really felt I fitted into, but I'm not entitled to belong to it any longer because of my education.' But he found himself without money, without a middle-class network of friends – his school friends had long gone (even John's school friends in Clay Cross had gone – one joined the army, one got a job in another part of the country), his university friends had gone on to the jobs for which they were always intended. He even found himself without the desire to continue or exercise his learning – 'the M.Litt put me right off reading German.' So Andrew was in limbo. Clever, articulate and personable he may have been, but in limbo nonetheless. 'I suppose when I get a job,' said Andrew, 'I'll be middle-class, but at the moment I'm suffering from social disorientation, I think I'm still emotionally working-class if you know what I mean.'

Perhaps the saddest thing about some of the unemployed graduates I spoke to isn't that they didn't get the jobs they'd been aspiring to for the previous decade, but that, with the onset of unemployment, the desire to learn seemed to evaporate. Formal education is, after all, founded on the principle of competition – when the competitive element is removed, the process of learning may lose a good deal of its appeal. Andrew competed at school and got to Oxford, he competed at Oxford and got a first, but now he was unemployed. He could still compete for jobs – he could draw up the best CV ever seen – but the subject he studied intensively is unfortunately now very secondary. I asked one unemployed graduate in modern languages and politics what he read. 'Not a lot,' he said. 'What about French literature – Sartre, Camus?' 'No, I never read literature, it wasn't part of my course.' University students are taught to compete, they're then blinkered and persuaded to jump a whole series of hurdles. When some of them get to the finish, they forget to take the blinkers off and they get lazy; all desire for locomotion, let alone running, has gone.

Another striking feature of the graduates I spoke to was how they attributed responsibility for their predicament. Talk to unemployed steel-workers about their situation and the first thing you notice is that their anger goes outwards and ever upwards. They *know* they're not really to blame, and they'll tell you so. The unemployed graduates I spoke to didn't think like this. If you ask them why they think they're unemployed, they'll not generally talk about government policy, (mis)management in education, or the recession; they'll personalise their failure, internalise it. 'It's the poor quality of my written applications,' they'll say. 'My CV wasn't up to scratch.' 'I did the wrong course.' Grammar-school boys are reared on the fine principle of accepting responsibility for their actions and credit for their accomplishments and achievements. They accept responsibility for every-thing, including their failure, oh so readily. They get very depressed as a consequence.

The collective consciousness of the BA (Hons.)

Not all unemployed graduates, of course, find themselves isolated when their courses finish. If you look around Britain today, you can find complete social units who have lived together as students, who have graduated together and who have failed to find jobs together. Students who have perhaps lived together for as long as three years and who have become close, supportive friends. Students who have helped each other through the rigours of finals (while competing simultaneously) and who can support each other through the rigours of unemployment.

I talked to three female graduates who had lived together since 1980. They were all social science graduates who had been unemployed since June 1983 – Jane, Sue and Melanie. The first thing I noticed about these graduates was that they didn't have the aura of depression which characterises many graduates in a similar situation. All were Sheffield University graduates and now lived in Sheffield but originally came from different parts of the country (Hemel Hempstead, Surrey, etc.). 'It's a great place to be unemployed,' said Sue, and Melanie added, 'The bus fares are so cheap – you can get into the country for 12p – we went on a lot of picnics during the summer in the fine weather.'

Apart from the absence of a debilitating depression, the other thing that struck me immediately was how busy they kept themselves. John had described life on the dole as like being in a coma, but here were some ex-students who were far from comatose. Jane, for example, was doing two courses, a typing course and a course on advice work, and in addition she was doing voluntary work in an advice centre and working on a voluntary basis in the Peace Shop in Sheffield (her father, by the way, is an army colonel). Sue was also doing a typing course, she helped in a school for maladjusted children, worked in the Peace Shop and helped in a youth club in Hyde Park Flats in Sheffield. (Hyde Park Flats is a notable area of social deprivation – Sue wouldn't have come across such flats in Hemel Hempstead.) Melanie worked in the Peace Shop and often spent lunchtimes working on the disarmament society bookstall. Together they formed a nucleus, a cell, of social commitment which shaped their days on the dole. For them it wasn't long afternoons of rerun westerns and *Play School*. I asked Sue to map out a typical week of her life on the dole. Her previous week ran something like this:

Monday morning	I usually spend at home.
afternoon	I work in the Peace Shop.
Tuesday ⎫ Wednesday ⎭	We went to an action in East Anglia. A peace camp was held for two days outside an RAF base. I've been to Greenham a few times. The women are great – just like us but the news cameras always pick out the oddest.
Thursday ⎫ Friday ⎭	I work on a voluntary basis in a school for maladjusted children.
Saturday	If there isn't a demo I'll go to a jumble sale and buy some clothes – I got this gabardine in a jumble sale.
Sunday	I'll do some sewing and knitting.

In the evenings I'll do my typing course or go to political meetings in the Students' Union. I'm a member of the Women for Disarmament Group, the University Disarmament Society, Sinn Fein and the University Anarchist Group. That week I also went to a public meeting for CND and a Grenadian Fellowship meeting.

Now the interesting thing about Sue's week is that (1) it was so full; (2) it consisted of a variety of practical activities (such as the typing course), commendable socially committed activities and a multitude of political activities; and (3) the political activities were arranged in the kind of classic and recognisable configuration that is reminiscent of the student radicals of fifteen years ago. (A kind of far-left-of-centre hamper – buy one, you get the lot. And rather a full hamper at that.) Sue clearly felt strongly about many of the issues. From a comfortable middle-class life in Hemel Hempstead, she had been changed by life at university and by life in a northern industrial town. What is perhaps interesting here is that in earlier times, Sue, a good graduate with an upper second-class degree, would have been propelled into a promising career, probably without time to linger, to brood, to reflect or to protest. Even as a student she hadn't had nearly as much time to explore the social and ideological jungles she found around her. But as an unemployed graduate she had the time, the energy and the motivation to do it. And, in addition, the credentials. The credentials deriving from her transition from privileged, middle-class schoolgirl and privileged middle-class university student to unemployed underdog in a series of easy moves. Her parents would have liked to see her settling down to a career, but she was happy at the moment with the work she'd got.

Jane, Sue and Melanie had become very close. They were all aware of how much they'd changed in the past few years, in terms of both their attitudes and their appearance. They came to university in C & A pencil skirts and Wallis tops but discarded them for jumble-sale coats and dresses and dungarees. The degree of transformation from then to now and the degree of congruence in their 'individuality' from one to another was striking.

But what about the future? How long would they stay together? Would they move in search of jobs? What kinds of jobs would they be prepared to accept? How long would the cell continue? The answers came back thick and fast. Sue said she was deliberately unemployed at the moment, but aimed to start working in Northern Ireland in the new year on a project to bring Protestant and Catholic children together. Jane would have liked a career in the social services. 'But failing that,' she said, 'I would take a job that was obviously for money, such as a checkout girl in a supermarket. I would never do something like a management course or a sales-rep job or some other compromise career.' And similarly Melanie, who had worked selling hamburgers – 'No one would think I was doing that for a career' – wouldn't consider any of the compromise careers, even if they were readily available.

Sigmund Freud, in his book *Civilization and its Discontents*, suggested that work is a person's strongest tie to reality. For the most part, the sixties' middle-class student radical activist eventually found a career and settled down to the reality of prosperous middle-class life, the angst of promotion and the struggle for material reward. It's amazing how many of today's thrusting entrepreneurs were yesterday's thrusting revolutionaries. But what about the eighties' middle-class student radical without that particular tie? Without that socially sanctioned bond (or form of bondage)? Indeed, what reality will they eventually find? The reality of Hemel Hempstead, or the reality of Hyde Park Flats?

Young, single and homeless

Wayne had worked in Tesco's. He had to get up at 7.30 to get there in the morning. His mates, he said, were out boozing at nights and they could have a lie-in. They were all on the dole. Wayne decided he was missing out, so he packed up work and stopped paying housekeeping to his mother. His father kicked him out. 'We never got on anyway,' Wayne said, 'but I guess I deserved it. I lived in a park in Sheffield for four weeks – it was bloody cold – it was October. One of my friends used to bring me old newspapers to put down my trousers. One afternoon, I met one of my father's friends. He brought me home for a cup of tea. While he was making it I nicked a fiver and a watch off his dresser. He got the police, but he didn't press charges.

He just wanted his watch back. My father worked shifts so I used to nip home in the evenings for my tea and then out again. It was four weeks before a mate I hadn't seen for a long time told me about a night shelter in Sheffield. I moved in there.'

Lorraine was sixteen but looked much younger. The first tentative applications of make-up, inexpertly applied, made her look like a child dressing up, pretending to be an adult. She had a slight speech impediment and was shy and unsure of herself. Her parents had picked on her because of her slight imperfection. She became the family annoyance, the scapegoat. Her father battered her. She had to leave home. She was now in a hostel for homeless teenagers.

John was a trainee hairdresser. He was seventeen, young and trendy. His parents were very religious. They didn't approve of his choice of life style or his choice of career. There had been a lot of tension in the family as they had tried to make him conform to their values and standards. He was beaten by his father on a number of occasions, and arrived at a night shelter badly marked. 'He wouldn't take his shirt off at first,' said the warden. 'It took me a while to work out why.'

Homelessness is on the increase, especially among the young. We know a little of the reasons. The Department of the Environment produced a report in 1981 called 'Single and Homeless' based on a survey of seven different local authorities. Among the young, parental disputes and family break-up were identified as the principal reasons for their losing their last secure home. What was alarming about the report was the identification of cycles of homelessness, with the majority of the young single homeless living in a variety of temporary accommodations and insecure homes. Few had managed to set up independent homes successfully. Homelessness, like cancer, develops and spreads.

It is impossible to put a precise figure on the extent of the homelessness problem. Impossible because to get even an approximate figure one would have to trawl all the parks and derelict buildings for those sleeping rough (called 'skippering'), tour all the emergency night shelters and hostels for homeless people, visit all the dosshouses and bed-and-breakfast dives and, in addition, go around neighbourhoods interviewing people to determine who was putting friends up. Nevertheless, it is possible to spot potential trends from the figures that are available. Centrepoint, the emergency night shelter in Soho, reported a 40 per cent increase in requests for admission from 1978 to 1981. In Sheffield, the number of people who approached the Housing Department claiming to be homeless more than doubled in the same period. Roundabout, an emergency night shelter in Sheffield for young people between sixteen and twenty-one, which opened in 1977, reported 153 people using it a year later (102 male, 51 female), and 247 last year – a 61 per cent increase in a five-year period. The proportion of girls using the night shelter had more than doubled in the same period. The Sheffield branch of CHAR (the Campaign for the Homeless and Rootless) rang round all the night shelters and hostels in Sheffield on one particular night in February 1984. They discovered a total of 362 single homeless people and 33 families (which included 53 children). And that was just on one arbitrary night in the coldest month of the year in a city of half a million. It is a major problem and a growing one, especially among the young.

There are a number of specific problems for young people. Council accommodation is difficult for them to acquire because they are not considered vulnerable under the Housing (Homeless Persons) Act, 1977, and therefore are not viewed as a priority group on the Housing Department's waiting list. In addition, young people under eighteen can't get council accommodation and, until recently, couldn't put their name on a council waiting list (the age limit of eighteen has now been lowered to sixteen in Sheffield). Furniture and household equipment also take both time and money to acquire. Young homeless people usually have little of either of these valuable resources. Grants are available from the DHSS but these are difficult to get. The alternative to council housing – private accommodation – is often too expensive for young people, and landlords are very reluctant to accept tenants who are unemployed. Consequently, the young single homeless have to turn to night shelters, hostels and bed-and-breakfast dives or derelict houses.

So what kinds of accommodation is available to young homeless people? I visited one emergency night shelter in Sheffield, Roundabout, and the Granville Road project offering longer-term accommodation. Both deal with single homeless young people between sixteen and twenty-one. (Roundabout, in emergency cases, will allow a fifteen-year-old to stay.)

Roundabout is both an emergency night shelter, open from 8 pm to 9 am for people who present themselves at the door, and an adjoining house of eight bedsits. The night shelter can accommodate seven (four in one room, three in another), but the number can vary in practice between two and twelve (couches are available). It costs £4 for a bed for the night but Audrey Waters, the warden, stressed that 'no one would be refused admission if they had no money' (at least for three consecutive nights). The maximum stay in the night shelter is two weeks; in the bedsits, one year (the licence renewable on a quarterly basis). Roundabout provides detailed statistics of the young people who use their facilities. In 1983, for instance, 247 young people spent a total of 1684 nights in the night shelter (the bedsits are in constant use and in great demand). The majority of people who use Roundabout hear about it through the grapevine or see Roundabout's adverts in youth centres. However, a proportion were also referred by the police, the Probation Service, the Family and Community Services Department, the Samaritans, the Salvation Army, even by British Rail. Nearly three-quarters of the boys who used Roundabout in 1983 were offenders, but only one third of the girls. If anyone is violent on the premises they are banned – for life, if necessary. (This has only happened twice since it opened.) Roundabout refuse admission to anyone under the influence of drink, drugs or, more commonly, glue. They are told to come back next day when they've sobered up. (I'm not sure what the correct expression is for glue here.)

When I visited the night shelter, it had five residents – four boys and one girl. Two of the lads had come to Roundabout after a period of 'skippering', after they'd left home because of rows. One lad had come straight to Roundabout after being thrown out of his home for getting into trouble with the police. The other lad had had a row with his family and then with the friends he'd moved in with. The girl had had a row with her mother and her new stepfather. So here they were. Belongings in Adidas sports bags or polythene carrier bags. There are no lock-up facilities at the shelter and petty pilfering, according to the warden, is rife. Belongings can, however, be left in polythene bags in the office. The shelter is locked all day, so the temporary residents have to find something to do all day long. As the warden pointed out, 'Sunday is a terrible day'. Tensions can also run high. One skinhead who stayed at the shelter, with HATE tattooed on the knuckles of his left hand and LOVE on the knuckes of his right hand, complained in a private moment about one of the drop-in centres in town. 'You play spot-the-white man in there.' The skinhead had moved from Plymouth to Sheffield. 'But I've only been in three fights since I came to Sheffield, which isn't bad really.' 'No,' I said, 'I suppose it isn't.' The lad in the bed next to his was a West Indian. You could see it wasn't going to be a comfortable night.

After the two weeks in Roundabout the trouble really begins. The lucky ones may get into one of the bedsits; the majority can't, of course. (A major role of the staff at Roundabout is to help them find some longer-term accommodation.) Only a fifth return home after their stay. The rest move in with friends, find a bedsit or a bed-and-breakfast place, get a council flat or leave Sheffield – sometimes to be homeless elsewhere. Roundabout's statistics have one note of optimism – only one person last year went back to sleeping rough after his stay.

The trouble isn't over for those who get bedsits or council accommodation. Betty Horton, from the Home Finding Unit of the Family and Community Services Department, said, 'It's one thing getting a young person a flat, it's another thing getting them to look after it, and themselves in it.' Living in a flat – cooking, cleaning, keeping it in order, paying the rent and finding the money for it, saving up for furniture, getting on with the other occupants and the neighbours – involves a set of skills which most of us take for granted. 'But,' Betty Horton said, 'many of these homeless youngsters haven't acquired them.' CHAR in Sheffield had been pushing for a 'homemaking' scheme for workers within the Housing Department to help young people settle into tenancies, to guide them through the Social Security maze and to assist them in setting up home. (A similar scheme was already working in Glasgow and in several other major cities.) Some people, however, don't see the problem or the need. Sheffield's *Morning Star* newspaper said in an editorial in April 1984, 'Young people do not need well-meaning snoopers telling them how to suck eggs.' It went on, 'Leaving home is a great experience for most young people.' It failed to see that for many, it isn't. Sucking eggs is one thing, understanding the Social Security system in order to get the money to buy them, being able to cook them and tidy away the shells afterwards is something else.

The Granville Road Homelessness Project is an attempt to smooth the transition from emergency night shelter to independent life in one's own accommodation. It offers accommodation for up to one year, mainly for teenagers between sixteen and eighteen. It has room for eight. The young people have a key to the front door and a key to their own bedroom. 'The aim of the project,' said Ruth Wallis, the warden, 'is to encourage and teach the youngsters to live independently but under some degree of supervision.' Ruth acted a lot like a surrogate mother – indeed some residents quite unselfconsciously called her 'mother'. 'It's easier than being their natural mother,' she said, 'you can view them more objectively.'

When I visited the project, it had four boys and four girls. Two of the boys came as dedicated glue sniffers. Ruth had to play the role of counsellor. 'When Jason came he was right into sniffing glue so we talked a bit and he said he'd stop, but he still sniffed glue; so we talked a bit more and he still sniffed it. In the end, he did stop – he gets drunk now instead.' The glue sniffers' parents (or foster parents in one case) couldn't tolerate them in the end. The other two lads – as were the four girls – were also there as a result of family breakdown. One girl had been ostracised by her family because she had a coloured boyfriend. Another was ostracised because of her speech impediment.

At Granville Road, they got the opportunity to learn some basic skills. One cupboard had holes punched in it after one resident had a temper tantrum. 'They have to learn to channel their aggression,' Ruth said. The kitchen had the remains of a pudding on the ceiling as a reminder of one resident's attempt at cooking. Ruth recognised the huge responsibility on her shoulders. For most of the kids, it's make-or-break time. Family life has failed them, or they have failed it. The easy options beckon. 'One lad used to flog stolen goods to the window cleaner. We couldn't do anything with him. He ended up in court.'

I heard that one girl when she came was on the fringe of prostitution. 'I don't know what it means, though' – Ruth laughed – 'whether you do it and don't get paid or you don't do it and you do get paid. We've had girls staying here physically pursued by pimps. I've told them to clear off.'

It's the last chance for many, in a different sort of family with the rules relaxed (residents can come and go as they please, and have a boyfriend or girlfriend staying with them for two consecutive nights in any one week). They need to develop new rules and standards about what is and isn't acceptable. 'They have to learn to live with others, to be considerate,' Ruth said, 'that blasting music in the middle of the night isn't on. On the other hand, some of them accept a bit too much – we've had a lot of trouble with girls being beaten up by their boyfriends. They've seen it at home and don't think too much of it. I have to persuade them that this isn't necessarily right or natural.'

Apart from the freedom, the teenagers often find themselves with money in their pockets for the first time. The vast majority are unemployed and they get a boarder's rate of £71 a week from Social Security; this leaves them £36 after the rent is paid. They have to feed themselves out of this, but it is still a lot of money for the average sixteen-year-old. Ruth stressed that they have to learn to spend it wisely, but some clearly don't. When I was there, the two glue sniffers in their stretch denims and Wrangler T-shirts were joking to each other about how they behave when the Social Security money arrives. 'He's always acting the big man with the Hamlets and the whiskies,' one said. One girl asked for a cigarette and insisted on a Benson and Hedges. Paul Young leered down at them from a poster on the wall.

Time was also a problem. Ruth said that the majority didn't get up until the afternoon and complain about having to get up one morning a week to sign on the dole. I asked one girl what she did with her time. 'What did you do yesterday, for example?' I enquired. 'Oh, got some green spray and sprayed it all over my face and head with a friend. We had to get a taxi home because we didn't want anybody to see us.' The remains of the green spray were clearly visible on her neck beside a large love bite. Ruth added when she had left the room, 'You always know when she's got up – she plays her favourite record, "Words Don't Come Easy", over and over again.'

But Ruth had to cut through this superficial gloss – no matter how irritating and off-putting – to get right beneath the surface. 'You should see her in the middle of the night – frightened and alone. That's when it really hurts, being without a permanent home. And I do worry about the future for them. What future have some of them got? And what would they be doing if it wasn't for the project?'

A history of homelessness

In everyday talk, we speak of an individual's 'life of crime' or 'history of mental illness', expressions which suggest longevity, even permanence. On the other hand homelessness is usually seen as a temporary state. But, in reality, a 'life of homelessness' or 'history of homelessness' seems not uncommon – like crime, or mental illness, it clings. Homelessness is on the increase, especially among the young. The principal cause seems to be tension at home. Unemployment undoubtedly plays its own little role; as one young homeless person put it to me, 'If you're all on Social, you can't afford to go out, so there's bound to be tension'. One warden of a hostel for homeless people said, 'They don't make houses the size they used to, people cramped in a small house all day are bound to get on each others' nerves.' Whatever the reason, rows develop and the young person frequently leaves. The short-term prospects are bleak enough – sleeping rough, finding an emergency shelter, moving into a hostel – but what about the long-term prospects? As a Department of Environment report, published in 1981 and based on a survey of seven different local authorities, pointed out, the majority of the young, single homeless spend considerable time living in a variety of temporary and insecure accommodations. Few manage to set up independent homes successfully.

So what happens to young people in the midst of a life of homelessness? I talked to three individuals, all in their mid-twenties. Lee left home after a row with his dad. He slept rough for three weeks in a park in Sheffield. It was September. His friend used to bring him food from home. A social worker whom he met by accident in the park told him about an emergency night shelter in Sheffield – Roundabout. He went to Roundabout, and got one of their bedsits for six months. At one point he tried moving to Yarmouth with another bloke and two girls. One of the girls gave him £200 for safe keeping. He left them all stranded. He got six months in Norwich prison. After he got out of prison, he moved back to Roundabout. He got a job as a glass collector in a nightclub and found some digs. Things were looking up. He was told by his employer that he would be considered for a trainee manager's position. But then he had an argument with his landlord and he packed his digs up. He went to work as usual that day and, at the end of the night, got chatting to one of the regular customers. Lee told him about his predicament, and John said he would put him up. John lived in a terraced house in Crookes, in Sheffield – Lee noticed that John was visited a lot by a West Indian whom Lee just calls 'the Jamaican'.

'The Jamaican and John used always to have little silver packages on the table, but when I came into the room, they'd always gather them up very quickly. After a while they showed me what was in them – "Paki black" and "red Leb". John asked me if I'd be interested in taking four packets down to the Students' Union for a guy. He said he'd give me seven pounds. I said it sounded OK to me – not bad for an hour's work. After a while I used to go to Newcastle and Birmingham to fetch some – a 'weight' at a time. It cost £360. I used to get £30 a go profit. I was making three trips a week. It was worth quite a bit and I felt quite flash. But then one of the dealers got busted in the Students' Union. I thought things were getting a bit risky so one night I just buggered off with the float – £280. I went to my granddad's in Edinburgh for a couple of weeks. After about three weeks I came back to Sheffield, to Roundabout, but they said I'd been there enough so they sent me to Pat Moss House – a probation hostel which had some space. John, in the meantime, had been going round pubs asking people if they knew where I was. He traced me to Pat Moss House – he'd got the address off a girl from the dole office – he said he was looking for a close friend and she gave him the address because she fancied him. John told me I had to leave Pat Moss House and come back and live with him. He told me I had to work the debt off. I did it in four months doing property repairs for Pakistanis in Tinsley. After I left John's I moved back to Roundabout. Then I met Carol, who's now my wife.'

Carol's history up to this point was very different. She had never been in trouble with the police (three-quarters of the boys who used Roundabout last year were offenders, but only one-third of the girls). Her mother had kicked her out for coming in late. She was sixteen. She went to live with an aunt and an uncle. At the time she was working in a shop. But her aunt thought that Carol and her husband were having an affair, so she kicked her out. 'We weren't,' said Carol, 'we were just close – he didn't have any daughters.' Kicked out not in any metaphorical sense – she was literally kicked out without her shoes and socks. She spent a week sleeping rough. 'I spent most of my time hanging about a bus stop,' she said. A friend told her to go to the Probation Service. 'I said "what for?" – I've never been in trouble.' But the Probation Service told her about Roundabout. There she met Lee. Together they got a council flat in Hyde Park Flats. Lee had made things up with his dad, and Carol and Lee started to set up house. They bought a suite, bedding, pots and pans, TV, fridge and so on. But one day Lee spotted the Jamaican at the flats.

'I couldn't go back,' he said. 'I was terrified – I hadn't paid him his half of the float.' So they sold some of their electrical equipment and gave the rest of their belongings to a friend for taking their key back to the council. They moved to King's Lynn. There they got lodgings. 'It was a disgrace,' said Carol, 'four blokes in one room – tramps and that – and there were bedbugs. Roundabout always had clean bedding.' They left King's Lynn because neither of them could get a job, and moved to Southampton. Things again improved. Lee got a job as a grill chef and Carol got two cleaning jobs (an hour a day each) and she was signing on. Lee was taking home £85 a week, Carol £24 from her cleaning jobs and she was getting Social Security. 'This was the best of times,' Lee said, 'we would go out for meals and everything. But the inevitable happened – Carol got pregnant.'

She wanted to go back to Sheffield but they had nowhere to stay so Carol moved in with her mother and Lee stayed at a friend's. But her mother threw her out again – 'We were always arguing about money,' Carol said. Together they moved to Roundabout before getting a council flat – their current home. They were married in 1982. They hated their present home. 'There's nowhere for the kid to play and there's loads of break-ins – we sold the music centre to buy an Alsatian.' (In the row of eight houses there are two Alsatians, two Dobermans and one mongrel.) They'd applied for a new house. 'I've told the Social this house is ruining our marriage,' Lee said. 'I can't stand this house and when I had a bit of drink inside me a couple of weeks back, I went berserk with a hammer – I smashed the colour TV, the cooker and the cocktail bar. I hit Carol as well, but not with the hammer – she called the police but when they got here they said there was nothing they could do – it was a family dispute. It feels like a prison here with that fence at the back. The factory behind us put it up because they said we were throwing rubbish over the wall. We weren't, though.' I asked what they did all day. Lee said he spent a lot of time redecorating – repairing the damage he did with the hammer. Carol kept the place tidy.

'I had an interview arranged for about a week ago,' Lee said, 'but I didn't go. I'm sure I would have got the job as well – it was a porter's job. I got all dressed up, but I didn't have any shoes. I've just got trainers. Carol said it wouldn't matter, but I told her everything matters in interviews. When I was in Pat Moss House, I got a £96 clothing grant but I haven't had any clothing money since. I can't afford any new shoes on what we get – £37.50 from the Social and £6.50 family allowance a week' (plus their rent, gas and electricity paid). I noticed that they both smoked Marlboro and I asked how much they spent on these a week. 'Oh, seven pounds between us,' Lee said, 'but it's our only pleasure.' As we finished talking, Lee complained about the system. 'It's all wrong,' he said. 'We've applied for a removal grant but they said we're not entitled to one – you have to be disabled or just out of hospital.' 'But couldn't your father help you move?' I enquired. 'He might be able to do it in his works van on a Saturday morning for us,' Lee said, 'but the Social should cough up.'

Kevin was their closest friend. He was also twenty-four. He had been put in a children's home when he was thirteen. He walked out on his foster parents in Chichester when he was seventeen, after an argument. He got a job as a trainee chef which was a live-in position. After six months, he got the sack. 'I didn't get on with the manager,' he said. He then got a job in a fair and travelled with it to London – to Croydon, where it was based in winter. He left it with a mate. They took £50 worth of tools, wires and bulbs with them. They slept in the YMCA for one night and then roughed it in Croydon for three weeks. They slept in multi-storey car parks, derelict houses and in the middle of roundabouts, under bushes. They didn't have any sleeping bags or blankets – just the clothes they walked around in. It was November and it snowed. Kevin said he knew nothing about Social Security at the time and so he nicked – cakes, biscuits and sandwiches – to survive. 'That's how I got into thieving,' he proclaimed (temporarily forgetting about the tools from the fair). During the day, he and his mate would walk around Croydon. 'It's a dump – like a smaller version of Sheffield. We'd look for somewhere good to kip – we'd wake up in the mornings with the bloody birds singing in our earholes.' He and his mate never made it into the centre of London.

Eventually, they met a lad from Mansfield who invited them to his house for a week. The police lifted them as soon as they arrived in Mansfield, but let them go. 'We were a bit scruffy,' said Kevin. He signed on for the first time in Mansfield but there were few jobs going, so he and his friend moved on to Chesterfield. They didn't have anywhere to stay for the first two nights but eventually they got a bedsit. In Chesterfield, they did some thieving. They were caught nicking a bottle of Blanc de Blancs from Marks and Spencer, and followed home by a store detective. 'I didn't even like it,' said Kevin. 'I had one mouthful and spat it out. I don't even drink. It's lucky the police didn't search the place, though. We had stolen clothes, radios and watches all over the place.' He got fined £30 for the wine, of which he paid £6. A few months later the police accused him of nicking lead from roofs. He insisted he didn't do it – 'I never do anything like that, I'm too big a coward' – but they warned him to leave town. He decided on Sheffield. Steel City – there's bound to be jobs there, he thought.

As soon as he got to Sheffield, he met a guy at the bus station who told him about Roundabout. 'It was right fantastic,' he said, 'but there were all kinds there – some were right snotty teenagers who didn't get on with their parents. Others were trying to get away from the law.' He got a job in a Wimpy bar as a pot washer and met a girl in Roundabout. She had the bedsit opposite his. She moved back home to her parents and he went with her. 'It was frightening,' he said, 'I never knew what to say or do. I got the sack from Wimpy for talking when I shouldn't have been, so I was signing on again. Her parents only charged me £10 a week for food and lodgings. This left me with £18 in my pocket. Eventually she went back with her old boyfriend so I had to move out and back to Roundabout.'

Here he met another girl and they got a bedsit together in Pitsmoor. 'And then the inevitable happened,' he said, 'she got sent down for seven months for fiddling the Social. She was two months pregnant at the time and she had the baby inside.

'When she got out, we moved in with her parents for two weeks, and then we got a council house. We got married – it lasted for two weeks. She found another bloke.' Kevin had his son Stephen living with him for a while but had to give him up. He's hoping to go to court to fight for custody of his child. In the meantime, he took his Alsatian, Sash, for long walks. He was unemployed. He was bitter about most things and critical of the system. 'People say we get too much money on the Social, but let them try it – I had to save up to go and see *Sudden Impact*. And the Queen is a right waste of money. Fair enough, she has to pay her own household bills. How much does she get now? Twice as much as the miners, I bet – at least two to three hundred quid a week for herself . . . The future doesn't look bright. Soon computers will be doing everything. One thing I do agree with, though, is cruise missiles – they're not wasting money. And the more missiles, the more people there'll be to guard them – the more jobs there'll be. Fair enough, it's only the army that guards them – but then the more people will be accepted in the army.'

And Kevin's strange logic gradually unfolded until his whole world view was laid out and tangled round my feet, and his. And as he got up I couldn't but notice the word HATE tattooed inexpertly on the back of his hand. He was the second person I'd seen that day with such a tattoo.

The management consultant

In the seventies we were always told that Britain was the *sick man* of Europe. It has been *suffering* from a recession and has endured numerous *bouts* of inflation. Mrs Thatcher chides those 'who talk and talk and talk about unemployment but say nothing about how in practical terms to *cure* it'. Trouble in the inner cities is seen by some as *symptoms* of unemployment. The nationalised industries need a *crutch* and continual assistance and, according to Mrs Thatcher, 'this has meant we have a real big *haemorrhage* on expenditure'.

The *treatment* is not going to be easy. 'We knew it would be painful, we knew it would be difficult but we cannot evade that long-term issue if we want a good future for Britain.' (Mrs Thatcher.) But worse might follow for the nationalised industries. 'We could have *cut* them off.' 'Does it really seem to be the time to say to them, "No, I'm going to chop you off at the stocking tops, when you've got a new car, you're getting enormously increased improvements in productivity and you are in fact not having more people than is necessary to do the job. You're getting rid of your wreckers."' (Mrs Thatcher talking about British Leyland in an interview with Brian Walden.) No, indeed, but the surgeon's knife is out on the table for all to see.

In this clinical economic climate with Mrs Thatcher and her cabinet as hospital chiefs, Jim Hatton is the surgeon on the spot. He has to be able to diagnose industrial problems, prescribe treatment and operate, often with some urgency. He is the director of Profile Management Consultants. The health metaphor slipped quite unselfconsciously into his speech. 'My job is to save companies and to help them survive in these difficult times' – simple as that.

He had worked in a variety of jobs in a number of towns and cities in the north of England and Scotland. In Liverpool in the fifties he worked as a design engineer for Lockheed but, he said, even then you could see the beginnings of decay. From Liverpool he moved to Manchester, which 'was a boom town in comparison'. Then he worked in an armaments factory for the Ministry of Defence but was worried that 'this might not be a future growth industry to be in'. So he moved again, to a job as chief industrial engineer at a factory in a new town – East Kilbride, south of Glasgow. 'East Kilbride,' he said, 'was full of English, American and Continental factories with no tradition of local industries or Scottish management. The senior executives, like the factories, were usually imported. The managers did their stint in the wilds before going home. East Kilbride was all right to visit but that was about it. This was the wrong atmosphere for healthy growth.' His time in Scotland in the late sixties corresponded with the rise of Scottish nationalism. The workers were starting to rise up. Jim headed south – to the Potteries as production manager. From here he got into management consultancy, his apprenticeship over. He'd been busy ever since.

'The needs for management consultants are quite obvious,' he said. 'Many firms are too small to have specialists in a number of technical, manufacturing or financial areas.' So Jim or one of his colleagues might be called in to organise a production system or effect some technical changes in a factory. This is perhaps the least controversial aspect of his work. He told the story of being called in by a government agency, which he refused to name (diplomatically, as it turns out), to check the technical and commercial viability of the products made by a small firm funded by government money under one of its growth-industry schemes. The product involved high technology for North Sea oil platforms. The government had already ploughed a small amount of money into the firm and was considering a major injection of capital to develop it. So Jim Hatton was sent along to the factory only to find that it didn't exist – the 'managing director' was just working on the prototype in his greenhouse. When he reported back to the government agency, he said, the civil servants found it hard to believe him. Most factories do exist but some of their methods, he said, are every bit as surprising as the factory in the garden shed.

Perhaps the most sensitive aspect of his job is in the 'human resources' end where the job evaluation and the wage and salary structuring takes place and where, of course, advice about redundancy is given. Jim Hatton's firm was called in to rationalise the salary structure of part of the British Steel Corporation with thousands of different staff jobs. 'The first stage is to get people to write a job description – not a generic title or what they're responsible for, but what they actually do. The next stage is to come up with a sample number of jobs from the population, say between twelve and twenty-four, which acts as a bench-mark sample. You then organise a steering committee of management and unions to compare these jobs in a paired comparison situation. Using this technique you rank-order all the jobs from top to bottom in order of importance, thus you rate a policeman higher than a porter and a doctor higher than a policeman so you have the order "doctor, policeman, porter". You then do a full analytic job evaluation of each of these jobs in terms of things like responsibility, skill, training, concentration, working conditions, manual dexterity, etc. You do an MRA – a multiple regression analysis – to adjust the weightings of each of these components to make the analytic procedure correspond with the subjective paired comparison one. You then know the importance of each of the components and each job can be analysed and assessed. Everyone can be assigned a number of points, and that leads to his position in the organisation which will lead to his pay.'

'But,' I replied, 'someone might naively say that because you're going through the statistical procedure to get your analytic scheme to force it to correlate with your subjective rank-ordering, all you're doing in the long run is reiterating people's prejudices about jobs. In the abstract, everyone is going to agree that the managing director is more important than the production manager, but some companies run quite successfully without help or interference from senior management.'

'Absolutely,' Jim said.

'Oh,' I said.

'I'm prepared to accept that; it's not the way that I'd put it, of course, it's precisely what we're trying to do. What we're trying not to do is to impose our own prejudices – such as, responsibility is much more important than working conditions – it's important for the people within the organisation to say it.'

So the man in the white coat steps in and with the technological wizardry of modern analytic methods lays your prejudices at your feet and with them your wage structure (but at least they're your own, not his).

Apart from rationalising pay structures, another major part of the human-resources aspect of management consultancy is the motivational schemes. 'Piece work,' Jim Hatton said, 'was the first generation of such schemes. The old carrot system – but that doesn't work for people who don't influence the output or the sales directly, such as the administrators. We're experimenting with PBR schemes – that's payment-by-results schemes, such as the added-value scheme, which was imported from the States – where you link the profitability of the company to the pay of the workers. This is good for corporate identity and good for profit but of course it depends critically on good industrial relations. If the employees don't trust the profitability figure, the scheme wouldn't get off the ground. When you have poor industrial relations with little trust, the more advanced remuneration schemes simply don't work. You're back to the carrot or worse.' He mentioned one multinational Dutch company, which operates with over 20,000 employees in this country and which with Jim's help had applied this scheme very successfully.

Jim Hatton had also visited Japan to see what we could learn from there. 'As far as the production systems and the quality systems go, there's nothing they can teach us. Their systems were all learned from the West and adapted to their special needs. Where of course they are special is in marketing and in their human-resources management area – their motivational structures, and the dedication of their work force. Many of the factories are organised around so-called "quality circles" which are teams of shop-floor workers who try to innovate improvement in quality. They elect a leader – usually one of their peers – and they all sit around a table with one of those bloody flowers in a pot and have brainstorming sessions. They then approach the management with their ideas and they make available the resources to implement them – design engineers etc. They have a league table representing the success of each of these small groups and at the end of the week the group with the best results are paraded on stage in front of all the workers and everyone applauds. They're the group of the week, and they're awarded an armband or a badge of merit. The amazing thing is that there's no financial reward at all for this – none. Just the esteem of their colleagues. It's also interesting that this doesn't work in Japanese factories abroad – not just in Britain and the West, but even in Japanese factories in the Far East such as Korea. It's not that it fails to work in Britain because we're not enough like the Japanese – it's the difference between the Japanese and everybody else. Like the ancient Greeks – everybody who wasn't a Greek was a barbarian. That's the crucial thing here.'

Jim Hatton pointed out that they have tried it in this country but with some changes. The first is that the 'quality circles' aren't necessarily about quality any more but about quantity and cutting cost. The second is that the democratic 'quality circles' no longer elect a peer as leader – 'It's better to build in a supervisory structure and have the foreman as leader of the group,' Jim said. 'The other important difference is that the success of the group has to be linked to pay. You could imagine trying to stage one of those award ceremonies with the funny armbands in Merseyside. The men would laugh in your face.'

And Jim sat back in his chair – himself clearly a survivor, from the decay of Merseyside in the fifties to the relative good health of Manchester in the eighties. 'Competition is the name of the game,' he said, 'and everyone including the workers has to face up to that fact. It's the survival of the fittest.'

3 · Bring on the night

**Bring on the night
I couldn't stand another hour of daylight.**
Sting, © 1979 Virgin Music

Dancing the night away

Steel was always the hard centre of commercial life in Sheffield – the foundation stone of its precarious commercial superstructure. When the steel firms found themselves in trouble, so did the scrap men, the car dealers, the fancy pubs for the scrap men, the fancy perfume shops for the car dealers' wives, and the clubs for all of them after work. A long complex daisy chain of commercial association was suddenly cut with giant economic shears wielded by God knows who. Too much work makes Jack a dull boy, too little work makes Jack an even duller one. Leisure costs and Jack simply couldn't afford it any more.

The clubs and casinos escaped for a while. 'Live today, for tomorrow we die/go bankrupt/are unemployed' drove people out for the evening for a drink or a flutter. But the recession was bound to catch up and sink its teeth in. When it did, it went for what many people saw as the fat rump of the leisure industry – the casinos and the expensive nightclubs. The profits of casinos in the provinces fell sharply with the onset of the recession (although this was partly due to the increased tax on casinos). Those in London continued to rise, protected by the steady influx of visitors from countries out of reach of the mad dog of recession. Clubs suffered badly as well. Several smart clubs in Sheffield opened with much publicity and ballyhoo and are expensively decorated but empty most nights. Expensive gambles that failed. They have to keep pretending it hasn't happened and have yet another opening night. But some clubs have escaped the squeeze and manage to pack them in night after night. Why?

Dave Allen must know the answer. He's a survivor. He's a local lad who is now in his forties. He started in the fifties with Viners, a cutlery firm (now

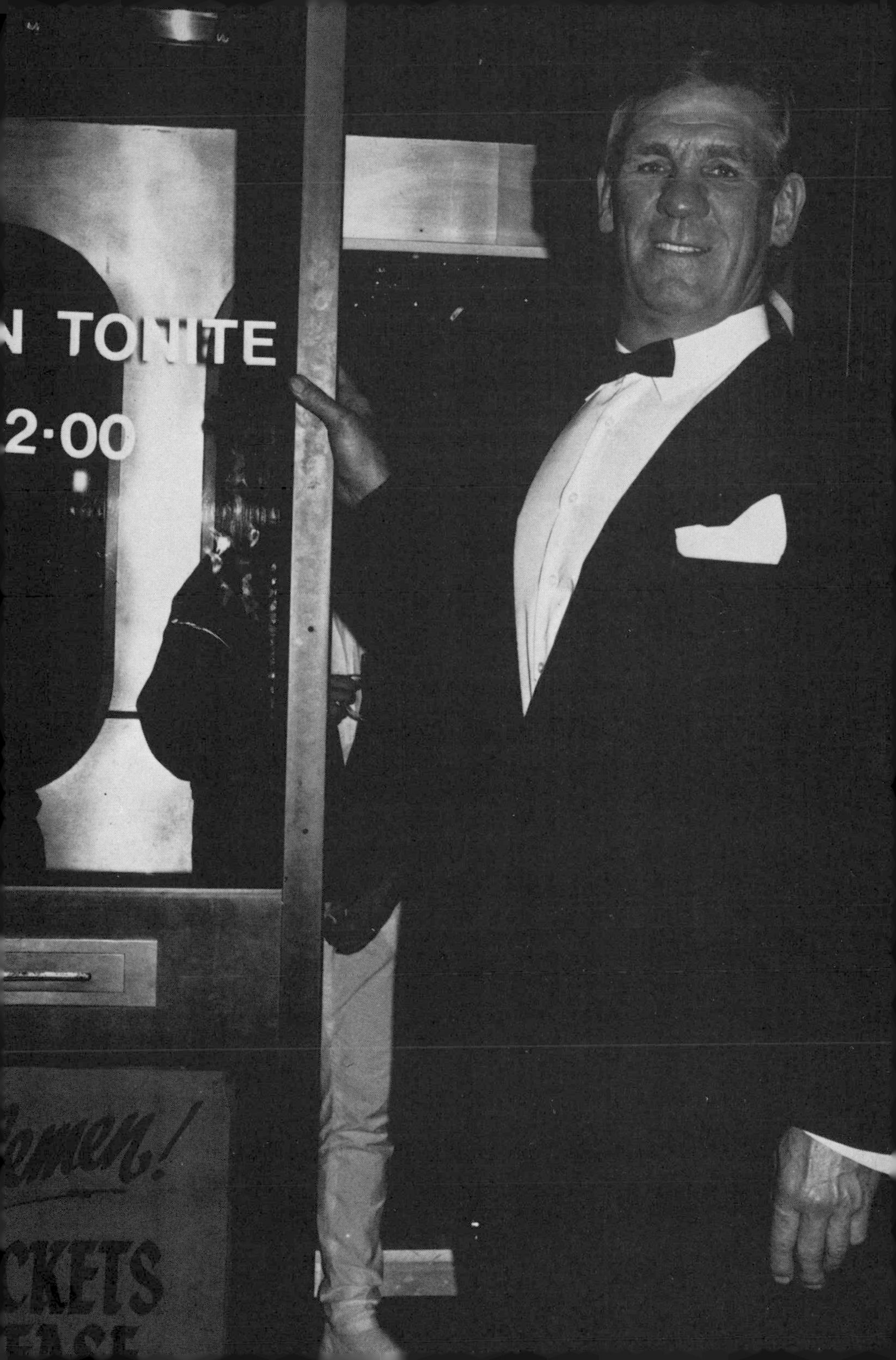
N TONITE
2·00
CKETS

bankrupt), and went on to become a band leader with the Mecca organisation (the nightclub side of whose business is now in grave trouble). He survived both. Now he's one of the directors and the major shareholder in A & S Entertainments, the biggest privately owned casino and nightclub company in the country, with six casinos and five nightclubs (and more in the pipeline). His company is still based in Sheffield but his operation is now expanding to the south of England. Some would say he's done more than survive. The annual turnover of the company is around the £5 million mark.

In a world of shifting fashion, Dave Allen went, he says, for 'timelessness'. He tried to market an image that wouldn't be out of fashion the next week. The image was the Martini ad suspended in freeze frame and suspended in Yorkshire of all places. Men in white suits, women in glamorous dresses. Suntans. The chink of ice. ('The first thing I did was buy three ice-making machines,' he said. 'Always plenty of ice, that's important.') Welcome to Martini Land. The Human League and ABC (both Sheffield bands) may provide some of the dance music, but Sinatra sends them home. The names of the clubs and casinos had to be right. No Locarnos, Roxys or Fiestas in Martini Land. Something with style, with panache – something French. And what's more French than Napoleon (except perhaps *liberté, egalité, fraternité*, and he didn't want any of the last two in his clubs)? The idea spawned an upmarket casino called Napoleon's, a middle-market casino called Bonaparte's and a nightclub called Josephine's.

Josephine's is 'Sheffield's ultimate nitespot' – it said so on the complimentary ticket. The ticket offered 'Nite life London style' – whatever that is – hopefully not mugging, rioting or arson, but music, bubbly, a good time. The doors opened at 9 pm – by 11 pm it was bursting. It took a good twenty minutes to thread one's way from one side of the club to the other. Solid people.

Hollywood films offered distraction to the unemployed in the thirties. The big stars with their glamour pulled them in off the streets. The big blondes in their glittering dresses. The suave sophisticated men, the champagne, the cars, the parties, the fun – fantasy land, American style. Drift off for a couple of hours. Sheffield's 'ultimate nitespot' offers a different kind of fantasy. You wear the glittering dress this time. You meet the suave sophisticated Sheffield men. Champagne by the crateful – drift off – wake up with a headache.

Bouncers guard the doorway. Big blokes, big as buses. They scrutinise you from head to toe. The management guarantee a 'select clientele'. 'Dress

A Member of Josephine's wine bar set

with style,' it warns on the door. The bouncers enforce the rules vigorously. Everyone is inspected. If they don't like the look of you, they turn you away. No longhairs, no jeans, no casual jackets, shirts must have buttons all the way down the front. In the club, men must keep their jackets on at all times. Plush carpets, mirrored walls, mirrored ceiling, flashing lights, scented loos with aftershave sitting out to be used, and an attendant to keep everything clean and to pursue the select clientele when they disappear with the aftershave. Loud disco music with a smooth DJ talking over it. On closer inspection he turned out to be a minute little person unkindly nicknamed 'Tattoo' by a rival DJ in the club, Tattoo being the dwarfish character in *Fantasy Island.*

The DJ tested the audience. 'The first girl to tell me the name of the baddie in *Buck Rogers* wins a bottle of champagne.' Someone obviously watched *Buck Rogers* and got a bottle of cheap sparkling wine, which they insisted on shaking and spraying a few dozen people with.

'Does any girl know what car James Bond drives in his latest film?' Another bottle of sparkling plonk. 'What's the most expensive perfume in the world?' Question after question – crate after crate of sparkling wine. A bottle for the most gorgeous woman in the club. A bottle for the best dancer. A bottle for the first woman to dance on stage. Two bottles if she'd strip. She did. Five bottles if she'd take everything off. She didn't.

Such a select club must contain celebrities. 'Tonight we have Alex Hurricane Higgins in the club' (during the Embassy snooker championships). 'Tonight, Steve Davis.' 'Tonight, Jackie Charlton.' 'Tonight, Bomber Graham.' 'The club where the superstars hang out,' announced the DJ proudly. Failing real celebrities, the DJ was forced to invent them or create them from more ordinary material. 'We have a superstar hairdresser in the club tonight.' One particularly bad night they even had a superstar car-stereo salesman.

'Would the owner of the Ford Cortina parked outside please move it – it's making my Rolls-Royce look shabby.' The DJ didn't own a Rolls-Royce but it didn't matter. Classical conditioning at work: associating luxury items – Rolls-Royce, Gucci, Yves Saint Laurent – with the club, without any connecting bridge of truth or web of reality. Just drop names and associate freely.

Josephine's is sexist ('Sex and booze, that's what people come for,' says Dave Allen): waitresses in leotards, go-go dancers in suspenders. Of the go-go dancers, one could dance, one couldn't. The one who could dance had a big bottom. 'Show us your tradesman's entrance,' ordered the DJ. She did.

The other go-go dancer flopped about in a fairly unrhythmic fashion – showing her tradesman's entrance at the mildest provocation. The stage on which they danced was lined with ogling men with their lower jaws undone. Occasionally the DJ invited one onto the stage to dance with the go-go dancer. 'Whip him with your feather boa,' he commanded. The nondancing go-go dancer did. The punter on stage loved it. His friends clapped. Lights, music, drink all went to his head. He started to remove his trousers. The DJ looked distinctly uneasy. Fantasy sex is one thing – this was something else. A bouncer helped the new celebrity back to his friends. The DJ dedicated the record 'Body to Body' to the go-go dancer who could dance. 'She's got a body like you wouldn't believe, she can crack walnuts between her legs.' The nutcracker strode on oblivious.

Many people who go to the club are regulars – some were so regular that it was difficult to imagine what they did the rest of the day if they were up till 2.30 am every night bombarded with music and drink. Many prosperous trendy businessmen seemed to go every night, as did others with irregular or late hours of work – nurses, footballers, shop assistants, the unemployed, a wide range of incomes but here everyone could be a superstar for a little while.

Thursdays are special, 'Bride-to-be nite'. Free admission for hen parties before 10.30. Hundreds of unattached women and brides-to-be. The men pour in. On the stroke of midnight the DJ invites the brides-to-be, one at a time, onto the stage. They perch on a stool and the assistant manager puts a garter as far up their leg as he (or she) dares. They get a bottle of champagne. The assistant manager doesn't smile, he looks as if he finds the whole thing a bit distasteful and mildly embarrassing. If the woman is wearing suspenders she gets two bottles, if she's not wearing any knickers she gets five (rumour has it that this happened once). The assistant manager picks them up and spins them round, giving the club a flash. The men go on Thursdays by the score, perhaps for their last chance to see up the skirt of someone else's bride-to-be. The assistant manager can hardly pick up some of the women – big, northern lasses, legs like tree trunks, the garters snap and break. If one is particularly attractive or wearing suspenders, she is forced to stand on a stool. Head touching the roof. The assistant manager looks anxious. Afterwards all the brides-to-be take part in a lottery. First prize is £50. Second prize is a canteen of cutlery – it reminds you where you are. The only thing is, the cutlery is made of imported steel. A sign of the times.

The club also acts as a barometer of international fortunes. 'In 1978 the wine bar was crammed with the Persian lads drinking Dom Pérignon, now you can see them queuing three deep for halves of lager,' said Dave Allen. Khomeini has a lot to answer for to Dave Allen. The Iranians who managed to escape feel at home in his clubs and casinos. The Martini ad is, after all, international. Revolutions may come and go but Martini Land goes on without even a street disturbance.

Dave Allen marketed an image. And when he walks about his clubs sipping champagne, bow tie on full alert, he is the living, breathing personification of it. 'Marvellous,' he says. Super, sophisticated style in Steel City. But he's too sensible to think that you can dispense with the programmes altogether and have one interminable Martini ad on the telly. His home life isn't all burgundy and pink (like his clubs). His passion in life is racing pigeons. Dave Allen drives a Jaguar. 'After all,' he said, 'I'd look bloody ridiculous taking the pigeons out of the back of a Rolls.'

Me and my Silver Shadow

It was 12.15 am, the nightclub was already full. He made his entrance. A vision in black and gold – black silk shirt unbuttoned almost to the waist, black trousers, black shoes and gold – everywhere. Three gold medallions dangling on his chest, two gold rings on the same hand. He was about forty, his hair was cropped short, he was smoking a cigar. He walked slowly in a cool, confident manner, scanning the faces. He greeted the bouncers, they greeted him. Don Corleone was back. He walked to the wine bar and greeted the owner of the club. The owner ordered champagne. Don Corleone kept watching, he kept scanning the faces. Strangers to the club stared back at this small dark man. But Don Corleone was not what he seemed. He was just an Italian waiter from a restaurant in a northern industrial town. He hadn't any money, he hadn't even got a car. He got the bus into town with all that jewellery hanging around him. He knew the nightclub owner from way back and he'd got a free pass to the club. If he hadn't, he couldn't afford to go. But there he was – six nights a week, laden with gold, almost certainly fake. But in the dim light of the club, all that glistened was surely gold and people assumed that he was somebody. When he was standing at the bus stop during the day, with a bag of washing for the launderette, he would jump into hiding if he spotted anybody he recognised. He lived alone in a bedsitter. Luigi, the waiter, by day – Don Corleone, the somebody, by night.

Another character strode in. He was also small but he'd gone for the

sailing look. Blue double-breasted jacket with a silk handkerchief in the pocket, his tie had a crest on it. He was getting on a bit and was balding. His hair was in the Bobby Charlton style and the long strands were weaved around his bald patch. But in here there were no cruel winds to give the game away; he could relax. He walked about as if his Rolls-Royce was ready and waiting to take some lucky lady off to his yacht on a moonlit bay. But there was no yacht and no Roller, just drizzle and a J-registration Hillman Minx. There was a flat of sorts – a little terraced house full of unwashed pots and pans (he lived alone and hadn't time to do them before he went out) and aftershave. By day he was a bus conductor, by night, well, he was a randy, old, rich seadog, four hours a night, six nights a week. He'd also got a free pass. He knew the club owner from the time when the club owner still used the bus service.

Anyone who had seen Don Corleone on a bus or Lone Yachtsman in his Hillman Minx could not take them too seriously, but John was different. He was thirty-six, tanned, fit, his hair streaked blond. He looked the part in a way that Don Corleone or Lone Yachtsman didn't. They had become submerged in images from the past; his was more contemporary. John got to the club about 11.30 pm in his brown Silver Shadow. He parked it in the underground car park just by the club. The car park is used by many of the club's customers. As he was parking it, he noticed that he was being watched by a gaggle of girls emerging from a white Mini.

'Did you see that car?' a tall blonde girl with buck teeth said to her friends. John pretended not to hear and turned round and walked to the exit. He walked slowly to give them a chance to identify his features. When he had left, the girls went over and looked at the car. They peered inside; one touched the paintwork, her sweaty palm leaving a thumb print on the door. 'He must be bloody well loaded. Imagine going home in that tonight.'

John went into the club and ordered a gin and tonic. He stood by the bar. The four girls, now arranged in two sets of two (a strategic configuration for picking up men), passed him at the bar. The girl with buck teeth gave him a quick smile, as did her friend (the one who had been admiring the paintwork). They thought he might buy them a drink, but he just smiled back. They ordered four Bacardi and Cokes. It came to £4.80. John looked nonchalant. A male acquaintance came over. 'Not much in tonight,' he said. 'No, not much talent tonight,' John replied.

It was Buck Teeth's round. She glanced over at John again. He was still sipping his gin and tonic. Buck Teeth forked out another £4.80. John was making his gin and tonic last. He went to the toilet; he took his drink with him and filled it up from a quarter bottle of gin he'd been keeping in his inside jacket pocket. He came back to the bar with his glass full. Buck Teeth assumed he'd been to the other bar. He quite fancied Buck Teeth's friend and he started chatting her up. Buck Teeth hung about until her friend started touching John's arm. At this point she felt really excluded and went in search of her other two friends. 'Joanne's got off with that filthy rich man in the Rolls,' she said. 'Lucky bastard,' they replied in unison.

Joanne had finished her Bacardi. 'Would you like a drink?' she said to John and they both laughed at the suggestion and the situation. Joanne had just told John that she was unemployed (she borrowed a tenner from her mother for the evening). John had just told her that he owned a company. One of them was telling fibs. John said, 'Oh, go on then.' Joanne didn't think he was mean, she just wanted to show him that she was not after his money, which she was. John accepted the drink and made this one last as well. The manager went past and said to one of the bouncers, 'I see John's got one on.'

The evening progressed. John went to the toilet and met a friend who bought him a drink. Joanne bought herself a double while he was away. John had told her that there might be a job in his company for her. Joanne had been unemployed for three months – she was over the moon and nearly under the table. They danced to the slow music at the end. John asked her if she'd like a lift home. 'Oh, have you got a car then?' she said innocently. 'Yes, a Rolls-Royce,' he said. 'You're kidding.' 'No, I'm not. Come and see.' They left together. The manager said, 'Goodnight, sir; goodnight, madam.'

The Rolls gleamed in the artificial light. The thumb print was still there. John let her play with the electric windows. 'Can we drive round past the front of the club so that my friends can see me?' she said. They did, but her friends had gone. 'Oh, it's a real pity,' she said. John asked her where she lived. 'Upperthorpe,' she said. John knew it was five miles out and not in his direction. He gulped but didn't say anything. All the way there, at every set of traffic lights, she looked around into all the taxis, hoping to see someone she knew.

They got home about a quarter to three. She insisted on waking her mother up to show her the car. Her mother came downstairs in curlers and stared out through the curtains. 'It's a real beauty,' she said. 'Yes,' said John. The mother made tea. It wasn't exactly what John had had in mind. After he'd gone, the mother said, 'What a nice lad, success hasn't spoiled him at all. He's very down-to-earth.'

He had promised Joanne he'd ring the following Tuesday but he didn't. Joanne went round to Buck Teeth's house. 'I'm not going back to that club, it's full of rich flash bastards who treat you like shit.'

But John hadn't meant to let her down or hurt her. It was just that she lived too far out. He simply couldn't afford the petrol to Upperthorpe. If she'd lived closer, he would have taken her out. John didn't own a company; he was a van driver, married with two adolescent boys. Most of his salary went on running the car. His wife worked – she paid reluctantly for the running of their council house. He had friends in the motor trade and he had got the car at a good price about four years earlier when he'd made some money selling another car. He only used the car at night. He couldn't afford the petrol to take it to work. He ran instead – five miles there and five back. One of the new set of marathon men, but out of necessity rather than choice. And it saved him going to a trendy and expensive fitness club.

But sometimes he did score. He had a two-year relationship with a girl called Debbie who worked in the make-up section of a large department store. Her make-up was always immaculate – a perfect mask. John's mask was more subtle. She was blonde and always wore white – tight white jeans or white dresses. Men always gawped at her and John loved the attention. They would drive out to pubs in the country and leave the car in the front car park. The customers would stare. 'It's all right for bloody some,' they would say. John saw Debbie every night from 10 pm to 2 am. They were a lovely couple. People in the club would enquire when they were going to get married. At weekends, Debbie said, they would go and look at £80,000 houses. 'We'd drive up in the car, and I'd get really made up. I used to have to loan John the money for petrol.' During this time, John had his electricity cut off for nonpayment of bills. John used one set of pubs for his wife and one set for Debbie. Everyone thought that Debbie and he were the perfect couple. 'We even went looking for an engagement ring,' said Debbie, 'a £500 job, but he hadn't a bean; it was all a bit stupid. I didn't even see his wife until after we'd split up. She was all right, a bit rough but even she's too good for him. She looked at me as if I was a real tart but he always told me the marriage was finished anyway.'

John was on his own now. He still missed Debbie but her absence didn't prompt him to take his wife out instead. 'People would wonder who she was,' he said. 'And I couldn't afford it anyway.' Instead he had one or two male friends. One of his friends had got a yellow Rolls-Royce with a TV in it. 'He's really cracked it,' said John. 'He'll pick up a girl on Saturday night and instead of taking her to the pictures on Sunday – that would be four quid at least – or for a drink – nearer eight quid – they just sit in the Roller and watch TV. All he has to pay for is the petrol and sometimes he can get the girl to pay for that.'

John only ever went to one club and one might imagine that after a short period, everyone would know that he was a van driver rather than a company director. But no, that kind of news seems to travel slow. It was almost as if people wanted to believe his story, despite evidence to the contrary. For, after all, the club was founded on fantasy for the Martini set and John came as close to the image (at least in terms of appearance) in this northern town as anyone. If he wasn't what he seemed, then who was? And he could always update his story to keep just ahead of the news hounds and the bloodhounds of gossip. 'Oh yes, I used to be a van driver when I went out with Debbie, but that was before I opened my own company, and have you seen my Rolls-Royce, by the way?'

The DJ

Tony was on stage, well, not so much on stage as in a control console. But he was dressed as if he should be on stage, white suit, red carnation, voice like syrup – 'and a very good evening, ladies and gentlemen' – smooth, rich and sugary. Mid-Atlantic syrup, with the odd Yorkshire word thrown in. His feet were on the same level as the punters' heads. He looked down from his elevated station, surveying the scene, sensing the mood swings, controlling the punters' every movement; or so he liked to think. He stood surrounded by all the switches and knobs of the electronic era – a little bit of laser here, a little bit of smoke there, and of course the next record – George Benson. Again. The laser show started in time with the record. 'The new technology is great,' said Tony, 'but you can't beat the old mirrored ball, it's timeless. You even have people reflecting their lasers off the balls.' Mecca and Star Wars reconciled.

Tony Habershon (stage name Tony Day) was thirty-eight and about to retire after twenty-one years as a club disc jockey. While many DJs started in the clubs and went on to radio or even dizzier heights (for example, his friend, the highly successful Peter Stringfellow), Tony started and finished in the clubs – he stayed close to the roots. 'I did a bit of radio work in the early days,' he said, 'in the old days of the pirate stations. When Tony Blackburn was doing Radio Caroline, I was on Radio North Sea International. It wasn't very glamorous or anything, it was anchored out in the

North Sea and you only got off once a week. I was always bloody seasick. I stuck it for six months. Then I did a bit of work for Radio Hallam in Sheffield. It was nerve-racking. My opening line was "Who needs an enema when you're doing a radio programme?" and I meant it. The producer really creased up.'

Tony started as a DJ in the Locarno in Sheffield in 1963. In those days live entertainment was an essential part of the evening. Disc jockeys filled the gaps in between. Tony started part-time for Mecca. 'Things were very regimented in those days – all records were timed and classified in terms of the number of beats per minute. You played all the records in strict order. You didn't have the flexibility in those days. That was the era of Petula Clark's "Down Town", which I thought was very appropriate as the Locarno was right at the bottom end of Sheffield – down the Moor. There were three different DJs working during the same evening. At the start of my spot I'd put on the *Doctor Who* theme because nobody could dance to it. It was a way of grabbing everybody's attention.

'Clubs were very different then,' said Tony. 'There wasn't a lot of attention paid to the decor – it was more a bar and a dance floor. People didn't look for a concept or a theme for the club. Guys would stand around the dance floor ogling the girls and on the whole girls would dance if you asked them to – if only for one dance. These days the guys just go and dance beside the girls and if the girl doesn't fancy him she'll just turn her back. And if you do ask a girl these days she might just as well say "piss off". There's no obligation to have a dance. Also the guys these days are the real poseurs, finding a good spot to stand and pose and get the ladies round. In the early sixties it was the girls who posed with their vodkas and limes. (Funny, they don't drink that any more.) In the sixties it was the lads who were expected to do the chasing. Now it's the ladies. I had a girl come up to me last week – she worked in the town hall, by the way – and say, "I don't know whether you're a tit man or not, but I've got nipples like raspberries." Twenty years ago it was the old glad eye and hint in the voice, not someone telling you that part of her anatomy was like a garden fruit. Or a few weeks ago a girl came up to me and asked when I got a break. I said, "I only get ten minutes." She said, "That's OK, I want you to make love to me." I said, "No thanks, I'm not into knee-tremblers." Twenty years ago no decent girl would have talked like that. I think this one worked for the council.

'There's also a big change in the way people dance, and I don't mean anything obvious like in the old films of the sixties where you see the girls in the black and white mini skirts doing the funky chicken or something. I mean in the attitude to dance. In the early sixties it was the start of the period when the guys and the ladies danced apart. They weren't as interested in posing when they danced, as trying to get some chat in. And during the smoochy dance – the old erection section, as I call it – the guys would really go for it. They'd really get into it. People kiss far less during the smoochy dances than they used to. I suppose there's more opportunity to kiss at other times now if you want to. You don't have to wait until it's dark and old Sade starts whimpering in the background.'

Tony had seen some dramatic changes in popular music during his two decades of disc jockeying. He'd had to keep abreast of the times. 'In 1963 Peter Stringfellow was DJing in Sheffield. Pete's strong point was that he was always aware of what was about to break. He had the Beatles and the Stones at his Mojo Club in Sheffield in the very early days. He had an eye and an ear for new trends. Mecca, in the early sixties, thought that things were going to go on much as they had in the past – dance bands and Petula Clark. The Beatles changed all that.' Mods and rockers, heavy rock, glam rock, punk, soul, Roxy, new romantics, electronic music – the nightclub and the DJ had to adapt to cope with it all. Onc year women feminine, men masculine, next year both masculine, next year both feminine. 'Peter runs a gay night in the Hippodrome in London,' said Tony, 'and some clubs in Sheffield have tranny nights [for transvestites]. But most of them are just young trendy poseurs.'

The biggest threat to the survival of the nightclub, despite its remark-able ability to change, was 'northern soul', according to Tony. 'Northern soul was up-tempo Motown – "Needle In A Haystack" by Martha Reeves and the Vandellas, that kind of thing. Its home was the north of England and particularly Wigan. This was in the midseventies. There were loads of all-nighters run in the Wigan Casino. These spread to Sheffield. In northern soul the guys would do spins, back flips and so on, a bit like break dancing today. The problem, of course, was that a couple of guys could take up the whole dance floor. You'd be having a normal night, put on some Motown and these guys would start doing back flips. We used to have to warn people about it – "One more and you're out." Wigan's chosen few notwithstand-ing, the clubs and DJs have learned to cope. You have to give the punters what they want – in the seventies, the rock era, nobody seemed to want a smoochy dance. Now it's back – the age of romance has definitely returned.

'The role of the DJ has also changed considerably,' he said. 'In the old days you did no promotion work – you just said a little about the record. Now the club owners want you to promote the club and its restaurant, welcome newcomers and regulars and generally get to know the punters. I'll say things like "I can see by the girls' nipples tonight that it's cold outside" or "I'd just like to say that, ladies, you're looking beautiful tonight" or "Would all the virgins put up their hands? Gentlemen, you know who to stay away from tonight." Just a bit of chat for them to get to know me. DJs have always played requests, of course, but in the seventies people wanted a bit more for people going to get married. So a lot of clubs started having hen nights on a Thursday when you get the brides-to-be on stage. I've done brides-to-be in most of the clubs in Sheffield. You get the lady to stand on a chair and have a garter put up her leg, for a bottle of champagne. They bring their mums and their mates and they're all egging the girls on. After this part of the show we have a quiz; it can't be too difficult, mind, for girls who have supped a lot. I've made up my own quiz at the moment. It's a bit like Trivial Pursuit, but a lot easier. I might ask them 'What colour is Bournville chocolate?" or "What is the most popular vegetable in Britain?" You may think these are a bit easy but to a girl on a hen night who's been supping all night, it's not. You'd been surprised how many get them wrong. To speed things up I might ask them "What colour would you paint white wood?" because no matter if you say "white" or "varnish" you still get it right.

'I don't just do brides-to-be shows – I do drinks promotions as well – Pernod, Skol, Malibu – that kind of thing. We have these drinks at half price and we give out T-shirts. Well, we don't actually give them out, girls have to do something for them. What I do is, I normally say, "You can have one if you get on stage and take off what you've got on and slip the T-shirt on." You'd be amazed how many girls will do it. Even girls without bras. But the last time I did this, some girl followed me back to the DJ stand and told me I was disgusting and perverted. She said, "Do you get a kick out of this kind of thing?" Well,' said Tony, 'it's just show business really, who takes offence anyway? The guys love it and the girls obviously don't mind. The T-shirts aren't even worth a quid. We're hardly tempting them into debauchery. Also,' said Tony, 'I pioneered the wet T-shirt contest in Sheffield.

'I also do promotion work for charity. We did a charity show for Mencap recently in the club. It's great – we just passed around buckets, we got £500. People in this part of the world are very generous. I was going to do a sponsored swim to raise some extra money. But this guy who's a regular punter said to me, "Go on stage and show us your bum and I'll give you thirty quid." Well, it was better than swimming, so I thought, what the hell? When I got up there, all these girls started screaming. They'd heard me shout "Get 'em off" a few times, so this time they were all set to get their own back. We really got them going – they were throwing coins and pound notes to get me to drop them. I really teased them along, then I did it. I even turned round – but I covered my privates. Well, it was worth it for charity, wasn't it?'

Despite his twenty years in clubs and despite the fact that watching out for trouble is part of the job, Tony had never really been injured. 'It's not my job,' he said. 'I just get the supervisors [bouncers] immediately. In fact, the only time I came near to being injured it was a supervisor who did it. He thought I'd made a crack about his girlfriend so he threw a punch. Luckily, I saw it coming, so I rode it and pretended to go down, and stayed down. I knew if I got up he would have torn me apart. The only real trouble I've ever had from a punter is from some guy who asked me to play a Led Zeppelin record. I said, "Sorry, we don't play that type of music in this club." He took it really personally, as a big insult. You'd think I'd called him a bloody wop or something. It's funny the way people identify with the music they like. He went mad. He grabbed the mike stand and tried to bash my equipment with it – several thousand pounds' worth. The supervisors got him just in time.'

So after two decades of this, Tony decided to throw in the towel. 'Well, I'm not a teenager any more,' said Tony, 'and I've always had a full-time job in the motor trade as well. I work every day from 9.00 am to 5.30 pm and five nights from 8.30 pm to 3.00 am. When I get to the club and get on stage it's fine,' said Tony, 'but it's getting the motivation to get into the car these winter nights. I always needed the money, though. In 1964 I was serving my apprenticeship as a car mechanic and getting £2 13s. 6d. a week. As a DJ I was getting 15 shillings a night, which wasn't bad. Now I get twenty-five quid a night plus unlimited drink. (But you can't drink that much because it shows in your voice.) I've enjoyed meeting the stars and being recognised myself. It's the old showman in me – people say "There goes the DJ" and I like it. Everybody knows me. Recognition. And I like performing up there. It's all part of showbiz, after all.'

Bridget (the midget)

The nightclub was jam-packed again. Michael Jackson was warbling, on record, in the background about the party people.

It was a slow and difficult business for the party people to get from their drinks to the toilets and back. It was all push and shove with beer spilling out of the tops of glasses down freshly laundered white jackets and newly bought cream dresses.

Little groups were all engaged in the rituals of the night – drinking, talking, living crazy, or trying to, with the little money that is about. One little tight knot of girls occupied a prime position just outside the ladies' toilet next to the side entrance of the bar – the side door for VIPs. They perched on stools drinking brandy and Babycham. They were laughing. They sent Andrea to the bar with a £20 note. She descended from her high stool into another world. She was transformed immediately from a small person on a tall stool to a midget on the floor, with men's crotches and women's bums in her direct line of regard. The brandy and Babycham had gone to her head. 'It's like a week's dole money here,' she said, handing the £20 note over to the barmaid. She was full of herself tonight, all her friends were in. The bouncer, all six foot two inches of him, bent down low and pinched her cheek. 'Ain't she lovely? I call her Bridget the Midget,' he said. 'We'll have a dance later.' She was beaming. Just one blonde registered something close to disgust as she pushed past Andrea to the ladies'.

'I'm not really a midget,' said Andrea. 'I believe the correct word is "dwarf". I'm a nineteen-year-old with a nineteen-year-old's body, but I've just got short arms and short legs. A midget has a nine-year-old's body. My mum's a dwarf as well. She had it more difficult than me – in those days it was really bad. I didn't even realise there was anything special about me until I was ten. I went for a hearing test at a school clinic with my mum and as we were leaving all these kids surrounded us. They were just junior-school kids but they were the same size as us. I thought they'd surrounded us because they thought I was deaf. Then it all suddenly clicked. Up until I was ten I could pass as a small ten-year-old. I'd always regarded myself as just being a little bit short, nothing special. It's only from that time that people started reacting differently. All of a sudden, people were staring and laughing at me. It was even worse if me and my mum went out together. My father is normal size, but he never walks with us – he always makes some excuse when we have to go to town, as to why he has to go first. He can't be ashamed of my mum, mind, or he'd not have married her, I suppose. My two older brothers are both normal size and they both accept it. My oldest brother first realised that my mum was different when he was about ten and she had to reach up to comb his hair for school. He thought it was great being bigger than his mum.

'It's just a bit of bad luck that it was me who inherited it, I suppose. My mum was told that there was always a 50/50 chance that she'd have a dwarf. I always thought I'd got it because I was the girl in the family. My mum told me that it would only run in girls. I always thought that if I ever got pregnant and had a boy it would be all right. Anyway, it turned out not to be that simple because I did get pregnant when I was seventeen by a boy who I'd been going out with for two years. He was eighteen and five foot eight. I considered getting rid of the baby myself and I said to my mum, "Do you want me to have an abortion?" and she said, "No way." I knew my dad wouldn't be too pleased, though, so I told my mum, if my dad gets mad at me I'll get rid of it. I knew if I said that she'd get round him. So I went ahead and had the baby – by Caesarean because of my size. I was praying for a boy and it was. He weighed five pounds 14 ounces. But when I finally came round the doctor broke the news – he told me the child was going to be a dwarf like me. It was like a smack in the face. I'd always been told by my mum that it just ran in girls. I couldn't believe it. I rejected the baby completely – I was pushing him away and all that. I didn't see him for a whole day. But then I came round and to be honest the next few months were the best of my whole life. I wouldn't leave him. You see, my family life was a bit empty at the time – my dad had been made redundant from British Rail, and my mum had had to retire as a domestic from the Northern General Hospital in Sheffield because of her health. We'd just been sitting around all day just staring at each other. The baby – Michael – changed all that. We all started living again. There was lots to do and my mum and dad were right fantastic about the house. But Michael didn't seem to be putting on weight. Three weeks before his first birthday he weighed only 11 pounds 14 ounces. He went into hospital and two days later he was dead. The house was empty without him, we went back to staring at the blank walls again.

'Since Michael died I've tried for hundreds of jobs – I tried for quite a few before I got pregnant with Michael as well. It's really awful when you go for an interview – most of the people interviewing you are too embarrassed to look you straight in the face. I went for an interview for a job as a cleaner in one of the poshest hotels in Sheffield. I went up to the reception desk and got an application form and I sat with two other girls filling it in. Well, I went upstairs to see the lady doing the interviews and before I even got a chance to sit down, she said, "Why do you want this particular job?" She couldn't even look at me. She went on, "You do understand that we have to have top cleaning here – we charge up to £95 a night. Why do you think you could do it?" I knew I could do it, but she just said, "We'll let you know." I knew what that meant. Another time I went for a job at a factory. The work involved putting handles on knives, the machine was fairly high up and I couldn't reach the handle, but I was prepared to stand on something to do it. My mum and I stand on stools all the time at home. We're used to it. But the manager was right embarrassed. He wouldn't look at me and he was making all these elaborate excuses as to why I couldn't do the job. They didn't give me a chance.

'But one time I went for a job and it was even more embarrassing. I was on the CB circuit at the time. I called myself "Smiley" and I had a friend called "Big T" – she called herself that because she was really fat but men thought she was called that because she had big boobs. We used to stay up all night talking on the CB and then sleep all day. We used to wind these guys up a lot. We used to talk to these guys, and then when we finished we'd switch to another band to hear them talking to their mates. They used to say, "Have you talked to Smiley and Big T – they sound lovely, they're right teasers." We even arranged to meet these two guys in a pub once. They were waiting for two right teasers and in walked a fat girl and a dwarf. They were a bit embarrassed. But through the CB circuit I got to meet quite a few people and I met this guy who owned a removals firm. He said he needed someone to work in the office to take bookings by phone and to talk to men in the vans over the CB. He said, "You're right experienced with CBs, you could do it." I was over the moon – my first job. I told my mum and she was so proud. I signed off the dole on Friday and went to see him on the Saturday. He just burst out laughing. It was just a joke, but I was so embarrassed. I had to go and tell my mum and my friends I'd been set up. He thought the whole thing was hilarious – a dwarf working in his office. But it wasn't so funny from my point of view – the dole stopped my money for six weeks because they thought I'd been messing them about.

'A couple of months after Michael died I started going out to nightclubs to get me out of the house. I know lots of midgets who never leave the house at night. I used to go on my own. My mum was really worried – she'd heard that in Australia they have competitions to see who can throw the midget the furthest. She'd seen it on TV. She was afraid that they'd start throwing me onto the stage in the nightclub. No one's tried that yet but people do spill drinks over me and quite a few either stare or laugh. When I first went out I used to clam up if anyone commented on my size, but through going out I've made some good friends – Jenny, who runs a private detective agency, and Paddy, who's a friend of hers. I only met them because there was this guy bothering me. Some blokes, when they're pissed at the end of the night, think that if they haven't pulled they might as well chat up a dwarf. I couldn't get rid of this bloke – he followed me to the taxi. Paddy had to follow him outside. But Jenny and Paddy are real friends. They're genuine, they accept me for what I am. If anyone stares when I'm with them I just say "Blow it", my mind is on other things. I don't like it when I'm on my own, though. Paddy and Jenny call me "Bridget the Midget" or "Dwarf". The other week when I said to Jenny, "Give me a shock to get rid of the hiccups," she said, "You've grown four inches in the last hour." You should have seen the other people's faces, but I don't mind it from Jenny. It's just a joke and I can laugh about it now. Jenny's done more for me in the past three months than anyone in the past nineteen years. She's even giving me some work experience in her office at the moment, answering the phone. I love it and it gets me out of the house.

'I like going out to nightclubs with Jenny and there's always the possibility that I might meet someone. The funny thing is I don't like other midgets, I can't really face them, but I met this bloke the other week. He was four foot eight – normal, just a bit on the short side. It was great being able to dance with him. I've danced with Paddy before but it was the first time I ever had a proper smooch. The only thing was, he was a bit embarrassed by everyone else's reaction. I haven't seen him since but I'd like to meet him again. His name was Charlie, by the way, and he worked for Sheffield parks. Paddy keeps teasing me that he was really a garden gnome.

'If I had the money I'd open a business for people like myself. I don't like going out with midgets but I'd like to be able to employ them – they deserve a chance like everyone else. We're not disabled or anything, just a bit on the small side, but people treat us like freaks. I definitely don't agree with midgets working in the circus. When I was young, my mum used to tell me that if I was naughty the gypsies would come and kidnap me and sell me to the circus. It really frightened me. I'm still frightened of gypsies now, and circuses.'

And I left Andrea dwarfing her friends with her smile, her personality and her chat. A three-foot-odd dwarf with a 10-foot personality, as Paddy says. I just glimpsed her on one other occasion that evening. Her friends had gone off for a smooch, leaving her alone. Charlie, the garden gnome, hadn't reappeared. There she was clutching her Babycham marooned in a corner of the club. The brandy had run out, and this time her mind wasn't on other things. And then some creep passed by. He'd been asking women to dance all evening and had a whole string of rejections. The chip on his shoulder matched the rest of his demeanour. But then he spotted Andrea. His face lit up into a sneering grin as he passed her in the corner. He tried to catch her eye with the same effort that others had attempted to avoid eye contact with him all that evening. He wanted to register his own personal triumph; he'd found someone to look down on, both literally and metaphorically.

It was Hazlitt's famous dictum that 'From the height from which the great look down on the world all the rest of mankind seem equal'. From Andrea's height – they don't. The creep kept up his sneer as she sank her Babycham – bubbles and all.

The bouncers

There are two sides to every nightclub, the up and the down, always poised in some kind of delicate balance. Up is music, bright lights, dancing, sparkling wine, sparkling conversation, laughter, champagne, beautiful women, handsome men, flirtation, love. Down is music that seems too loud, lights that dazzle, women who refuse to dance, men who refuse to ask, too much sparkling wine, morose conversation, tears, wind from too much champagne, ugly women, ugly men, no flirtation and finding oneself alone at three in the morning. Drink can lift you up and drink can pull you down. In most nightclubs, the bar is open from 9 pm until 2 am – plenty of time for someone to be hoisted up and dragged down several times in one evening by the alluring liquid.

Nightclubs are designed to get people together. Beautiful people packed in a small space, the drink, the laughter, the conversation flowing. Closeness, togetherness, intimacy. Or so the theory goes. But these same features can work in the opposite way. Hundreds of people violating one's personal space, pricking one's small, protective bubble. Sweaty people bumping and grinding, pushing and shoving. Bad smells. Aggravation.

Any successful nightclub has to be able to keep people up without letting them fall to earth too quickly. It's a difficult job. A nightclub manager has to be genteel host, discreet acquaintance and public protector. Most people don't go to a nightclub for the aggro. Managers and doormen have to be able to spot trouble a mile off and stamp it out – wham, bam, dead, no messing – without in any way harming the individuals concerned. It's a very difficult job.

The burden of making things run smoothly in Josephine's falls on Rod Johnson – a director of the company, A & S Entertainments, that owns the club – the manager and, usually, four bouncers. Rod Johnson supervises at the door. He uses his instinct to sort people out, to decide whom to let in and

Big Jim and Rod Johnson (Rod is six foot)

whom not to. An instinct supported by considerable local knowledge. His heuristics seem straightforward enough at first: 'No large all-male coach parties from out of town, no drunks, nobody in jeans, nobody without a jacket, nobody without a proper shirt, nobody whose hair is too long, no troublemakers.' But then, 'Nobody with scuffed shoes – you can tell a lot about a person from his shoes – and nobody with the wrong attitude.' Rod Johnson said he could pick out those with the 'wrong attitude' straight away. He has to get it right – his livelihood depends on it.

Rod's seen a bit of trouble in his time. He's been attacked with hammers, darts, screwdrivers, knives, axes, stiletto heels, even animal legs (he didn't say what animal they belonged to). His teeth have needed redoing a number of times. He has to stay sharp. He started his working life as an electrician, but he and his brother got jobs as part-time bouncers in a small club outside Sheffield. A club renowned for trouble; but they 'sorted it', he said. The local police were impressed and asked both him and his brother to join. His brother did, but he stayed at the door. Later, he worked for the Mecca-run Locarno ballroom in Sheffield. Part-time doorman, box-office manager, assistant manager. All these jobs involved standing at the door watching and learning. Looking at people's faces; looking at people's shoes. Ejecting the yobs, and stopping them from getting in. Twenty years of petty aggravation and real aggro.

He picks his fellow doormen carefully. Big Jim – six foot nine, square, an ex-professional wrestler. Hands like grappling hooks. A voice several octaves below the bottom of the pitch range. You can't even see past Big Jim, let alone get past him. But Big Jim is gentle with it. There's no point in having a bouncer that can't handle people. Violence for bouncers in a club like Josephine's must be a last resort. The majority of the bouncers are ex-wrestlers or boxers, but occasionally the odd hard nut is employed just in case things get out of hand. The secret is the promise of menace. Big Jim threatens the punters with his body; Mick with his reputation. People still talk about the time when Mick worked for another club and he headbutted somebody who ended up across the street. Apocryphal maybe, but the story works. People watch out for his nut.

A & S Entertainments also owns a nightclub in Chesterfield, a town with a reputation for being 'hard'. A reputation which many of the residents enjoyed. Rod insists that his doormen keep an incident book to report any trouble, no matter how small. This book catalogues the other side of the nightclub world – the world away from the champagne and the bright lights. The down side – the drunks, the irritations, the violence.

Friday 24 June, 11 pm, Chesterfield
About 12 men stopped at door – too much drink and untidy. Police called to move them on – no physical contact but they kicked door several times.

Signed Max and John

Thursday 12 August
Two males ejected – jumping over dance floor rail repeatedly. Refused to go therefore escorted out. Usual abuse at door.

Signed Max

A world in which females are not always ladies. Two females found the club too quiet and wanted their money back. This was refused.

The lady then started throwing abuse at everyone in the foyer. I [the manager] intervened and asked the lady to leave with her friends. After a few 'No, not without our money back', she tried to grab my neck at which I prevented her from doing so by grabbing her arms and putting her out of the club. During this she ripped off a gold chain round my neck. While I was busy with this lady, her friend was shouting, swearing and generally not acting in a ladylike manner to one of my door staff.

All of a sudden the smaller one of the two kicked the glass in the door and it went through. She then proceeded to kick the others in and kicked two more in.

A world in which the police don't always arrive in the nick of time:

Saturday 23 July, 11 pm
Ball [a local criminal] refused entry. A large gang were with him and threatening all the staff. Police were called – they took 10 minutes to arrive (3 calls were made to them in that time). Ball had to be forced out – all the windows were then smashed out by his gang. One of them was taken away but later released. 3 staff made statements.

Signed Sugar

Tuesday 26 July, 11 pm
Ball came to the door to start trouble. Police called. One car, 2 police, arrived. They asked if it was the same people who damaged the door on Saturday – it was! The police then said 'You can handle this can't you? If they come back give us a ring'.

Signed Sugar

Thursday 17 November, 11.30 pm
Police called to disperse crowd at the door (under-age). They never came. Crowd eventually went away.

Signed Nev

A world in which the police are sometimes not very polite when they do get there. Two doormen had just been arrested at the Adam 'n Eve in Leicester on suspicion of actual bodily harm:

He [the sergeant] told Mick and Leroy [the doormen] their rights and took them to the van. Dave Lemon said he had to leave someone in charge and the police told them they didn't want to know, or as he put it, 'He was not fucking bothered'. Mick said he could get the sack for not leaving anyone in charge and a bobby said, 'He couldn't give a fuck; take them to an industrial tribunal'.

When Dave was released, some of the staff had waited for him, and one of the policemen said, 'Take your disco friends and piss off'.

This is the other side of the nightclub business. The side the ordinary punter, it is hoped, never sees. Drunken men kicking doors through frustration or anger. Local criminals trying to get into the club for the hell of it. The police not getting there on time. And then suddenly out of the blue comes real violence. Real nasty violence. The bouncers again have to put their necks on the block. They can't get reinforcements or ring the SPG. They have to hold firm.

Saturday 9 September
About 11.30 pm. I stopped Lincoln Penn at the Door. I did not think him suitable for the club (along with his brothers). The doors were closed. When I next let some customers out, Penn wrenched the door open and he and two friends came into the doorway. Max, who was on the right-hand side of the door, moved to the door and was hit in the face by Penn. (This punch broke his jaw in two places and closed his eye.)

In the next instant I was confronted by one of the gang (Rogers) with his sleeves rolled up. He said, 'I have a score to settle with you' and proceeded to kick at me. Both doors had been pulled open by this time, and the entrance to the club was filled with his gang. (The Welsh brothers (2), the Penn brothers (2) and about 6 of their friends.) Rogers drove me into the foyer with his kicks. When I moved forward to punch, he went back into the crowd at the door.

The police arrived at this point (Constable Jim Dury with a policewoman). Their presence broke up the trouble. After a few moments, Jim took me into the back room and told me to stay there for a while. He came in again later and said a serious incident had occurred and he would have to take me to the station for questioning. I offered to make a statement to two different CID officers. They did not seem to want one. I was released three hours later on conditions of bail.

Signed Nev

Nev was later charged with stabbing Rogers. He was acquitted on a charge of wounding at Leicester Crown Court.

Rod Johnson treats his bouncers like personal friends. He stands by them. When incidents like this happen and a bouncer is charged, he goes to court with him. He is an expert on the judicial system, he's been through it so many times. He can give potted biographies of most local crown court judges and many police superintendents. At the opposite end, he knows the men who are 'a bit naughty'. He has to be able to keep an eye on them.

His social life is affected by the job. Like policemen, he's a marked man. Policemen often go out together after hours. But who can he go out with, where can he go? Over the years he has turned many people away from his clubs. Many people owe him one. When he's out on his own, some of the people he's turned away bump into him. How does he cope? He bluffs his way, he said. 'You have to be firm. I just tell them to get out of my way. I don't threaten them, I'm just firm. Most people are like dogs. Give them an order and they'll react.' He told a story about being surrounded by a gang of eight in Chesterfield who aimed to do him some harm. He talked firmly and walked straight out past them.

Needless to say, the social lives of his doormen are also affected. People do bear grudges. Following an incident on a Friday night, Dave Lemon, a doorman in the Loughborough club, got a phone call described in the incidents book as follows:

On Sunday morning I was out playing football when at home my father received a phone call from one of the girl's husband. He said that I hit his wife and blacked her eye. Then he said he would kill me. At about noon, five of his friends came to my house with pick-axe handles with which to hit me. My mother phones the police to which they said nothing could be done until they actually harmed me.

Rod Johnson uses the calming technique in his clubs. Perfect politeness. He calls everyone 'sir' or 'madam', he talks quietly but firmly. If all else fails, Big Jim carries troublemakers out through the nearest fire exit and deposits them outside. 'Girls are more difficult for Big Jim,' said Rod. 'Where do you grab them without causing offence?' Mick follows behind. Most punters leave quietly, their eyes glued to Mick's head, lest his head is given the chance to propel them across the street and back into reality.

Casino Royale – Yorkshire style

It was Sunday afternoon, five past four in a casino in Sheffield. He was playing blackjack, alone. Just he and the croupier – attractive, with beautiful white teeth. But she'd stopped smiling. He was playing all seven boxes and he was good, perhaps too good. The £1000 set float had disappeared in about twenty minutes. The inspector and the pit boss were keeping a careful eye on him. Blackjack has a 3 to 10 per cent edge in the house's favour (depending upon the strategy of the player) but this punter didn't seem to know it. The other blackjack tables had a few mug punters scattered about trying to buy cards in every deal and looking for five-card tricks, as if they were in their living room playing pontoon, but not this table. This punter was different. He watched the croupier dealing from the shoe with the utmost concentration. He bet with confidence. And he was winning. The pit boss rang reception. 'Guy in a grey suit, red striped tie, about fifty, gold-rimmed glasses. Who is he?' The receptionist had noted him as he went in. 'He's not a member – he came in with Bob, you know, Bob Jones, and he gave a Leeds address.'

The pit boss called the gaming manager over. He'd been in the business for twenty years. He watched the unknown punter's style of play. 'Definitely a card counter,' he whispered. For the uninitiated, a card counter is someone who tries to work out the relative probability of a high or low card being dealt in blackjack by memorising all the cards from the four packs used. Not illegal, but not desirable from the casino's point of view. Good card counters invariably win. The gaming manager had a word with the pit boss. 'I'll let him win another £500, then I'll have a word with him.'

It didn't take long for the unknown punter to acquire his next £500. The croupier was starting to perspire, just a little. A small crowd had gathered. The gaming manager intervened. 'Excuse me, sir, could I have a word with you. Would you like a meal in the restaurant or a bottle of champagne? Perhaps you'd like a break?' No deal. 'I'm sorry, sir, I've got the greatest respect for you, you've definitely beat us with your brains but this casino simply can't afford you. Why don't you go down to London where they can?' The unknown punter didn't want a trip to London – he could afford the fare, though, he was sitting with six grand in front of him. He just wanted to know whether he was barred. 'Well, sir,' said the gaming manager, 'I'd hate you to come all the way down from Leeds next week only to find that you're not welcome.' The unknown punter got the message. He and the gaming manager shook hands and he left amicably. Six grand for an afternoon's work wasn't bad, and he'd been barred from most casinos in the country anyway.

As he left, the gaming manager said to the pit boss, 'There are only about half a dozen really good card counters in the world and he's certainly in that class.' Normally when a guest wins the kind of money the unknown card counter had just won, the casino will make sure he signs up as a member before he leaves. That way, as one casino owner said to me, 'As long as we can get him back through the doors again we can look upon his winnings as borrowed money. We make sure we have all the details about punters who influence the results of the casino by as little as £100. We make sure we get them back.' But nobody wants a card counter in the club either as a member or a guest.

Harry Sharpe just smiled at these goings-on. He was a bookmaker, and a semiprofessional gambler of a very different sort. 'I'm not a card counter, I wouldn't play blackjack – it's the worst game in terms of odds for the punter. I play Punto Banco and I reckon I've won £50,000 tax free in the past ten years. My method is simple – "controlled gambling". I come in to win £20 in a night from each of two casinos. I gamble five nights a week. When I've got my £20, I stop. I gamble with £100 maximum. If I lose that I stop. At least 75 per cent of punters will be winning at some point in the evening, but they're too greedy. If they win £90, they want to make it up to a hundred. I just go for £20 and I play Punto Banco because the house edge is lowest. The gaming staff all make jokes about it. They'll come up and say, "Have you got your wages yet, Harry?"' And Harry went on his methodical and controlled way. Elsewhere in the casino, control just wasn't working.

Brian Dooley, the gaming manager of Napoleon's, Sheffield's poshest and most popular casino, told me that on occasions he had actually intervened with punters, who were also friends, when they'd been ahead. 'I took two grand off a punter and told him he wasn't going to get it until he left and got into his car. He wasn't too impressed at the time but was extremely grateful the next day. You have to intervene sometimes. If we make a good profit, I like to see a regular punter take a couple of grand off us. On another occasion, though, there was this punter called Dave who used to like gambling on afternoons when I was working. He'd lose a couple of hundred quid a couple of days a week. One of our better punters. When I was put on nights, he switched to nights, he liked a bit of a chat afterwards. So one night he started gambling with £30 and he was up to £960. I walked over to the table and took his arm and said, "There's always tomorrow, Dave, get yourself out, lad, while you're ahead." But he said he just wanted to make it up to a nice even figure, an even grand. The same old story. He lost the lot and £1500 of his own money.

'I used to be a real softie,' said Brian, 'this job used to depress me. You can see the despondency on people's faces. But if I wasn't doing this I'd probably be on the dole now. Life in Sheffield has got hard. When I started as a croupier in 1965, I had a job as a milkman for Express Dairies. I used to finish at the casino about 5 am and go straight to my milkround. I used to

sleep in the afternoon for about three hours. I did this for five years before getting into casinos full time. The pay was better in casinos than in the milk trade but sometimes it is difficult.' He knew all the regular punters by name and could suss out a newcomer with considerable skill. He reckoned I'd be worth about seven quid to the casino.

On Saturday nights, though, the scene is somewhat different from Sunday afternoons. It's a night for small fry and spectators. The gaming room is full and big punters can't get near the tables. There are as many people watching as playing; it's a good night for poseurs. The poseurs get their money changed into 25p chips and sit with their huge columns of chips in front of them. Other punters can't tell the value of the chips. As one casino owner put it, 'They could get £5 or £10 chips but they prefer these enormous phallic symbols of 25p chips, and they like to put a lot on a number. I suppose it makes them feel big for the evening. My name is Bond and all that.' And when you watch them play you can see all the glamorous images of a hundred movies and a thousand newspaper articles flooding through their minds. They risk all, or at least 25p, on the spin of the wheel. 'Luck be my lady tonight. Frankie babe, here's looking at you.' The croupiers look bored in return.

Casinos are run as a tight ship, they have to be, because they're all about money and money, as we all know, is a serious business. The figures are astounding. In 1982–83 the total drop (money changed for chips) in casinos in this country was £1,219,000,000 – a 21 per cent increase over the previous year. The major portion of the cake (£894,000,000) was gobbled up by only twenty London casinos. The other £325,000,000 was fought over by the remaining ninety-nine clubs in England, Scotland and Wales. Provincial gaming is in a different league from gaming in the capital. As Brian Dooley said, 'What we call our big punters, they wouldn't even buy them a drink down in London.'

Casinos are also a scrupulously honest business. As Mario Puzo (of *Godfather* fame) notes in his book *Inside Las Vegas*, 'After fifteen years of watching and trying to figure out how they cheat, I reluctantly came to the conclusion that Vegas has honest casino gambling and it may be the first time in the history of civilisation that gaming houses have been straight.' And this from a self-declared degenerate gambler and inveterate loser. But the simple fact of the matter is that casinos can't afford to cheat – they've already got the 'edge' and they can't gamble their licence, and their huge capital investment, on trying to increase the edge in any way. Some punters, of course, think otherwise (and we have Hollywood and natural paranoia to blame for that). They ask for croupiers to be removed, balls to be changed, and wheels to be spun in the opposite direction. The fact that the two different types of ball used in roulette have somewhat different properties, with the Teflon ball spinning faster, bouncing more and making more noise than the ivory ball, reinforces the punters' belief in the casinos' hidden and devious influence.

Punters are notoriously suspicious and, of course, superstitious. Some will only play when a certain croupier is in the room, others only when they're out of the room. They sit marking the sequences on their cards for roulette, desperately seeking to find order in randomness. But entropy unfortunately always increases. Even Mario Puzo has a theory when it comes to roulette. 'Red and black paint differ in their chemical properties and reactions. Black paint tends to make the wooden fibres of the slot hard, making the ball bounce out. Therefore red is the better colour to play.' Puzo's system hasn't done him a lot of good – he tells us in his book that he's been losing for thirty years. Max Silverman, one of the directors of the company that owns Napoleon's, said, 'The advantage of a system is that when you've lost all your money, you've still got it to hang on to.' He mentioned the famous gambling aphorism, 'System going well, send more money.'

So how do casinos go about attracting custom and building up a regular clientele? The obvious answer, since the Gaming Act of 1968 came into being, is: with some difficulty. The Gaming Act aims to keep the supply of gaming facilities at a level only sufficient to satisfy any 'unstimulated' demand for them. What this level is, of course, is a matter for dissent. The holder of a gaming licence isn't permitted to stimulate demand by either advertising, providing live entertainment, dancing, or offering credit for gaming. Clubs can lose their licences and a number of well-known clubs in London were closed in the 1970s for a variety of infringements of the act. In addition, the 'hard' gaming areas have to be kept physically distinct from the areas in which the alcohol is served. Severe constraints indeed.

So how does a club like Napoleon's attract custom? Basically by creating an environment which nongamblers might like to frequent, with an excellent restaurant and fashionable bar. Max Silverman says, 'In the first instance it's just a case of getting bodies through the front door, like Harrods' sale. After that it's a whole series of contingencies. Maybe they'll venture into the gaming room, maybe they'll try a bet to impress a girlfriend, maybe they'll come back.' And maybe they won't, there's nothing certain in this game. Nevertheless, relying purely on word of mouth, the number of people coming through the door at Napoleon's (not necessarily entering the gaming room) increased from 1200 a week in 1978 to about 2000 a week in 1985. The good punters, of course, receive special treatment, special in that they get extra courteous attention from the staff, if not downright respect, and more. For example, the ten best punters were recently treated to a Variety Club do at the Cutlers' Hall in Sheffield to see some amateur boxing, plus a meal, then returned to the casino, presumably for them to say thank you in return. But even Napoleon's best punters wouldn't be noticed down in London. 'Money is tight,' said Max. 'In the old days before VAT there was a lot of loose money around, now it's all in the till rather than in the back pocket.'

But let's finish with the $64,000 question. Why do people gamble at all? As Mario Puzo notes, it seems like a vice without any redeeming feature. On the other hand, 'drunkards are tragic or romantic, murderers interesting, gourmands and sex aficionados are approved of, as at least getting something for their money.' But gamblers, what do they get? I put this question to a wide variety of people who worked in casinos, from the men who worked on the door to the owners. Interestingly, the majority of employees did not gamble. Why do others? Some talked about the 'charge' involved in gambling – the 'high' and its addictive nature, the excitement. Some pointed to the concentration required and argued that it was a good way for the successful businessman to forget his worries. Some argued by default – what else could a fifty-year-old, too old for discos, do in the evening for excitement? Some suggested it was just because it was fashionable – Monte Carlo and Frankie baby. But all of these explanations, while containing a grain of truth, in my opinion fall a little short of the mark (to mix metaphors a little). When you walk into a casino in a depressed town in the 1980s you can see what it's really about, at least here – there are good punters and there are mug punters and there's a long, winding social scale in between. The mug punters try to climb this social ladder with their 25p chips and their studied nonchalance. The good punters, without really trying, get respect and deference from the staff. The mug punters don't, and respect is a very valuable commodity. Money may not be able to buy you love but it may be able to buy you something just as valuable. The good punters by definition have money to burn, and up in Sheffield in the 1980s, that really is something.

4 · Just a bit of bobbing and weaving

Education is an admirable thing, but it is well to remember from time to time that nothing that is worth knowing can be taught.
Oscar Wilde, 'The Critic as Artist', 1891

Cockney

I first saw 'Cockney', no, let's start again, I first heard 'Cockney' in Josephine's in the section reserved for VIPs. He was loud, brash and very verbal (as I believe they say south of Watford). He was introducing someone to his 'very best pal', Terry Curran, the ex-Everton and ex-Sheffield Wednesday and ex-Sheffield United footballer (and arguably one of the best-known footballers in Sheffield). Cockney was drinking 'a little shampoo'. Cockney had a silk suit and a Cartier watch, a diamond earring and a pair of handcrafted shoes. Terry had some of these things as well, but not all. They made a formidable couple, with Terry's fame and Cockney's loud voice. Someone asked Terry for his autograph. Terry signed.

'That's the thing about Terry Curran,' said one watchful bystander. 'He may be the Sheffield George Best, but he's always a gentleman, even on his night out.' Terry passed the signed napkin back and the eager autograph hunter passed it to Cockney. He smiled and signed 'Cockney Richard'. The eager autograph hunter wasn't quite sure whose signature she'd managed to acquire – she knew he was definitely a somebody, she just wasn't sure exactly which one. Cockney went back to the 'shampoo'.

'I think I'll get another bottle,' said Cockney, 'or what about another two? I feel like a right good drink.' He turned to a hanger-on. 'This is nothing, what I'm getting through tonight. Last week me and a few mates got through nine bottles of champagne, and a while ago I was in Stringfellows with some lads and one of them ordered eight butterfly cocktails – they're one hundred guineas each – there are two bottles of champagne in each one, and they're meant to be for eight people. But my mate ordered one for everyone in his company. The barmaid said, "Excuse me, sir, are you sure

Out on the town; out in the scrapyards

you haven't made a mistake here?" And he said, "You're quite right, luv – I have made a mistake – I forgot you – make it nine." Nine hundred guineas for a round of drinks – that's style. Mind you, he got barred a week later for running up and down the bar with his trousers down. He was a scrap dealer, by the way, and he looked a bit ridiculous when he dropped them. Even though you buy all that drink you can still get barred. You have to have genuine style as well. It's not enough to be a big spender, you've got to have class.'

Some of the younger Sheffield Wednesday players arrived. One had just been given a transfer. His large doleful eyes were like basins full of dishwater, slightly discoloured. He looked a bit like a Disneyfied fawn gone a bit wrong. It was obviously an emotional moment and he certainly wasn't over the moon about the whole thing.

'How much are you getting again? . . . Bloody hell, is that all? . . . What about a car? I don't care whether you've got one or not, ask for a car. You never get anything unless you ask . . . Do you know how much Terry got when he went from Wednesday to United? . . . and all you're getting is that . . . I was down at the PFA dinner last week as a guest of the Everton lads and Andy Gray was telling me . . . You don't want to be taken for a mug, do you? . . .'

The fawn was beginning to resemble a parrot. He had gone a bit green and he was only able to repeat back the odd word that Cockney was firing at him.

The slightly surprising thing about all this is that this particular fawn was a well-known footballer, difficult to imagine in his role as victim. But in the concrete jungle, Cockney was the ultimate survivor and he'd got proof. He pulled out a wad of photographs. 'Here's a photo of me and Freddie Laker on his yacht in Palma and here's a picture of me and the Everton lads at the PFA dinner in London.' He was keen on Everton (after all they did win the First Division) and Fred, before the collapse. His verbals started again.

'See, Everton and Liverpool, they're in a different class from other football clubs. They don't even bother training – they run around the pitch five times and that's their lot. Sheffield Wednesday have to run ten miles on a Monday, never mind the rest of the week. And Wednesday have to stay in nearly all week – the only time an Everton or Liverpool player doesn't drink is the day before the game. But I'll always support Wednesday. Wednesday and I go back a long way. When I was eleven I broke my arm playing football and I wrote to three England players, and only one wrote back to me – Ron Springer from Wednesday. He sent me a load of autographs so I started supporting them. I only moved to Sheffield because it was cheaper to get to the games. It caused the break-up of my first marriage, though. My wife said to me, "You prefer Sheffield Wednesday to me," and I said, "I prefer bloody Sheffield United to you." She was a millionaire's daughter, you know. I met her on 11 July, we got married on 11 August – Sheffield Wednesday played Swindon away and got beaten 4–0. She first left me on 11 January, Sheffield Wednesday were playing Portsmouth away. The second time she left me – when she gave me the ultimatum, Sheffield Wednesday or her – it was the 11th again – they were playing Portsmouth again – at home – this time Wednesday won. I love this club, I'll always support them.' Cockney's magnanimity was clearly impressing his audience.

The group was joined (improbably) by an Irish academic. 'What poets the Irish are,' Cockney said, and launched into Oscar Wilde's *The Ballad of Reading Gaol*:

> 'He did not wear his scarlet coat,
> For blood and wine are red . . .'

He got to the fifth verse before he was stopped. The audience was clearly impressed by his literary knowledge. His offer to recite 'the first three verses' from any Shakespeare play was, however, graciously refused. What scholarship! What adaptability! What verbals! From extravagant consumerism to football mastermind to English scholar – all in the space of one large swig of 'shampoo'. A lord of the concrete jungle who could change his spots.

In a city of moderate public behaviour and moderate, if not downright dour, talk, Cockney's colourful and adaptable hyperbole, like a well-known brand of toothpaste, got him noticed. 'I'm the most famous man in Sheffield,' he said.

But what exactly did Cockney do? My question met with a stony silence, then evasiveness. 'Let's just say I'm a man with no visible means of support. I get by but don't worry, when I'm out with the lads, I buy more champagne than they do.' How did he get promotion into the first division of champagne cocktails, famous personages and public recognition? 'Let's just say I know everybody who's worth knowing. I've introduced Terry to quite a few of my famous mates. Sheffield's just small-time. As to what the celebrities round here think of me – maybe they just wonder how I can get out every night of the week drinking champagne.' How did he get to know Freddie Laker? 'I saw Freddie in Palma – I'd never met him before – I just went up to him and said, "Hello Fred, long time no see." He said, "It is a long time, please forgive me but I seem to have forgotten your name." A friend and I were with a couple of birds he wanted to meet so we got invited out to his yacht that way. I've been out with loads of famous people. What's that guy from the Who called? I'd go up to anybody. I've been out with some right upper-class birds but I haven't met old Prince Charles yet.'

But who financed the old shampoo? What were the invisible means of support? He agreed to explain. We met back at his small flat – 'my little palace', bursting with all the expensive ephemera of the consumer age. A video with a screen that wouldn't shame a cinema, silver cutlery, expensive carpet.

'It's handy living here,' he said, 'right in the centre of town, since I got done for drinking and driving in my XJS.' He'd been on the dole for the past two years. 'I get £60 a fortnight, but I can spend that on a Friday night. Who could live on that?' And he showed me his wardrobe with its seven silk suits and twenty-odd pairs of expensive shoes. He looked at my clothes. 'You're a right scruff bag, you know. You can always tell a man by his shoes, and look at yours – they're a bloody disgrace.' I had to agree. His weren't. So how come, in the style wars, he was a fighter ace and I was trudging around like a refugee?

'Well, the first thing to know is that I've been in trouble a few times. But who hasn't? Scratch any rich man and you'll find a thief. I was a thief since I was fourteen until last year when I was thirty-two, but I've come to the conclusion that it's just not worth it. I've had six custodial sentences but I've been nicked thirty-seven times in all. I've been out of prison for nearly a year. Nothing heavy, mind. I got into trouble for the first time when I was at school for stealing by finding a motorbike. But the first time I got sent away was for stealing from a dwelling house (they didn't call it burglary). I nicked some cufflinks from a house in which my girlfriend was baby-sitting. I got five quid for them and then ten weeks in a detention centre. Ten weeks of marching up and down. When I got out I started hanging about with some lads who had never worked. We used to buy something small in a Marks and Spencer's and as the girl opened the till we'd grab some money out and run. I don't mind talking about these things – I've been done for them all. The lads I knocked about with then got into armed robbery but I never got into anything too heavy. I got into deception, you know, buying stolen chequebooks for four quid a page and passing the cheque.

'The person who nicks the chequebook never tries to pass the cheques off himself. He sells it. People always wonder how you copy the name so well – you don't. You take the original name off in a solution of warm water, brake fluid, washing-up liquid with a little bleach and you just sign the name yourself. I've had Sheffield police puzzled as to how I did it. In fact I even explained it to them. They're making it more difficult now by having a patterned strip where you sign the name. My wife and I got done for passing off these cheques. We used to go to DIY shops because they cash cheques there so you don't have to queue at the till. They were easier than banks. I used to do a lot of this in London as well – at one time I was making ten grand a month. I got my wife involved – I think she was just doing it to impress me.'

His wife interrupted. 'Tell him where you got your Cartier watch, though.' He declined. 'I came back one day and he'd sold my Mini. I paid 600 quid for it,' she said. 'He bought himself a Cartier watch.'

'What are you complaining about?' he said. 'I bought you a gold sovereign from the sale.' Cockney clearly brought his worldly ways home with him.

'Look, I admit I've been a thief and a con man but who isn't bent? I'm making a bit of cash at the moment through some people I know who work for the council. You can get anything fixed, you know, if you know the right people. Housing lists, anything.' He winked. 'I hate this bloody council as well, by the way – talk about the blind leading the blind. I'm Margaret Thatcher's biggest supporter. Anybody who wants to earn a living can earn a living. I'm on the dole through choice. I'm taking a break from work, that's all. I do keep myself busy – I use my contacts. I know all the big jewellers in Sheffield and I'll sell things for them. See this gold chain – it's worth nearly 500. I paid one and a half for it and I'll get two and a half. I know the kinds of people who would want a chain like this. I also sell tickets – I know all the famous ticket touts down in London – Stan Flashman, David Brown. I was selling £15 Bruce Springsteen tickets recently for £30 and £25. Live Aid tickets for £50.'

Didn't he have any reservation about making money out of the latter venture? He looked at me as if I was some kind of idiot. 'Nobody, nobody does anything for nothing. Those bloody groups got an audience of millions – a good free plug. Do you think they'd have done it if it wasn't for that?' Cockney was proselytising now – the doctrine of the free market economy and the sanctity of the entrepreneurial spirit, unhampered by common morality or civic law.

'I also do a lot of Cup Final tickets. I give the players who get them five times their market value – that's thirty quid. I get fifty quid for them. Just a bit of bobbing and weaving, that's all I do now. But, as you know, I'm well in with the footballers – I also sell them clothes, for example snide [false] Lacoste shirts, even suits. I once sold a load of suits at fifty quid each to the

Hillsborough players. It's all right, they weren't nicked or anything. It's all down to who you know and what you know. I'm not ashamed of what I've done. Why should I be? The world's full of bent people – in any section of society, just look at the judges and the police. How come the police can afford to go out to nightclubs every night? You just have to have the cheek to get by. I had my eyes done recently by one of the top cosmetic surgeons in Britain – the bill was 600 quid but I didn't pay – they weren't quite right. So why should I?' And then he returns to his second favourite subject (his first is naturally himself). 'I learned Wilde's *The Ballad of Reading Gaol* when I was in prison. It was Oscar Wilde who said "There's only one thing in the world worse than being talked about, and that is not being talked about." That man had real style; he didn't have any money, just plenty of style. If I don't have any money I'll just get things on account – meals, champagne, anything. I've even had bets on account at a racecourse, believe it or not.

'They made a scapegoat of Wilde, he wasn't really a queer – he just had syphilis and he didn't want to give it to his wife. Half the bloody aristocrats and half the judges in this country are bent anyway. They just wanted to victimise him. All great Irishmen are sent to prison – look at George Best. Only Barry McGuigan has got to go. God help him if he gets into trouble. When you're in the public eye you have to expect trouble of this sort, especially if you're Irish. My grandmother's Irish so I'm watching out.'

And as I left, Cockney was just fixing up the use of a friend's apartment in Marbella for his holidays. He then requested a fee for the interview. 'Five hundred pounds will do nicely,' he said. 'Well, you don't do it for nothing, do you?' But, as I left, he looked at my shoes once again with the look that said, they can't be paying you very much anyway.

The minder

Sheffield was full of ex-steelmen with shopping bags. You could see them in the supermarkets in the afternoon. They didn't talk a lot, even to each other. It was embarrassing. Straight in and straight out; back to the house; back to Wimbledon, cricket, old films and the housework. Many of them quite liked the housework – they didn't like to be seen doing it, mind, but it was still all right; it was still something. One former steelworker I knew had just got a job on a building site, so his brother, another unemployed steelworker, slipped in to do the housework one day a week. He slipped out again as cautiously as he went in. Burglars would have envied his stealth. A new brand of domestic help, bred of frustration and resentment. There were no jobs for them to go to. They were in limbo.

Patrick had been in limbo many times – or perhaps purgatory is a better word for a good Catholic lad. He'd had a number of periods of unemployment between joining Brown–Bayley's, the Sheffield steel firm, at sixteen as an apprentice electrician, and his current unemployed state at thirty-four. But he was confident something would turn up – it always had. 'Well, it's not so much a matter of something turning up,' he said, 'it's what you can get, it's what you can grab for yourself. I made a list of all the jobs I've had – it's thirty-two different ones so far, and I've got a few ideas at the moment. I've been everything from store detective to chauffeur, plumber to debt collector. My size helps of course – I'm six foot two and fifteen stone. It comes in handy.' He sat back to expose his great bulk. He was accompanied by a formidable French bulldog. 'Don't worry about the dog,' he said, 'it won't bite you – it may suck you to death, but it won't bite.'

Patrick was from Irish stock. His father crossed to Liverpool with his brothers in 1949. They made their way to Sheffield for the industry and there they worked on the roads, the ubiquitous trade of his class from Belfast to Barnsley. Patrick was born a year after the family exodus. He always wanted to be a policeman, 'but my father distrusted the police; well, they do, don't they – my father liked a drink. He couldn't stand coppers.' His father meanwhile had progressed to steel erecting in Brown–Bayley's and got his son an apprenticeship there. 'He wanted me to have some security; he was laid off not long before I started.'

Like most steelworkers Patrick had a love/hate relation with the mills. 'The noise and the dirt was bloody awful – I used to sit with my hands in neat bleach for half an hour when I got home, to get rid of the grime – but the men were great. When I started I was six foot two but really skinny. I worked with a guy called Arthur Smith – he asked what they called me at home. I said "Paddy". He said, "We're not going to call you Paddy, you look like a big daft lass; we'll call you Pat," so Pat it was. They used to take the piss because I was Irish, of course, but I never took offence. Any time I made a mistake it was always "What do you expect from an Irish bollocks?" or "We'll never educate you as long as your arse points downwards", but it was just part of the crack. It wasn't so funny, though, when someone painted WOGS and IRISH BASTARDS GO HOME on our wall. Before they got into black men, we were the wogs, weren't we? But the men at work weren't like that. When they called you an Irish bastard you knew it was just a joke.'

The Irish bastard finished his apprenticeship in Brown–Bayley's but not without a struggle. 'I'd discovered nightclubs and was going out until 3 am and getting up at 6 am. Pete Stringfellow was a DJ in Sheffield in those days and used to run all-nighters at the Mojo Club. When I finished my apprenticeship I packed it in. Well, you could in those days – there was a lot of work about.'

He got a job house-wiring before being unemployed for a bit. During this period of unemployment, he got a job as a bouncer. 'It was cash in hand three quid a night, but it was rough –' he laughed – 'because I was basically rough, I created a lot of trouble. In those days I'd just say, "Would you mind leaving?" If they said no, I'd just clip them.' Pat had metamorphosed into Paddy. 'Yeah, I'd put on a bit of weight in the meantime. And I was young and fit and keen; really keen. Well, it's part of growing up, isn't it, of proving you're a man.' (His father had meanwhile died of cirrhosis of the liver.)

'I got the odd hiding, of course. One night a girl came up to me to say she'd just tried to get some cigarettes but some guy wouldn't let her near the machine. So I went with her and there was this bloke with long hair leaning up against it. I said "Excuse me, please" but he just thumped me. He didn't say a word. His friends grabbed me and he gave me a good going-over. I shook free and ran off. I found the other bouncer and we worked out a plan of attack. I sent him round the back to corner this guy. The owner of the club then came out and saw what was going on. I'd lost my tie, my shirt was torn, my clothes were all over the place. He tried to stop me. I just knocked him aside. He thought I'd gone mental. Me and the other bouncer got hold of this guy and gave him a taste of what he'd been giving me. This guy was wriggling all over the place and eventually he got free. He tried to run off and my friend tried to get hold of him by the hair – it came off in his hands. My friend and him both shrieked. It was a bloody wig. He ran out clutching it, blood everywhere.'

Patrick then went self-employed as an electrician for a couple who were opening a nightclub and they offered him a job on the door in the evenings. 'It was outside Sheffield and people would go to the club just to have a crack at the bouncer. I was getting four pounds a night plus a meal. But the wages went up from the first fight. I seemed to be on bonus. In the end I was getting seven pounds a night. But one fight finished it. They were all little blokes as well. The chef had to help me out. I went wild, though. It ended with the nightclub owner's wife jumping on my back because she thought I'd gone mental. I was hitting everything in sight. I thumped one guy and he ended up against a grandfather clock. It chimed and everyone stopped, just for a second. The owner wasn't too pleased because he'd just been offered 150 quid for the clock. I was really keen in those days, though. One Paki pulled a knife and I just kicked it out of his hand. Now I'd just walk off. It's not worth it for that money.'

Patrick eventually went back to Brown–Bayley's, only to be made redundant when it closed. When he was made redundant he signed on for a diploma course in construction and land use at Shirecliff College, but at nights and during the holidays, he tried his hand at different jobs.

'I was a cocktail barman first, but the owner tried to diddle me out of my wages so I threatened to stick him to the wall. He paid up. Then I was a waiter. Then through my work on the door I was offered a job by a rich Arab to chauffeur him about. Then I got a job as a chauffeur–handyman at a garage – delivering cars and cleaning the toilets. People used to see me sweeping up and think I'd got what I deserved. Then I got a job as a debt-collector – licensed of course. It's usually debts for small businesses. If cheques bounce, I get 20 per cent commission if I get the debt. The secret is not to go in as a heavy. I often send a female friend who's also a debt collector. It's embarrassing if a girl asks you to cough up. The last debt I collected was for a cheque for a car. The last instalment – £300 – my commission would be £60. It was a guy in the haulage business. I called on him and he said, "Have you come as a heavy, then?" I said, "No, it's just a job." I'd a smart suit on – no sleeves rolled up or any of that bollocks. He said he hadn't paid because there was a fault on the car and he'd been threatened three times by a heavy. You have to be subtle,' Patrick says. 'I couldn't hit anybody in cold blood anyway, could you?' (I grimace – probably not even in hot blood, but that's beside the point.) 'Most pay up. It's embarrassing for them.

'I've also tried my hand at painting and decorating, plumbing, carpet fitting, car breaking, window cleaning and I've done a bit more chauffeur work. I met this businessman in the club where I worked and he said he was looking for someone to drive him around a couple of nights a week in his Roller. So I said I'd do it. I put on a grey pinstriped suit and drove him up to Leeds. I was sitting in the front seat with him and he was telling me about how many birds he'd pulled. Two in one bed, the whole works. I thought this was going to be a right boring job, hearing him rabbiting on all the time, but he was right chatty, calling me Paddy, telling me all his tales. So we get to Leeds and he gets me to park in this back street and he says he'll be back in a minute.

'He comes back with this bird. All the way there he called me Paddy, now he suddenly starts calling me "driver". His voice had completely changed – he'd gone real posh. He's saying "Driver, take a left" and all this bollocks. I get a bit annoyed so I turn the mirror round to give the bird the eye. She's a bit tasty and he's got a face like my dog.' He points to his obedient French bulldog sitting morosely at his feet, its slobbering jaws a grim reminder of the perils of the business lunch. 'So he directs me to the hotel and he tells me to park right in front of the reception. I'm doing the business, opening doors, saying "sir" and "madam". They leave me for three hours. A couple of coppers came by and I'd noticed that the car wasn't taxed, so I had to lean up against the window as they walked by. After they came out, we set off through Leeds, we drove through this council estate and then on to this private estate. He said "Driver – pull up" and they got out. He told me to wait there but I followed them in the car. He escorted her back to the council estate. He went mad when he saw me, but I loved it – he was pretending that she was higher class. He offered me six pounds for the night – I asked for a tenner and got it.

'I bumped into the girl a few weeks later in the nightclub where I worked. She'd met him through the lonely-hearts column of the local paper. The funny thing is he's broke – he can only afford to go out two nights a week. I saw his house – the curtains are in tatters. I've only ever seen him in one white jacket and red shirt. It's pathetic really – just bullshit, but she was impressed. She asked me for his number because he hadn't contacted her again.'

Patrick's most recent job was store detecting. He'd formed an agency with a female friend. They'd found work in some of the big shops in Grimsby and now they're looking further afield. 'Scunthorpe is a likely place,' he said. 'It's all psychology really, looking for those little signs is a bit like being a bouncer. You have to notice things. It's not without its dangers, though. At Christmas I got glassed by this skinhead with tattoos all over his face. He and two girls nicked a nine-pound dress. I followed them outside with another store detective. He threw a punch, so I nipped the nerves on the back of his neck and he passed out. I learned this trick from a guy in the steel mill who'd been in the army.' He offered to demonstrate it, but I declined. The dog, whom he called Fat Man, declined as well. 'I drag him inside and he comes round in the lift and he goes for these two women shop assistants. So I nip him again and he passes out again. In the manager's office he's really groggy but he had a go at the manager, so I pulled him back and he picks up this ashtray and hits me in the face with it. There was blood everywhere. He got four months for it though, and he was only seventeen.

The kids today have got it hard, though. If I'd had no work when I was their age I'd have been a real tearaway.'

The boxer

Boxing is a traditional way out of the street. But there are a lot of bums even in the boxing world. As one young hopeful put it, 'It's not a world for losers.' It's a world of bright stars (Marvin Hagler), rising stars (Bomber Graham, perhaps), falling stars (Ali), and bums.

Vincent Vahey (Vinny to almost everyone) was on the ascent, he hoped. He'd been boxing for eight years but he was still only twenty. He had left school at sixteen with four O levels and got a job as a steel erector. He did this for two years before he was made redundant. When this happened, he turned professional boxer. As a fourteen-year-old amateur, he won the South Yorkshire championship, the North Eastern championship and the Northern championship, but he missed the National Association of Boys' Boxing Clubs semifinals because of a cold. His interest in boxing then waned a bit, but at sixteen he began visiting Brendan Ingle's gym in St Thomas's in Sheffield. Brendan was building up a squad of boxers with real potential. The squad included Herol (Bomber) Graham. Brendan saw some potential in Vinny – a skinny waiflike boxer with quick reflexes and real boxing ability. Vinny enjoyed boxing and even liked the training. When he was made redundant, boxing offered a convenient, if gloved, helping hand. A hand to get out of the street. The route for hungry kids for a century or more.

Boxing ran in Vinny's family – his father had been an amateur boxer as was his older brother, Vernon. His family were originally from Ireland but they moved from Belfast to Sheffield when he was six. He was part of a large family with five brothers and two sisters (whose names all began with the letter V). He said he was a bit of a devil at primary school. His father taught him to look after himself. On his first day at his new comprehensive he was picked on by an older, black kid. They had a fight outside the school grounds watched by a large crowd.

'It really got the adrenalin going,' Vinny said. 'I was really scared at first before it started, but as soon as it got going I was okay. I really enjoyed it. I won but I ended up with more cuts than my opponent because his sisters kept kicking me from behind. But it was great fighting in front of all these people.'

These parts of his background fit the traditional, if stereotyped, image of the professional lightweight. But they were never a poor family – his father was a self-employed businessman who produced madonnas for a living, so Vinny was not really the classic hungry kid fighting his way up out of the streets with his eyes on a title. Rather, he saw economic potential in his boxing ability and wanted to see what he could make from it. He wasn't interested in flash cars or gold rings; just savings, property and investment. He seemed to have inherited as much of his father's business acumen as he had of his boxing ability.

Since turning professional, he has had twelve fights of which he has won ten. His most recent fight had been against Jimmy Bunclarke from Liverpool, for the Central Areas lightweight championship. He was fighting on the same bill as Bomber Graham, in front of his home crowd. Boxing crowds are notoriously partisan, and Sheffield is certainly no exception. At the time, he was ranked ninth in Great Britain and a win would have virtually guaranteed him a crack at the British title. He said he hadn't been nervous at all about the fight.

'It was the only boxer who I've had to fight who I'd seen boxing before and I really fancied my chances against him. I'd been living with Bomber at the time and we were both really optimistic about our fights. On the night, we shared a dressing room. Bomber brought his stereo in and we were playing all this disco music, George Benson and the like. I'm usually really nervous before a fight – always off to the toilet – but that night I was laughing and joking and had Bomber really in stitches. Anyway, the fight started. It lasted two and a half minutes before he put me down. I got up at four but the referee stopped it. I couldn't believe it, I wasn't cut or anything. The crowd was booing and chanting. I was really depressed and didn't want to talk to anybody. I was *almost* hoping that Bomber would lose in his contest, but of course he didn't. He picked up the European championship. He got £5000 for his fight. I got £500 for mine, of which £80 went to my manager. It might seem like a lot for two and a half minutes' work – in fact people keep taking the piss out of me about that – but six weeks' training went into that – six weeks of getting up for a run at half past five in the morning and training in the gym twice a day.

'Of course it also means that I won't get a crack at the British title now, at least for a while. But the funny thing is because I lost, I'll probably get more fights and earn more money. When they're looking for a fighter for a contest down in London they don't want someone from the north who wins every fight and is going to give their boy a good hiding. They want their boys to look good. They don't want a real dummy either from the north, but they definitely don't want somebody who is too good. I've fought in the Café Royal in London, the Grosvenor and the Hilton. You can be rung up the night before a fight and told to get your gear ready and then it's off to box in front of a crowd of several thousand who want your blood.'

I asked him about the fixing of fights – Hollywood had taught me that boxers are sometimes offered huge sums of money to caress the canvas. Did this go on? He laughed.

'Not really,' he said. 'There are easier ways of fixing a fight than bribing the boxers, like putting a boxer in with someone in a different class, or even in a different weight class.' He reckoned that lightweights (less than nine stone nine pounds) sometimes found themselves up against light welter-weights (less than ten stone two pounds), or even welterweights (less than ten stone nine pounds). Welterweights are big boys compared with light-weights. But, I asked, how can this happen? I'd seen the Muhammad Ali weigh-ins on the telly, with the officials, the TV cameras and the reporters.

'Well, it's not always like that,' he said. He told the story of being weighed in on kitchen scales at the Café Royal and on another occasion a friend of his simply being asked his weight (because he wanted to go off to get a hamburger). The weigh-in isn't always terribly formal, it seemed, and in some cases it doesn't take place at all.

Since becoming a professional, Vinny said, he didn't enjoy the training so much. Since his latest fight in May he had done no training at all for three months. No running, no press-ups, no sparring, no nothing. He'd got another job – bouncer in a pub in Sheffield. He reckoned to get about £3000 a year from this job and about the same from boxing. So for three months he had just been working in the pub. He was a bit of a local celebrity. Men came in and bought him drinks and persuaded him to go to nightclubs with them so that they could get in free. 'It almost pays you to go,' he said. Vinny had only started drinking since his latest fight. He could see the irony in the situation, though. When he was training, he got up at half past five in the morning to run because the air is clearer at that time ('if a bus passes you at that time in the morning you can really smell its fumes – at any other time you can't') but here he was four nights a week in probably the smokiest pub in Sheffield (the Metro, one of the most popular, in a basement). He knew that working in such an environment is probably the equivalent of smoking about twenty cigarettes a week, so he tried to stand outside when possible, even if it was raining. It might look like real dedication to the job – scrutinising the punters as they came in – but it was just that the night air, even in Sheffield, is preferable to the air inside. He'd had other part-time jobs as well – before his latest fight he worked on security at York racecourse for three days. He laughed when he remembered it. 'It was pouring down with rain the whole time and I had to stand in it for six hours a day. I missed three days' training just before the big fight.' All the professional boxers from his gym had other jobs to make ends meet – most worked in the building or steel industries.

Vinny didn't look much like a professional boxer. He said that he sometimes overheard people talking about him and saying 'Who, him?' in disbelief as he walked past. He's the kind of guy bullies pick on, but 'they usually regret it,' he said. One week he was coming out of a nightclub and some ox picked on him, punching him on the back of the head for being too friendly with his girlfriend. Vinny tried to get into a taxi, but the ox took a swing at him. Vinny started dodging and rolling and the ox was getting angrier and angrier. A crowd had gathered – it was after all a good deal cheaper than the £30 ringside seats at his last bout. Ox wouldn't give up and Ox's girlfriend also joined in. 'One minute she was giving me the eye, the next she was trying to scratch mine out.' Vinny ended up having to slap the ox and set his girlfriend on the ground before slipping off. 'Some boxers would have just punched the pair of them, but I wouldn't do that. His girlfriend kept signalling her lunges so on one of them I just picked up her leg and set her on the ground.' Ox's pride of course was greatly hurt, because some waif had humiliated him in front of a huge crowd. So Ox now threatened to blow him away. Such are the rewards for having some real skill which generalises to the street. Most people want everyone else to be what they seem, and Vinny obviously isn't. On the mean streets you don't expect someone to weave and dodge and roll and then to land you with one. And you certainly don't expect it at two in the morning.

Vinny wanted to be out of boxing before he is twenty-seven. Seven years to get some collateral for acquiring property. Seven more years of watching out for left hooks in the ring and hooligans with broken glasses and knives outside it. It's a risky, even perilous way of saving money. 'Bomber wants to be world champion and to be a millionaire. I just want a steady stream of fights with nice regular payments, so that I can buy some property and rent it out. But you can't get a mortgage if you're a boxer; your income fluctuates too much and is too unreliable. So I really need some good money. The British title would be nice, but I'll probably make more money in the long run if I'm not too hot. My stoppage in my last fight probably did wonders for my bank balance. It probably makes me really attractive to the London promoters.'

The pimp

Pimps are targets of moral outrage, usually pictured as sinister, callous manipulators, heartless, gutless and loaded. But what is the reality of the pimp? On the streets of New York or even Marseilles may walk cool dudes with chunky gold bracelets, handcrafted shoes and fedoras, but not, thankfully, on the streets of Sheffield. Sheffield is no Miami when it comes to vice; it's not even a London. It does have massage parlours, it does have a red-light district (where the Yorkshire Ripper's career came to its sticky end) and, of course, it does have the demand. But it doesn't have the sheer size or volume to provide the anonymity which successful vice seems to require. The women on the streets are the same women as in the pubs or nightclubs. Ordinary women with ordinary needs and desires. They can't so much hide their guilty secret as laugh it off. Few women, when you ask them why they do it, blame the recession. 'It was the recession, luv, honest.' But a surprising number metamorphosed into sluts, having failed to become anything else. 'I just wanted to work in a bank,' said one, 'but I couldn't get in anywhere.' Now she was used to depositing sums that the cashiers could only dream about. 'I'm afraid there's no going back now,' and I could see her gold tooth when she smiled. I didn't know whether to feel more sorry for her or for the penniless cashiers.

But I thought I'd start with the infrastructure of vice. After all, whores may come and go, so to speak, but pimps, like acne, are harder to remove. So I decided to meet someone who fixed blokes up with women. Not too flash. Just an ordinary working type – like the women themselves. A normal chap who made a bit of money out of fixing blokes up with women and perhaps looked after the women as well. I came to interview him with my stereotypes and prejudices simmering, my moral outrage under control, just. Then Bill walked in – six foot two, 15 stone, twenty-eight, ex-bouncer, ex-blacksmith, a professional heavy who almost joined the army. So far, so good. And then we chatted. How did he get into it?

Bill originally worked as a night porter in a hotel outside Sheffield. Life wasn't easy. 'Long hours for fuck-all pay. I was fighting a lot and getting all my exercise that way. But when I moved to a hotel in Sheffield, I wasn't getting enough exercise, I was getting fat. So after I finished work in the early morning me and a friend would take some weights and a punch bag out to the country. We'd tie it up to a tree and work out every morning. Oh, it were beautiful. Fantastic. My friend had a bit of a bad back but I knew enough about weights to help him out with different things. We'd wash in the cold stream afterwards. Oh, it were beautiful. Then I'd take my friend back down to the station to get the train home. But then the weather got bad so we were missing a few mornings. So we mentioned this to a guy called Bob we vaguely knew, who's very interested in boxing. We were telling him about our training and how it was disrupted by the weather. He told us that a friend of his had got a sauna with a gym so why don't we go down there. So we went down to see the bloke who owned it, and he said we could put us punch bag up, use the weights, the sauna and the jacuzzi. Fantastic. All free. He also said if there were any trouble could we help out. We said of course we can. That's how I got involved and got to meet the girls. I knew most of them from around town anyway.

'I started looking after four girls, finding them customers and all the rest of it. I used to take one of the girls out. I told her she had to get herself smartened up though. I've got a big car, you see, a bit flash. I used to go round the clubs finding her good punters, you see. Earned a bit of money for myself and them as well. I used to go to a lot of blues as well – you know, the all-nighters for blacks. I started mixing with these black guys and their girls. You should see them up Spital Hill in Sheffield on Tuesdays.'

Bill was critical of women with black pimps. 'They're the low-life girls; they've got a way of talking. They imitate the black men's patois, they develop a sort of accent. It sounds so cheap. You can always tell them, they always say "You know", "You know what I mean, right". They slur on the "right". It's just me that notices these things, I think. "Do you want a cup of coffee, you know?" slurring all the time. Or "He's my man, you know, you've got to leave him". They slur all over the bloody place. They try to talk like black men.'

Bill had his own views on how women get into this line of work. 'Well, a lot of them have a rough background and leave home. And often, a lot of black men are out looking for these young girls that leave home. The blacks have got the run of it, for some reason. I wish I knew why! They take half their money, or even two-thirds of it. He then protects them against other pimps. But it's all a bit of a joke. The pimps get their mates to harass the girls and the pimp will come up and say "You leave my woman alone" and she's thinking "Oh, thank God for that", and it's just a game the pimps play for each other. It's psychological, I suppose. And these guys will be dealing in hash as well.

'In the saunas the atmosphere is more relaxed but quite a few of them have pimps anyway. I look after some of the girls there. In the saunas, they only let in the people they want. They've more control; but to be honest, they let anybody in. They don't really know what they're like until they get in. Some get a bit violent and slap the girls about.'

Bill had had to step in on a number of occasions to help the woman he was going out with. 'There was this guy, he was a bit mucky and my girlfriend didn't want to do anything, you see. He smelled; she wanted him to go and have a shower and all that, and that's what started the argument. So I went up and he was standing at the back with a wine bottle in his hand. He wanted to have a go, you see. So I took it off him, but he got that violent, I had to let him have it. When I say let him have it, I don't mean I brutally made a mess of him, I just sort of knocked him semiconscious.'

'But,' I said, 'weren't you a little worried for your girlfriend's safety?'

'Not really, I wasn't thinking of her as a steady girlfriend. She was just a steady fuck.'

'But weren't you a little worried for your steady whatever's safety?'

'It's part of the game,' said Bill, 'the same as what bouncers do or anybody else. You can't worry about things like that. The only difference was I was getting a tenner a night when I was a bouncer, she was picking up a hundred a night.

'Our relationship was quite simple. We both knew the crack. There was none of this "I'll take you out for a meal because I might be able to give you one afterwards". You know what I mean. I could give her one any time I wanted. It was nice to go out for a meal. It was nice for her to take me out for a meal. We could talk plainly to each other. I just lined up some punters for her. In the sauna she pays the owner £20 a week to work there, anything else she makes is entirely on her own back, to coin a phrase. It's £10 for a gobble, £15 for a fuck. But I've arranged for girls to go to punters' houses. Then they get up to £100 from one punter. The majority of girls who work on the streets are the girls who don't know what they're doing. They've got young pimps who think they're a bit clever, who are trying to work their way up the pimp scale, shall we say. They've got a few girls working for them who are often under age, who don't know anything else. Some of these girls in winter try to get into the saunas. The only way to categorise girls really is those who are working for blacks and those that aren't. Those that work for the blacks might go to the blues with them but they've no real social life. The girls who do it for themselves and any girls I know do have a social life. They're nice clean-living girls that you wouldn't think were on the game. They know the crack, they're very wide. They know what all the chat's about.'

Bill was especially useful for fixing women up with punters from out of town, through his other work in the hotel. 'When the snooker's on at the Crucible or when there's businessmen's conferences there's a lot of visitors to the town. It's entirely on your own back – it's nothing to do with any place you work for, it's entirely as a bloke to a bloke. They don't want ripping off and it's got to be a decent-looking girl, otherwise they'll think, who the fuck's he? What's he doing to me? So rather than send him to a sauna, I'll fix him up with some nice-looking girl I know that he can take out. And nobody will be saying "Look who's out with brass". They can go out with some nice company who can talk, present herself well and even associate with his friends if necessary. She'll get £100 and I'll get a drink from the business-man. The last bloke gave me forty-five quid for looking after him. He was worried, you see, that he'd end up with a right dog.

'The art is not to be known as someone who is always mixing with prostitutes. The art is to get people to say "He's all right and he can even fix you up with a bird if you want". That's the difference. Do you understand? I want to keep myself on that middle line. I'd hate to have a bad name for anything.'

The masseuse

Anita was a woman with a lot of 'oomph', a real go-getter. In Thatcher's Britain with unemployment at nearly 4 million Anita had managed to hold down not just one job – but three. She was simultaneously a part-time beauty consultant and a part-time secretary and she worked in a massage parlour. The last job was the most lucrative. 'You can earn up to £600 a week,' she said. 'Well, most girls earn a bit less but you can if you want to. It depends of course on what you are prepared to do. In this line of business hard work is rewarded.' Living proof that effort will get you somewhere in these times of recession.

Anita was twenty-three, blonde and pretty, but she had bad teeth. 'I could have been a photographic model,' she said, and she pulled out a wad of black and white contact prints. In them she looked very pretty indeed, she pouted and teased. You couldn't see her bad teeth. She would have liked to have been a model but the massage-parlour job came along. 'It probably pays better anyway,' she added. But what did her family think of the job? 'Oh, they don't know anything about it, they think I'm just a secretary. They're not my real parents anyway, they're my foster parents. They're in their seventies – very prim and proper, very strait-laced. They'd die if they

knew. I had a very strict upbringing. Some of the girls are a bit rough. One of my friends worked on the streets in London before she came here. But I had a very proper upbringing. I hardly ever went out. I was very shy with boys. They'd just die.' But what about her friends? 'Well, most of my girlfriends know because they're in the business too, but I never tell my boyfriends. Well, how do you think they'd react? They wouldn't respect me for a start. They'd think I was an easy lay, and the funny thing is I'm not.'

Anita worked in a sauna/massage/adult-movie emporium, open twenty-four hours a day. Hers was a 'bent' sauna. Massage plus extras. They're always very busy. 'A lot of men call in on the way home from work and a lot on the way to work. Well, you know what men are like in the morning. Then we're busy at two o'clock in the morning when the nightclubs empty and even at five o'clock in the morning when the punters come from the casinos.' Anita's best friend was the receptionist in the massage parlour. Anita had been doing it for three years.

'Two of my best friends were in the business at the time. This was in Leeds. They brought me along. When the first customer came in I wouldn't go anywhere near him. He had picked me for the massage but I just couldn't do it. One of my friends had to do it for me. They were both mad at me, my friend and the punter. He thought it was something to do with him. My friend said, "How are you going to earn any money like this?" The first customer I did massage was a gentleman about fifty – very toffee-nosed, very prim and proper. He really put me off with his manner. The massage lasted about two hours – it's only supposed to take about fifteen minutes. He was lying on his stomach all that time. I didn't want him to turn over. But as soon as he did, he came out with the line I was dreading. "Any extras?" I could have died. I told him it was £15. I hoped he'd say he couldn't afford it. But he didn't. I had to go through with it. He said he knew it was my first time. I did it without looking at him.

'Most of my regular customers are between about thirty-five and seventy. I hate doing younger ones. Especially ones I fancy. I find it really embarrassing. Loads have asked me out. I've even been out with a few although I make it a rule never to go out with clients. I can't respect them. One of my older clients – he's sixty-three and called John – says he's in love with me. He comes twice a week – that's £7 to get in and £15 for the massage with extras – twice a week. That's £44 per week and he's retired. He's not that well off. He sends me letters nearly every week and keeps saying he'd like me to marry his son. But he never brings his son with him! He says I'm different from the other girls and should be doing something else for a living. He says I'm a very complex person. On one occasion he even asked me to kiss him. But that's something I would never do. Kissing is an emotional thing, it's not a sexual act. I hardly ever even kiss boyfriends! If I go out with a boy a couple of times I'll let him feel my tits – that's because he fancies me – but I won't let him kiss me. When you kiss someone you show your emotion. When John asked me I told him to get stuffed.

'I sometimes see clients when I'm out – well, you can't avoid it in a small place like Sheffield – but I never say hello unless they say hello first. It might make explaining who I am a bit difficult. It's amazing the number of girls who'd like my job. See the girl there – that barmaid [we were talking in a pub] – she was asking about a job last weekend. The money is so good. I did it first when I split up from my boyfriend. He was a Jewish wheeler-dealer, whizz kid making a bundle, some of it illegally. We lived together and he supported me completely. We lived on a kibbutz in Israel for a while. When we split up, I wanted to be independent – my own flat, nice clothes, a car. It was the only way I could achieve independence. I thought I'd just do it for a little while – all the girls do – but it's addictive. It's not the sex, it's the money. You get used to having it.

'But there's something else about the job which I really like. It's the status. In the massage parlour the girls are right high up in status and the men are so low. They know it and we know it. You get respect from the men. It's a good service and we have to be professional – cool, calm and collected. The men respect our professionalism. I've been offered a number of jobs through my work – selling, modelling, one client even offered to make me a director of his company. He said that I was good enough to be able to handle anything. But he also said that he wanted me to fall in love with him first. I told him I couldn't do that.

'Working in a massage parlour has done a lot for my self-confidence. I used to hate my body and be really shy with boys. But all the clients say that I've got a lovely pair of tits. I love compliments. I've also become a bit of an actress – I can act dead sexy, watch.' She narrowed her eyes and pouted her lips and Bardot circa 1960 shone through. 'You have to be an actress. I do a two-girl massage with my friend Debbie. I've learned a lot from her. She's been doing it for much longer than me. She can act dead sexy and she really turns the punters on. It's great to watch. The first couple of times I nearly burst out laughing, though. But Debbie's a real professional, she never laughs.

'I really respect the girls at work. The ones I don't respect are those that hand their money over to a pimp. They're as bad as the prostitutes on the street. But the other girls are real professionals. They're making a bomb. One or two have even opened their own businesses.

'All the men want to chat to you while you're giving them a massage. They tell you about their wives and their businesses. They always say the same thing. "What's a nice girl like you doing in a massage parlour?" I tell them I'm just saving up enough money to go to university, which is true in a way. I used to want to do psychology in order to sort myself out, but now I want to do law. We get a lot of lawyers as clients and they're all very nice. I moved flat recently and John sent me a card with a little note inside telling me about visiting Bristol with his wife and how he missed seeing me. Wouldn't it be a laugh if I bumped into him one day with his wife and son? I wonder who he'd say I was. He says I'm a complex person and he'd like to sort me out. Perhaps if I study psychology I'll be able to sort him out.

'Working in a massage parlour hasn't put me off men. I've got lots of boyfriends but they don't know what I do for a living. God knows where they think I get my money from. I'm very clean. I don't do sexual intercourse. I have about three showers and one bath a day. When I get home from work I always have to have a bath to wash the dirt off. Sometimes I feel really filthy. I always like talking, as you can see. I never stop. I chat the whole time I'm giving a massage. Some of my clients can't get a word in. Just as well, some of them are a bit quiet.'

5 · The professionals at work

> 'Well, in our country,' said Alice, still panting a little, 'you'd generally get to somewhere else – if you ran very fast for a long time, as we've been doing.'
>
> 'A slow sort of country!' said the Queen. 'Now, *here*, you see, it takes all the running *you* can do, to keep in the same place. If you want to get somewhere else, you must run at least twice as fast as that!'
>
> Lewis Carroll, *Through the Looking-Glass*, 1872

The burglar

I have only been burgled once, and the burglar wasn't even successful. Indeed, so unsuccessful was he that he ended up leaving me some goods rather than leaving with mine. I could hear him pottering about. I shouted, he ran, leaving a typewriter behind, undoubtedly removed from a neighbour's house. I considered myself very lucky because like most people I have heard and read the stories about the mess burglars make when they're on the job – the ransacked rooms, the broken furniture, the meals they cook themselves, the urine, the excrement.

Crime-prevention advertisements exploit and propagate such images to persuade people to lock their windows. But my burglar wasn't like that – he was careful, meticulous and tidy (even if a bit noisy), he didn't try to cook himself a meal or use my house as a toilet. Apparently he's like many other burglars, contrary to the popular or sensational image. Research by Mike Maguire and Trevor Bennett (1982), which involved interviewing several hundred victims of burglary, revealed that in less than one in a hundred cases was wilful damage caused and only in one in 300 cases was a 'nuisance' committed in the house (that is, the burglar 'excreted, masturbated, urinated or vomited').

Nevertheless, my personal experience got me thinking – what kind of person could go into the home of a total stranger and, firstly, have the skill to find something of value (certainly difficult in my house) and, secondly, have no twinge of conscience about removing whatever he could lay his sticky little fingers on? And what other myths about burglars had I been fed on, and digested? How did the burglar, in fact, select my house – was I a prime target (or a 'prawn' target as one burglar subsequently put it to me)? Was it easy to get in? And what was the probability of it happening again?

According to Maguire and Bennett's research, the answer to the latter question is 'very likely'. They reckon that the 'average British citizen' can expect to be burgled two or three times during his or her lifetime. To arrive at this figure they considered both official police statistics *and* interviews with the public, because many burglaries involving quite small sums are never reported to the police. *House* burglary is also more popular today than ever before, presumably for a variety of reasons. Insurance companies now often insist on tight security for shops and warehouses, and safes are more common and better designed. Houses, on the other hand, nowadays are full of expensive and highly marketable goods such as TVs and videos (as one burglar put it, 'some houses, even on council estates, are bloody Aladdin's caves inside'). Sentences for house burglary can be quite stiff – the maximum is fourteen years but many burglars today end up in magistrates' courts facing fines. As another burglar put it to me, 'I'd enough in my piggy bank for the first fine.' (In the seventeenth and eighteenth century, house burglary carried the death penalty.)

But what are burglars really like? I needed to meet some personally. I originally made some enquiries to a group of acquaintances who were at the shady end of the used-car trade. Surely they would know someone who did a spot of burglary. They received my enquiry with a mixture of surprise and disbelief. 'But everybody does a little, don't they?' they said in unison. 'Do you really mean that if you were passing a house on the way home and its windows were lying open and you could see a wallet on the table that you wouldn't nip in?' I gulped my lager. 'Certainly not.' Their collective faces, like so many one-arm bandits, registered 'MUG, MUG, MUG'. It was clear from the outset that I had to make a distinction between my used-car friends – merely opportunist thieves who couldn't resist temptation when thrust in their face – and real burglars who made their living from it. Pros with good *markets* for their *goods*. Pros who had learned the *trade* and knew the ropes, who did *jobs* that were good *earners*, and who someday may *retire* to Marbella. That is to say, then, who viewed it as *work*, in more than a metaphorical sense.

A chain of association eventually led me clanking along to Danny (name changed). Still only twenty but already a pro – he'd served his time at his chosen profession in more ways than one. (Several hundred burglaries in five years and two stretches in borstal and one in prison.) In official terms he's a recidivist. He put it bluntly: 'Money, clothes and having a good time is my life. If I got a job I'd have to change my whole life style. What would I do with £80 a week? I can spend that in one night. Burglary is the only real skill I've got.'

Danny's profession runs in the family (his father was at the time on the run for an armed robbery offence) but he said his family had nothing to do with it. It was his mates. He was fifteen, they were sixteen, he was their eager pupil. He started with a warehouse. 'We were careful to choose one without a burglar alarm. We got in through a ground-floor window. It was dead easy. We all had a look about and I found a cashbox in a drawer with a hundred quid in it. I couldn't believe it. It was money for old rope. We blew the money in two days on Indian meals, taxis and drinks. Then we went out again about three days later. We'd just get the bus a couple of miles down the road to the Moor or Bramall Lane and have a wander about.' (Research done in Sheffield suggests that nearly three-quarters of burglars travel less than two miles from their homes to commit the crime.) Danny enjoyed his new pastime. 'Some nights we'd do three places in the one spot. Sometimes of course you'd find nothing but occasionally you'd hit the jackpot.'

Within six months Danny had graduated to houses. 'We'd usually get the bus to Gleadless, which was a good spot because it borders on a wood. Dead easy to get away. We'd go up in the afternoon and just pick a house that looked empty. My two mates would stay in the next street and I'd just go up and knock the door. If anyone answered I'd say, "Is Paul in, please?" Nobody was ever suspicious. They'd just say, "Sorry, you must be at the wrong house." If nobody answered I'd just go and get my mates and we'd go round the back and steam in. If the windows were locked we'd just put a coat up to the window and knock it in. When I was in, I'd head straight for the bedroom to look for the jewellery case. I'd also look under the mattress straight away. Then it was down to the kitchen. You'd be amazed how many people keep money in the oven, but I've even found money stashed in cornflakes boxes. We never made a mess, at least deliberately – some houses would look a bit untidy afterwards but that's because you're looking for things in a hurry. You haven't got all day. The most I ever got from a house when I was a kid was eight and a half grand in goods from a house in Lodge Moor – at least that's what the local paper said. Me and another kid only got a grand and a half for the jewellery and stuff. Our fence was a market stall holder – a friend put me in touch with him.

'We also did quite a few electrical shops – well, some of them used to have eight videos in the window at the one time. The first time a mate of mine told me about this shop in the Ecclesall Road with eight in the window. We were in a nightclub at the time. So we get a taxi back to my house – I told the driver I had to get some stuff for work in the morning. Then we got the taxi to the Ecclesall Road and we got let off about a hundred yards from the shop. It was about three in the morning. I just kicked the side window in – the shop didn't have an alarm. I climbed in and passed the videos out. We hid them on some wasteland nearby. Early the next morning we rang our fence and he came and picked them up. We got one hundred and fifty quid for each one. Nobody noticed the broken window until the shop opened. The display must have looked a bit bare, though.' Danny laughed. 'The only problem was that I cut my hand badly getting in through the window. I showed it to my mum and she was really concerned. She said I needed to go to the hospital. But I couldn't go in Sheffield. I must have dripped blood all over the shop. So I got the train to Hull with the Sheffield United supporters. The hospital in Hull is very close to the station so I went there and gave them a false name and told them my mum had locked me out, for coming home late, so I had to smash a window to get in. My hand needed fourteen stitches. I went on to the match, but Hull City won 3–2. But what happened next was that the lad I did the electrical shop with got caught on another job. He grassed on me. I got a £554 fine plus probation. Of course, the fine wasn't that bad. I'd made quite a lot by then. My mum had to pay the fine, though. I'd spent what I'd made.'

After his court appearance Danny eventually got on a Youth Opportunity scheme but was dismissed for fighting. He then got on a building course and landed a job on a building site. This time he was sacked for being late. He kept up with his burglary and explored new avenues of thieving. At away football matches when his friends were congregated in a pub, he'd nip upstairs to the private quarters to take what he could find. On one occasion he found £600 in a cash box. But one lunchtime in York as he was trying to slip back into the pub, the landlady spotted him and grabbed him. 'I nearly crapped myself,' he said. 'I had to slip out of my coat and run off. Luckily my friends could see what was happening so they created a bit of a disturbance so that I could get away.'

At about this time another of his friends was arrested and the police started calling at his mum's. 'Just a few routine enquiries, madam.' Danny was off – to a little town in Wales. 'It was great,' he said, 'none of the jewellers or cigarette shops had alarms. They weren't used to crime. I was staying in the best hotels and coming back to Sheffield to sell the goods.' But on one visit home things went badly wrong. 'I'd arranged to meet this fence in a pub. He wasn't someone I'd ever done business with before – he was a friend of my dad's. So I sat there waiting, but he didn't show. The next minute the place is full of coppers – but they run straight past me. You see, I used to have a perm but in the meantime I'd had my hair straightened and streaked. I also had a good tan from a sun bed. The coppers didn't let anybody out of the pub, though, and the landlord identified me. He said he didn't know I was on the run. The fence must have grassed on me – to do himself a favour with the coppers. At Sheffield Crown Court the judge said I was a professional burglar and if I'd been older I would have got five years. As it was I was sent to Everthorpe borstal. I did thirteen months.'

Danny went back to burglary within a week of getting out of borstal. 'I'd got even more bottle now,' he said. 'I went into this jeweller's in Sheffield and asked to see some gold chains. When the assistant went to get her calculator I just grabbed the tray and ran. She started shouting, "Stop thief!" I thought they only did this in films. She ran after me and so did three passers-by. I ran all the way to Park Hill Flats where a friend of mine lives. I lost the people chasing me in Pond Street. The chains came to £7600 and I sold them to a fence in Birmingham for £2800. When it eventually came to court, by the way, the jeweller claimed it was £10,000 worth of stuff. They're all bloody bent.

'The really funny thing was that they had all these eyewitnesses giving different descriptions. I had a really good suntan at the time and a customer in the shop swore I must have been a Paki. But the shop assistant gave them a good description and I was eventually spotted in a hairdresser's. They pulled the hairdresser in as well because I'd been talking to her and she had a big gold chain on. She started bawling. They asked me to go on an identity parade but I refused. The police kept saying that all they were interested in was getting the stuff back, which wasn't a hell of a lot of good because I'd sold the stuff and spent the money. But when I was in the nick, this old bloke gave me a bit of advice. He told me to tell the coppers that I'd take them to the stuff but do a runner instead. He said that if a fit young lad like me couldn't get away from two fat CID men, who could?

'So I told the coppers I'd do it, but I didn't want ten big CID blokes tramping up to my mate's house. So they said, "That's OK, Danny, there'll only be two." So they picked me up about nine o'clock and handcuffed me. I told them that I wanted to ring my friend from the telephone box on the corner to make sure he was in. So they undid one of my handcuffs. So I went into the telephone box and pretended to make the call. They let me walk to the house with one of them, a sergeant, holding the end of the cuffs. He said to me, "You're not going to try and do a runner or owt like that, are you?" I said, "Of course not." I told them the stuff was in the bin in the back garden. I knew that part of Sheffield really well, and as soon as I got to the garden I sprinted off across this wasteland. The sergeant was just standing there shouting, "Come back, you little bastard!" I ran straight to one of my friends' houses and he sawed the cuffs off. They sealed the whole area off and got dogs, Land Rovers, the lot. As my mum said, "It wasn't bloody fair, all this for one kid – Jack the bloody Ripper doesn't get this treatment." I sat up all night watching them search this wasteland from my friend's bedroom.

'In the morning the coppers called at my friend's at about eight o'clock. I was still in bed and his mum had to waken me up. I climbed out of the bedroom window with no shoes or socks on. It was December and it was bloody freezing. I was going to nip back in when they'd gone but some cleaners from a pub spotted me so I had to leg it. I saw this woman in her garden and told her my dog had run off and I was chasing after it so she loaned me some socks.' He hid with his cousin for a few days but the police went round all his friends and relations and Danny was eventually found hiding in her cubbyhole. 'The police told me I'd really done it this time. It was a really serious offence – what would have happened if the shop assistant had got hold of him? I was also charged with escaping from police custody and theft of handcuffs. Could you believe it? I was really crapping myself. Anyway the case eventually came to court and all I got was a "recall" to borstal – sixteen weeks. I'd been on remand for thirteen weeks so I only had three to do. My relatives in the public gallery all started clapping. The police weren't too happy about the sentence, and the two CID men who I'd escaped from got demoted to the shoplifting squad. I saw them last week – they gave me a real evil look.'

Danny went back to burglary within a few weeks of getting out of borstal. He started nicking Capo di Monte figures. 'Some people do collect them, you know.' Within two months he was back in remand. 'This time I got a really bad judge – I got fifteen months this time and spent the last eight in Armley prison in Leeds.'

Danny leaned back in his chair. 'It might seem to you that I haven't been that successful, but I've done hundreds of jobs and I've never actually been caught on the job. It's usually people wanting to do themselves a favour with the coppers. I know I've got the bottle and the skill. In ten years' time I'll either be doing a ten-year stretch or living it up. I'm not going to change my life style.'

And as he got up to go, suntan, streaked blond hair, expensive leather jacket – all the trimmings of the pop star – I asked him the question I've always wondered about, 'Do you ever think about your victims?' (Again, research by Maguire and Bennett suggests that burglary has a considerable effect upon people's lives, leaving them 'uneasy', 'insecure', even feeling 'violated'.) Danny doesn't think about this. 'Why should I? The people I burgle can afford it, and jewellers are all bent and bump up the insurance claims. Another thing, I never burgle poor people or old people.'

Danny was beginning to sound like Robin Hood. 'But just a minute, you've burgled council houses, isn't that right?'

'Yes,' Danny said, 'but loads of ordinary people have stacks of dough stashed away.'

'But do you really mean that if you went to all the trouble of breaking into a house and then discovered that it belonged to an old person, you wouldn't take anything?'

'Well, not nothing,' said Danny, 'but I wouldn't leave them broke.' And Robin Hood had, before my very eyes, started to metamorphose into the Sheriff of Nottingham – just enough left in the kitty to survive, when Danny's high demands were met.

The nurse

Hospitals are scrupulously clean, sanitised affairs washed through with soap and disinfectant and washed out by the soap opera. So many series have been set within their walls – *Doctor Kildare*, *Emergency Ward 10*, *Angels* – all offering glimpses of possible, imaginary worlds behind the closed door of the hospital. *Doctor Kildare* gave us glamour and the dashing man in the white coat, *Emergency Ward 10* gave us drama, *Angels* gave us bitchiness and nurses feuding over boyfriends and failing to cope with the demands of the job. Greater realism? And an attempt to show that inside every cool calm nurse there is an ordinary person with normal fears and anxieties wildly signalling to be let out. *Angels* attempted to give glimpses into both the public and private worlds of its fictional characters and to trace their interconnections.

Jane was a 25-year-old black nurse in a 750-bed northern hospital. It's an enormous modern building which dominates the area in which it is situated. She used to watch *Angels*. 'It was a load of crap,' she said. 'All that rushing about when someone had a stroke. It's not like that at all. All the nurses were real stereotypes as well. The problem with nursing is that there are so many different types. There are no stereotypes and they don't dash about like that either.'

Jane came originally from Jamaica. Her parents moved here when she was seven. She had always wanted to be a nurse, and her parents were very proud when she qualified. Her older sister was a nurse, her younger sister wanted to become one. Her younger brother, however, was unemployed and a Rastafarian. He was the only one interested in black culture, the rest were all 'forward-looking' and white-oriented.

Jane worked nights from 9.30 pm to 8 am, eight nights on and six nights off. Her take-home pay was around £95, she reckoned. It was a long night. *Angels* would have trouble reflecting its sheer length, the sheer boredom, interspersed of course with pure drama of the kind that wouldn't have shamed *Emergency Ward 10*. On nights she was usually accompanied by two other nurses, most commonly a student nurse and an auxiliary. Together they were responsible for about twenty-eight patients. There wasn't a sister on at nights but a sister was assigned to a surgical block of six wards. A doctor on call covered for two wards. Between 10 and 11 pm the doctor came in to check the patients and their fluid charts. The nurses did the drugs rota between 10 and 10.30 pm. They began in the TV room. It was lights out at 10.30 pm.

By 11 pm everyone was settled in bed. Jane worked in a surgical ward – they got direct admissions from casualty and also people who have been waiting years for an operation. People who were in hospital to have a toenail surgically removed and people who were in hospital to have half their stomach removed. Men who wanted to feel their bums and asked for a goodnight kiss ('my wife always gives me one') and men who wanted to hold their hands because they were dying. Men and women who went quiet because they were terrified of their operation and men and women who went quiet because a black nurse had just tried to tuck them in. The patients were a very heterogeneous bunch and the nurses had to be tactful, patient and really perceptive. 'Some patients feel a bit sorry for themselves and I try to help them, but some, once you start, try to get you to do everything for them,' said Jane. 'I tell them to do it themselves. Some, of course, can hardly manage to do anything for themselves but some people are just plain lazy. One old man asked me to wipe his bum yesterday because he had arthritis. I asked him, "Who does it for you at home?" He said "I do", so I told him to do it himself.'

The night was long and boring. The first meal break was at half past eleven. The most junior nurse went then. Jane, being the senior nurse, went for dinner at half past twelve. Breakfast was at 4.30 am. There were regular checks on patients throughout the night and some patients were regularly turned to prevent bedsores developing. Jane reckoned that about a third of the patients on a surgical ward have catheters inserted to drain urine. These had to be emptied at midnight, 4 am and 7 am. It was not terribly glamorous.

People also die on surgical wards so death was always something that the nurses had to face. One day on Jane's ward there was a death on every shift – one in the morning, one in the afternoon and one at night. 'That was the worst it's ever been,' she said. She still found death distressing. 'We move any patients who are doing poorly on to a side ward. Side wards are usually kept for those about to be discharged or those about to die. It's less distressing for the other patients, it's more private; their relatives can stay. When a person is doing poorly and moved to a side ward, a senior nurse is sent to "special" them – this means give them all the necessary cares; take their temperature, pulse and blood pressure, measure their urine output in the catheter; check the intravenous infusion every few hours; turn them every two hours. They also have to make sure their mouth is clear and free of blockages. And of course, they have to look for signs of imminent death – "cheyne-stoking" with long pauses in their breathing, their extremities turning blue or the skin on the arms and legs developing a motley appearance. I've become very good at estimating someone's likely time of death on the basis of these signs,' Jane said proudly. 'But you need the experience.' Death, according to Jane, was a bit of a noisy business and very distressing to all concerned – the nurse, the relatives and the patient. 'The patient most of all,' she said. 'Quite a few of them know when they are going to die. They look terrified and they really fight for air. It's sometimes a relief when they've finally gone.

'When someone is dying we have a nurse with them all the time to "special" them and hold their hand.' But didn't the relatives sometimes wish to be alone with the patient? 'No, not really. They want help. They want us to take over. They're very cooperative. They leave when we tell them – it's almost a relief for them. It's our responsibility to care for them until the very end. You only stop caring for them when they go to the mortuary. It's not our job to tell the relatives when they've died, though. It's the doctors'. Even if we know they're dead we just tell the relatives that their condition has deteriorated until the doctor comes to certify death. He then has a talk with the relatives. On nights there can sometimes be a bit of a delay, because there are fewer doctors and if there is an emergency on somewhere, the doctor can be tied up for quite a while. We keep the relatives in the sister's office until he arrives. We have to just keep saying that their condition is getting worse. Even when a patient is doing poorly you have to be very careful what you say in front of them. One nurse said about an elderly patient, "I'm glad she's nearly gone, she was a horrible old bitch," and the patient recovered. She'd even heard it. It was very embarrassing.

'We have a lot of people in this ward the night before an operation. They are always very anxious. The men go quiet, the women have a good weep. It's our job to reassure them, to explain what's going to happen to them. The doctors explain it to them as well but it's always over their heads. They'll say things like, "You're going to have a choleysystectomy, and a redivac drain is going to be implanted." We tell them they're going to have a tube put inside them for a couple of days to collect the gunge. They feel better when they know what is going to happen.

'The operating days in this hospital are Monday, Tuesday, Thursday and Friday. List admissions (those on the waiting list) come in on Sundays and Wednesdays. Serious operations are on Tuesdays and Fridays. Patients are "prepared" and "starved" the day before. Most patients are very co-operative, but you get the odd one who isn't. We had one man come in with an acute appendicitis. He hadn't had food for five hours so we were going to operate immediately. But we had to put back the time of his operation by a couple of hours because of an emergency road-traffic accident which took precedence. He was really annoyed, really angry, and just for badness he ate a load of food he'd brought into hospital with him in a brown paper bag. We had to postpone the operation, and ring theatre control and ring the surgeons and tell his doctor. We gave him a good bollocking.

'Our hospital has got very bad security. Anybody can walk in here. We've had a number of intruders. One nurse was attacked a while back by someone dressed as a doctor. It's very scary going to collect blood in the night because there are so many places to hide. There's also a lot of ghost stories that go round hospitals about old grey ladies appearing in the wards in which they died. I've never seen one but I do get a creepy feeling in some wards when somebody has died. It's always really cold. Even though this is a modern hospital it can have quite a scary feeling to it at night. And when someone you've been looking after for weeks has just died, the atmosphere is strange. Especially if they've made a real fight for it in the end. On nights it's usually so dull but sometimes I get really clear pictures in my head of patients who have died gasping for air and so on. It can really be quite frightening. But of course you can never show patients you're scared.

'We even had an obscene phone call last weekend. There was a heavy breather on the line. We asked the operator to trace the call but she said it was an internal call. We still don't know whether it was a doctor or a patient.

'I wouldn't try to persuade my sister not to become a nurse. Occasionally you get the odd patient who you can see really hates you. Just after my training I was helping one old woman and she shouted at me, "Go away, you black bastard!" I didn't go near her again. But they're exceptions. Most people don't notice your colour, they're too grateful for what you can do for them and some of course take a fancy to you. Some of the old men are always asking me to bathe them. I give them the sponge and tell them to get on with it. Well, I suppose it's better than them hating me.'

The store detectives

There she stood, surrounded by a huge wall of belts. Belts of every description – red, green, white, leather, suede and shiny shiny plastic. All glittering, all beckoning. It was obviously too much for her. She was almost fourteen, fat and untidy. She selected one little leather number and ran her fingers along its machine-crafted seam. And then the buckle – chrome, real chrome. She lifted it down from the stand and started to try it on. 'Watch it disappear,' the store detective, Jenny, said. All eyes were on the belt and suddenly, like a float in water, it went under; it dipped under her voluminous coat. The fish had bitten.

But it resurfaced again; it didn't fit. She selected another from the glittering display – a larger one that might fit around her considerable girth.

'This time we'll get her,' Jenny said. We were waiting for a second bite. Jenny nodded to another store detective – Paul, dressed unobtrusively for the day in pink vest and pink socks – 'He's gay, you know,' said Jenny. 'The fat lady,' she whispered. Paul looked confused. 'You're standing beside her – fat girl, I mean,' she said, correcting herself. Paul started flicking through some scarves – just another gay boy out for some Saturday shopping in the ladies' department of a large store, or so it seemed. He stood right beside her. The fat girl, who was now trying on another belt, was visibly perspiring. But whether this was from the anxiety of an imminent bout of shoplifting or from the sheer effort of getting a belt around her large waist or even from the fact that an obvious member of Sheffield's gay community was violating her personal space was much less clear. Paul didn't take his eyes off the scarves. 'He's watching her every move, though,' said Jenny, and I started wondering about the exact properties of Paul's eyes.

The fat girl struggled with the belt before giving up in despair. She put it back on the rack, her reputation intact, just. Saved by modal fashion. We left Paul, still examining the scarves.

No one doubts that shoplifting is a serious and prevalent form of crime in Britain. Newspaper headlines insist that it's the equivalent of a Great Train Robbery every day, even allowing for inflation. But it's hard to put an exact figure on it because 'shrinkage' in retail includes all the pilfering by everyone from the warehouse staff (through the delivery drivers, the sales assistants, the shelf-fillers, the managers) to the people who operate the tills. The customers play some role in 'shrinkage' but it's clearly not the whole story. It's nevertheless a sufficiently important part to warrant a boom in the growth of security services and store-detective agencies.

Jenny Brough and her partner Sylvia Woodland had operated a store detective agency (SYLJEN) in Sheffield for the past five years. They had about twenty employees, nearly all women, Jenny said that before the recession, men wouldn't really have been all that interested in spending an entire day in ladies' fashion. They had been billed as Sheffield's Charlie's Angels but without any hidden male master behind them. Store detecting is a cut-throat business, in more ways than one, and the only way to make a decent profit was to have a reasonable number of employees because they only charged shops around £3.85 an hour. Syljen operated in many of the large retail stores in Sheffield, Barnsley, Rotherham, Scarborough, even Lincoln.

I met one of their best store detectives, Ron Teskowski, twenty-six, an ex-miner. He'd been a store detective for the past five years. 'He's good,' said Jenny, 'he can blend in anywhere. I've seen shoplifters look straight past him.'

Ron interrupted. 'There have been loads of times when I've arrested a smart-looking lady and the police have been called. When they arrive they say, "Right, madam, tell us what he did." I have to say, "Hang on a minute, I'm the bloody store detective, she's the thief," and on one occasion I was standing next to this old lady in a chemist's and she slipped a bottle of shampoo into her bag and said, "Don't say owt, love, I'm a pensioner." I had to nick her, of course.'

Ron said store detecting was like a hobby to him. 'I've caught thirteen shoplifters in one day, if I don't catch anybody I feel really guilty. My thrill used to be in catching people nicking large amounts but it's the unusual ones I get a kick out of now – I get a real thrill out of catching a company director or a policeman.' All 'stops' were recorded in his little notebook and this register chronicled the full gamut of human greed, rapacity, weakness and folly. 'Here's a good one,' he said. 'I caught these four unemployed lads from Liverpool with £350 worth of stuff. They were coming out of a store as I was walking in, and I heard one say, "Let's do Burton's now." So I followed them there. Two of them just picked this rack up and ran out of the shop with it. Their mates just walked slowly out behind them. I followed them to this multi-storey car park. They put everything in black bags in the boot of this car and set off back to town. So I phoned the police and me and the police hid in the car park and we pounced on them when they got back. They had sixteen pairs of cords and seven shirts in the boot.' The bulk of this stuff came from Burton's, but Burton's still declined an offer of this agency's services.

'Or look at this one. I saw a bloke nick a small toy train from one shop so I followed him. He went into the next shop and nicked a portable television. We got the police. When they searched his house they found that his cellar was set out like a mail-order catalogue. He kept a book of all the things he'd stolen and there was more than £30,000 worth of stuff recorded.'

These cases contrast markedly with some others in Ron's book.

Girl aged 10. Stole 39p lip gloss. Slipped it into left-hand pocket of coat. Parents called.

Charge hand aged 64. Stole one pair of socks	99p
one plum	3p

TOTAL £1.02

Police called.

Some of the entries were just plain embarrassing. 'This woman said hello to me as I went into the chemist's. She lives on my estate. I saw her slip two packets of Durex into her purse. I had to stop her, but I let her off with a verbal caution. She can't look at me straight now.'

In some shops in which this agency works, calling the police is at the discretion of the store detectives – luckily for the woman with the Durex. In many others it isn't. If the shoplifter is under twelve, however, the parents are called instead. When they have discretion, what affects whether the police are called or not?

'Well,' said Jenny, 'if you're between say fifteen and sixty-five you've no chance unless you're on day release from Middlewood [a local mental hospital] or something like that. Between these ages we get the police. With kids or pensioners you like to give them a second chance. Some kids don't know any better, with pensioners they usually nick for attention because they're lonely. But you can't feel too sorry for pensioners – I haven't met one yet who has stolen out of necessity. And they've all got excuses, of course.' She showed me some letters written to her by people they'd apprehended, blaming the slight deviation from the straight and narrow on (variously) 'intestinal infections', 'sudden bereavement', 'high blood pressure', even 'flu'. 'Most people are very upset when you stop them, although some couldn't care a monkey's,' she said, 'and it's amazing how many women urinate on the spot when you stop them. One even pretended to have a heart attack. Five minutes later, though, she was asking me for a fag and pulling down her knickers to show me the scars of an operation she'd had. There's one pensioner in Barnsley who's seventy who we've caught loads of times. The last time I caught her she'd nicked two bottles of cough mixture. You'd probably think "poor old dear" but when I stopped her she ran off, and I had to chase after her through the middle of Barnsley. When I eventually caught her she thumped me with her shopping bag. She's tough as an old boot – she's been in Holloway three times.

'Shoplifters are definitely getting more violent,' said Jenny. She was just getting over a badly bruised face. 'I stopped this lad going out of a shop with a stolen ski jacket on under his own coat. He tried to get away so I grabbed his arm and we fell to the floor. He had three mates and they doubled back and gave me a good kicking while I was down.'

Jenny did not underestimate the seriousness of being caught shoplifting, but, she said, 'If people want to risk it, that's their business. I caught a lawyer nicking a packet of disposable razor blades from a chemist's. He'd even nicked two tins of dye and a book from an Oxfam shop. The police searched his house and found more stolen property. Ron caught a Bradford policeman who had been in the force for thirteen years nicking a brass switch plate worth £5.28 from a DIY store. He had to resign. A Sheffield Crown Court judge, Mr James Pickles, even admitted in a court case in Sheffield that he had once, earlier in his career, walked away from a souvenir shop without paying for some postcards. When he suddenly realised what he'd done he went back immediately to pay for them. But he says he's had considerable anxiety over the years about feeling a hand on his shoulder when he's in some stores. What occasioned the confession was his instructing a jury to find a manager not guilty of stealing some batteries. The judge knew how easy it was to absentmindedly leave without paying.'

But what about Jenny – had she ever shoplifted? 'Well, I once tried to nick some snowdrops perfume from Woolies when I was about ten. But I panicked and dumped it in a woman's shopping bag.' Panic had kept her record clean.

John, another store detective, knew what it feels like to have a slightly soiled past. His nose had been rubbed in it enough times. He'd been a store detective for three years and by all accounts a very good one. When he got the job he didn't mention his 'criminal record'. When he was eleven, he and a group of friends threw stones at some greenhouse windows. Some windows broke. 'I don't even know if my stone broke a window,' he said. He was fined two pounds. Two years later he nicked a Mars bar, and got a verbal caution from an inspector. When he was fourteen a friend (also fourteen) gave him a lift in his dad's Reliant Robin. They got stopped by the police. They had to say that the father hadn't given them permission, even though he had. Again a verbal caution.

Hardly notorious form, and all at least twelve years ago, but it was still on file. 'I caught a retired policeman who was seventy-two in Barnsley nicking. I got the police and went with them to the station to make a statement. When I was just about to sign it the station officer suddenly said to me, "Have you ever been in trouble yourself, lad?" I just said "Why?" and he said, "Well, I'm just asking you a question, have you ever been in trouble?" Well, I wasn't really expecting him to say this so I said "no" at first. He got up and went out of the room and came back with this piece of paper and started reeling off my three convictions, one after the other. He'd checked me out, even though you're not supposed to do that unless you're suspected of being involved in a crime. All I'd done was catch a bloody ex-cop nicking. So I said, "I don't think you should bring this up," and he just said, "I don't think we'll be seeing you around Barnsley again." I just got up and walked out.' The statement was never signed.

The police then phoned Jenny and asked if she was aware that John had been convicted of shoplifting and criminal damage. 'We were flabbergasted,' said Jenny. 'We had him up in the office but when he explained how long ago it was, we stood by him. They'd no right to use this against him.'

John broke in: 'It's because of my brothers – they've been in trouble with the police quite a few times.' 'It's also because he's too good at his job,' said Jenny. 'John caught a superintendent's son who's thirteen nicking £57 worth of stuff. And would you believe it, a couple of months later we caught the same superintendent's dad shoplifting as well. Both got an instant verbal caution. That means nothing went on record. Neither file was processed. No criminal record, no blemishes on their character. No nothing. And who says crime doesn't run in families?'

The shark

The room always felt cramped enough when there were just two people in it, but tonight there were five. All were gathered around the low plastic table with just a single new car catalogue lying on it as a possible alternative focus of attention to the salesman's face. Not surprisingly, everyone was looking at the catalogue. The light in the room was unusually bright, like something out of a fictitious spy drama, but the pressure was real enough. It was now eight o'clock, the showroom closed at 5.30; the salesman had gone out of his way to arrange a test drive after hours. He'd taken a lot of trouble to show the car to the customer's wife (this latter act of generosity had, unfortunately from the salesman's point of view, meant that the customer's wife and children returned to the showroom with him, thus swelling the numbers and the pressure). The salesman had spent weeks getting the customer, who had expressed some small, some would say insignificant, interest in the car weeks ago, back to the showroom.

The stage was now most definitely set. The salesman knew it, the customer knew it, even the customer's wife and children could feel the tension in the room. And the two-year-old child reacted to this tension in the customary way. 'I need to do pooh,' he said quietly, between sucks of his thumb. In such a small, cramped room the statement was nearly redundant, the only uncertainty was the person concerned. Everyone was relieved that it was the two-year-old. The wife and both children (she couldn't take chances) disappeared to the toilet. The customer was now temporarily deprived of the usual familial support network. In other words he was alone; the salesman pounced.

'Well, Bob.' (They'd been on first-name terms since the first introduction, the salesman had made sure of that.) 'You've inspected the car, you've had the customary test drive. Are you prepared to buy this car – not tomorrow or next week, but tonight? I should have been home for my tea three hours ago. Why don't we get it all over with?'

Bob blinked back. The pen was pushed in front of him. A clock ticked in the background. His hand made an almost involuntary movement towards the pen. He couldn't bear the tension. He stared at the salesman, Tony with the smooth moustache. What a shark. He'd set the whole thing up, the late test drive to arrive back at the closed showroom, the little bright room with no distractions, he'd probably even engineered his two-year-old son's sudden panic reaction. All to get him under pressure. Crafty devils, these used-car salesmen. Tony wasn't oriental or anything but he had that same hard gleam in his eye as the Hollywood Chinaman, the same cold expression not ameliorated in the slightest by the warm soft tone of voice. 'But –' Bob was starting to stammer – he hadn't done that since his youth-club days – 'what about the torn thing that holds the gear stick?' Anxiety was making him unable to find his words.

'It can be fixed, believe me,' Tony replied, his reply starting before the question was finished, indeed seeming to begin before the question even commenced.

'What about the accelerator which was sticking?'

'It can be fixed, believe me, believe me. It'll all be fixed before you get the car.' Bob started to sweat, he noticed that there was even condensation on the face of the clock. The pressure was unbearable.

'I can't, I just can't,' Bob blurted out. 'I want the car. I'd love to buy it, I don't want to be a time-waster but there's too much wrong with it. I'd love to sign the form but I just can't. Please, we must go. I'm sorry and . . .' Bob hastily departed, picking up his family on the way, relieved to have escaped from the salesman's grasp.

'They're such sharks,' he said as he got into his own car, 'such bloody sharks,' and he felt all sticky with sweat as if he'd somehow managed to heave himself out of its cavernous jaws.

The shark looked quite forlorn. It was ten past nine. It had been a long day and he'd only managed to sell one car. The figures flooded his mind: his basic salary is £2000 – that's less than £40 a week before stoppages. If he sells five cars a month he gets an extra £100, for the next five an extra £125, and so on. Last month he sold twelve cars – if he kept that up he'd be earning less than five and a half grand before stoppages. If his sales drop at all then his income drops – to social security levels. He could feel the tension inside and he pressed the accelerator, just a little too hard – it started to stick like the one on the car he'd been trying to sell.

Tony was twenty-six, he never wanted to be a salesman – let alone a used-car salesman. He trained as a foundry technician and worked in the steel industry for a number of years before being made redundant. His time in the steel industry wasn't entirely happy – he'd been the management's blue-eyed boy, he won the student-of-the-year award. 'When the management said "jump" I was in midair jumping before they'd even finished their command.' He was sent into one section of the factory where he worked to sort out a piecework scheme. The workers treated him with considerable caution and downright suspicion. 'They thought I'd been sent in to find ways of reducing their money,' said Tony. When the scheme was worked out, he had to implement it, taking over as foreman. There followed two years of acrimony and bitter dispute about the scheme. 'Everyone thought they were being fiddled,' he said, 'and then the recession got bad and the order books shortened.' Piecework was abandoned and they moved over to a scheme of average earnings.

'When that happened,' said Tony, 'the workers started taking longer and longer breaks. The management told me that it was my responsibility to ensure that they took only those breaks to which they were entitled.' Tony was piggy-in-the-middle and everyone likes to try to stick the pig. The workers sent him to Coventry. 'They just explained to me that it was okay for me to talk to them about work but not about the weather or the football results, or anything else. It wasn't a happy time. It was hardly my fault.' And then Tony opted for a rather unfortunate metaphor. 'I was just like a guard at Auschwitz, I was just carrying out orders. Those at the top were really responsible for all the changes.'

The recession bit deeper. 'The order books were going down and down, and the management called for ten voluntary redundancies. Nobody stepped forward.' Nobody was that keen to join Maggie's army. The management said they were going to get out a blindfold and a pin, but they made sure that Tony was first to go. 'It was a real kick in the teeth,' said Tony. 'They'd started blaming me for the bad feeling which existed between workers and management. I'd only been carrying out orders.' And jumping every time they wanted him to.

'I wasn't unemployed that long – just a matter of weeks before I got onto a short-term community project as a supervisor. This gave me the opportunity to attend interviews for more permanent jobs. Then the car salesman's job came up. It suited me because I wasn't going to be blamed for other people's schemes any longer. It was all up to me. I didn't mind the hours and I wanted the chance to earn some money. I wasn't long married. I'd no background in selling, mind, except when I was a little lad I used to sell conkers. And when I was twelve I used to go out to the sweet factory near my school and buy sweets to sell in the dinner hour. The problem with this was that I used to eat the sweets I couldn't sell. As a consequence, I got quite fat and became very shy and self-conscious. It wasn't the only reason I was shy, though. In class I was a bit of an introvert. My parents are from Italy and I was a little slow at school. I remember once in class pronouncing "OK" as "Ock" instead of "Okay". The whole class fell about laughing, but I was really embarrassed. I felt like hiding under the desk. This kind of incident had a profound effect on me, and when I got fat from all those sweets I couldn't sell, I just thought, that's it, I'm going to be stuck like this for ever. But I realised even then that if I was going to get on I'd have to change my personality, that I'd have to become as wild and as extroverted as everyone else. So, I just changed my whole pattern of behaviour. I just really came out of myself. I even went a bit over the top – in terms of clowning about in class. In reality, I'm still very shy but I just act differently. That's how I got the job selling cars – by showing them this side of my personality, by showing them how outgoing and confident I can act since I've stopped being that other person. It can get a bit difficult sometimes at work because some of the salesmen are exactly how they appear. They've always been full of chat and never been shy in their lives. I have to make that extra effort to sell cars, even to talk to people.

'At work, it's really competitive. We have a league table showing who's sold the most new cars, the most used cars and the most accessories. We divide all this by the number of people we've spoken to, and the number of demonstrations we've given, to produce a "conversion ratio". There's a microwave oven for the person with the best ratio this month. I don't think it'll be me. There's usually about seventeen salesmen working at any one time and we all take turns sitting at what we call the "up-desk". As soon as someone enters the premises, the person sitting at the up-desk automatically attends to him or her and then someone else takes his place at the desk. It's awful when you're at the up-desk if you see some right tyre-kicker come in, you know, the kind of bloke who's just come in to pass a bit of time over his lunch break. You've wasted your turn. Earlier today, there was a young girl of sixteen came in, and she was looking at these nine-grand cars. She hadn't even passed her test. I tried to direct her to cheaper cars, but she just wasn't interested. I suggested to her that she came back when she passed her test, but she just said that her dad could afford to buy her a car before she did her test. Anyway, she had a good look round and got me to take her out for a test drive. I suppose it was a good hour out for her and a good laugh but it wasn't so funny from my point of view. I lost an hour of my time and my chance at the up-desk.

'I have to sell a car a day to live. I can't afford to waste time. There's one bloke at work who once sold thirty cars in a single month, but that was back in 1979. I keep touching him, hoping that I'll catch something. I have to make a success of this job. There's really nowhere else to turn. And perhaps if I just act outgoing and confident, if I just get my act together and forget about my past, it'll all work out.'

And as I departed, Tony was just leaving the up-desk to attend to two more cackling and diminutive seventeen-year-old girls. The minnows looked as if they could swallow him whole.

The dancer

There they all were – or, at least, seven of them were; three hadn't turned up. They all looked Gary's way. 'Come to check us out, yeah!' They were all warming up – in their own way. The tallest ran through his robotic moves – hands on pivots, arms on pivots. It wasn't so much a warm-up with him – he looked as if he couldn't stop doing it. The smallest was laying out the lino on the dusty floor – he positioned it just between the handball nets. He taped the lino down. Gary stood motionless. The leader came over.

'What would you like us to do?'

'Just run through your routine,' said Gary.

'We haven't got one,' said the leader.

'Well, just do a number then,' said Gary, a little impatiently. They'd already kept him waiting for an hour. 'That's the trouble with these black lads,' he said, 'they're never on time. It's just not good enough – it's just not professional.'

The music started – break-dance music hot from the streets of New York and here we were in a dusty hall in the middle of wet Sheffield. The seven members all started moving to the music at the side of the lino. They weren't in time and they had to check each other's hand movements to see what they should be doing. They all had tracksuits with SMAC 19 on them, except the smallest, the lino-fitter, who was all in black – for no real reason. Some had caps – New York circa 1930. Recession, street-wise fashion, again. The leader approached the mat gingerly and then something took over – it's not clear what, but it was impressive.

'You've got to hand it to black people,' said Gary, 'they've just got natural rhythm. How many white men, or women, could move like that? My group excluded, of course.' I nodded.

Then it was the turn of the small one, the one with the black tracksuit – he

Joanne – Gary's latest signing, training and practising

assaulted the mat headfirst, spinning on his head – 'break dancing' is the right name for it. Then, by mistake, two came on at the same time. One did a few moves and then stepped back in some embarrassment. Gary grimaced. And then came the robot – tall and angular in form and movement, but with a certain fluidity of style. He made you look for the wires.

'I'm a professional robotic dancer and I've never seen anything like it,' said Gary. 'The big question is, could he do it in time with others – in my group we can.' Then the robot went into a break routine, on his head, but the coins in his pocket tumbled out onto the mat. He had to stop and gather them up before the next could continue. The rest kept moving, but looked a bit embarrassed. 'He should have just left the money lying there,' said Gary. The robot repeated his spot. You could see Gary was impressed – he was trying to imitate his moves, surreptitiously. At the end of their dance, they finished not so much with a bang as with a nervous, exhausted whimper. Beads of sweat on their foreheads, all eyes fixed on Gary, the old pro – at twenty-four.

'I'm impressed. I could get you work. In Finland they'll go a bomb for it. There's not many groups like you there – not even that many blacks – you'll go down a treat. Just a couple of things – are you all over eighteen?' Nods all round. 'Have you all got British passports?' 'I have one,' one piped up. The rest were silent, clearly not so sure. 'Get the passports sorted and I'll get you work,' said Gary, 'but you'll have to divide up into two groups of five each. I couldn't send all ten of you to one club – there'd be no room.'

You could see that SMAC 19 were ecstatic even though they were trying to act cool. They got out their big (empty) diary to write down Gary's address. A pro had given them a nod, and everyone knows that a nod's as good as a wink to a teenager blind with ambition. Today, break dancing outside Top Shop in Fargate in Sheffield to the music which blasts the customers – tomorrow, the land of the midnight sun (or thereabouts), and the midnight cabaret. Gary strode off – cool, confident – he'd already earned his spurs and he knew it. You could positively hear them clanking.

Gary Jones (stage name Gary Check) had been a professional dancer since he was nineteen. He belonged to the post-*Saturday Night Fever* generation. When John Travolta strutted down those New York streets, a thousand golden dreamers from London to Lurgan tottered after him. Teenagers kicked and bobbed and weaved in front of their bedroom mirrors, some even did it in public. *Flashdance* and *Staying Alive* kept the fever burning. Gary lived the dream. Long drab days on the building site – short exciting nights in the disco. He and a friend won the Yorkshire final of the

World Disco Dancing Championship in Doncaster. A dance teacher spotted him and whisked him off to join a group and perform at such heady locations as the Civic Theatre in Doncaster. And that was about it. The members of the group got frustrated and four broke off to form their own group – Bodycheck. They acquired a professional manager and got gigs up and down the country for around £80 a night between them. Out of this came the rental for their transport and petrol. They averaged one gig a week.

'They were hard times,' said Gary. 'I lived with someone at the time – it was just as well.' They changed to a new manager who got them more gigs and entered them for a dance competition for professional groups. They won the northern region and got to the final in Windsor. The first prize was a car, which they desperately wanted. Their style of dancing had changed somewhat. The group had started off with robotic dancing, but now Gary said it was getting a bit 'raunchy'. The tinfoil suits were getting smaller – the routine was getting sexier. 'That's what people wanted,' said Gary, 'entertainment.' At the final in Windsor, the judges refused to score Bodycheck. 'The competition was organised by a religious company,' said Gary, 'it wasn't what they had in mind.' Their applause, however, stole the show. But applause wasn't enough for the two female members, who got despondent and left some time afterwards. 'I sacked them for their lack of commitment,' said Gary.

Gary advertised for new female dancers and found two with exactly what he was after. 'Good faces and good figures – we could always work on the dancing later.' Both were, however, trained dancers. Their manager then came up with their first international date – Nigeria. 'I didn't even know where it was,' said Gary. 'The week before we went, we got the map out. Nigeria was some experience,' he said. The two women in the group – Angela, twenty-one, and Babs, seventeen – had never been abroad before. 'They spent the first two weeks crying, wanting to go home,' said Gary. 'We saw bodies lying in the street, one day we nearly drove over one.' The food didn't agree with them. 'I spent the first three days in the toilet watching the lizards in our hotel room changing colours for camouflage,' said Angela. 'I could only eat tinned food in the end. We lived out of tins.' They performed in a nightclub in front of wealthy Lebanese and Syrians who would throw money at them at the end of the show. Sometimes, several hundred pounds would finish up on the stage. The act had definitely got raunchier – the men, one white, one black – would perform in tiny briefs, the women 'with flames covering their private parts', said Gary. 'It went down a bomb,' he said.

The ordinary Nigerians, of course, never saw the act. They couldn't afford the entrance fee or the £75 for a bottle of scotch in the club. They did, however, catch glimpses of the group in training. Every day for between two and seven hours they'd train on the roof of the hotel. Crowds would gather to watch. 'We could see all these rats scurrying about on the roofs of the other buildings. The locals didn't seem to mind. But they'd even do their business in the streets,' said Gary. 'It was a filthy place.'

Their contract was for three months but their employer didn't want them to leave in the end. In fact he refused to let them go. Gary got out of it by lying. 'I told him we had to do a TV show and we'd be straight back.' Through some careful arrangement they managed to get some money out of the country (it's illegal to export Nigerian nira) but they agreed that the £8000 they were owed in back pay should be transferred into their account in England. It never arrived. Three months in Nigeria for a couple of hundred pounds, a few bracelets and snakeskin handbags. And the experience, of course. 'It changed us all,' said Gary. 'We knew that if we could survive that, we could survive anything.'

Survive it they did. They changed managers again and got more bookings. Black members came and left. Gary's girlfriend Alison joined the group. Sometimes they did four shows in one night in clubs all over London. One week they did twenty-three different shows. 'It was bad management, though,' said Gary, 'we were only getting £50 a show – that's why we had to do so many.' They also travelled to Ireland and the Channel Islands. Their raunchy show apparently went down well in rural Ireland. 'Their eyes would pop out,' said Gary. 'We're the only dance group in the country which wears G-strings. I try to leave things to the imagination, though.' They got other bookings – in Norway and Spain – and managed to support Smokey Robinson on one of his British tours. They have also supported Freddie Starr and Jim Davidson.

'Dance groups start and finish every other week,' said Gary, 'but we're survivors. Every manager we've had has told us we'll never make it, but we're getting there.' Gary now managed the group himself. 'We got fed up with managers sending us to clubs on the wrong night and booking us in clubs with no dance floor. We're prepared to work at it to be successful. We train every day and we keep changing. The girls eat what I tell them to eat – Babs can hardly eat anything because she puts on weight so easily. We keep changing our style. We're always compared to Hot Gossip, but they stood still – the only thing we have in common with them is sex. We made a guest appearance at the last World Disco Dancing Championship. You should have seen the kids asking if there were any openings, but most of them won't be able to stick at it. I manage one other group at the moment – Vibrations – three white girls and a half-caste. I've got them gigs abroad. Kids are always contacting me, asking me if I can manage them. It's one thing being able to spin on your head – it's another to get your act together to please the punters. If those break dancers are late when I'm their manager I'll fine them. That'll smarten them up.'

The clairvoyant

It was the women's big night out. There were six of them all huddled in one room of Wendy's beauty salon, drinking wine, smoking and giggling. There were Wendy, her mum, Joy; Wendy's assistant, Trish; her mother, Pamela; her grandmother, Ivy; and an ex-employee of Wendy's, Kath. The air was thick with Estée Lauder and cigarette smoke. It had been Wendy's idea (although she kept denying it) – instead of going out to a pub or a wine bar to hear the same old guff from single men, why not get a clairvoyant in for the evening to do a party reading to hear something a bit different?

'Just a bit of fun,' said Wendy. But with his arrival imminent, the seriousness of it all had started to descend on the proceedings.

'This clairvoyant who's coming tonight is very good,' said Wendy, 'he's been well recommended.' There were clearly some believers in the audience and talk was now getting round to matters supernatural and spiritual – to things that go bump in the night – ghosts, husbands. Kath was definitely a believer. 'I go to a clairvoyant every couple of months,' she says. 'I've got my own tarot cards and a book on predictions. I believe in the spirit world, it's nearly always right what they say.' Trish wasn't so sure. 'They always just tell me I'm going to get married soon and live happily ever after and have two children. They always predict wedding bells for me but they always get the month wrong.' Trish's engagement ring was, however, so large and so obtrusive that few special gifts would be needed to predict an imminent transition for her into a matrimonial state. Trish's mum, Pamela, had had good and bad experiences with clairvoyants. 'Just as with men, really. A lot of them have told me that men are like boats in my life, they sail in and out, which is quite accurate, really. I hope this one doesn't go too deeply into my past.' And Trish threw her mum a stern but concerned look. Trish's mum's anxiety about possible revelations concerning past and very private experiences got them all thinking. It's one thing being told that you're going to meet a tall, dark, handsome stranger, it's quite a different matter to have one pulled screaming and kicking out of some dark forgotten cupboard.

The wine was flowing a little more copiously now, as much to calm the nerves as to set the stage for an evening's fun. Trish's grandmother, in her seventies, didn't usually drink and the wine was starting to produce some very nonspiritual effects in her. 'I think I'm going to go to the other side right now if I have any more of this wine.' Drink was loosening her tongue. 'I normally don't tell people this but I've had a ghost in my house. My husband didn't believe me but I believe in things like that. I saw it, it came right to my bedside. I left the house where I saw the ghost but I've seen another one since. It's like a ring around the ceiling which follows me around at night. My husband says it's my imagination; he doesn't believe in anything like this, he's an atheist, I think. He laughs everything off. When I told him I was going to a clairvoyant he just said he wanted to know whether I was going to marry again. He said not to keep it back from him because he wants some peace.'

The talk was now getting heavy. Joy interrupted. 'What your dad always says to me is that "if there's something, there's nothing, and if there's nothing, there's something", if you can work that one out. It's rather deep. You can get into deep conversations with Albert.'

Kath looked puzzled. 'But what does it mean exactly?' Joy started to explain. 'Well, if there is something – some being or whatever – it virtually is nothing – but if it's nothing then it can still be something. It always makes sense to me what he says.' 'Oh,' said Kath. 'Albert also says if there's a God why does it have to be a good God, why can't it be a bad God; why can't it be a God that eats biscuits in bed?' 'Oh,' said Kath again.

Grannie, in the meantime, had sunk into a deep philosophical state aided by the wine. 'I've had a lovely life. I wouldn't care if I died tomorrow. I believe it's a good God. I prayed for my dog when it had some teeth out, to make it better, and he did.'

The philosophising was disturbed by a knock on the door. Clairvoyant Glenn had eventually materialised – very wet. He'd obviously had to walk from the bus. 'It doesn't pay to look too prosperous,' whispered Joy, 'that's what Albert always says,' as Clairvoyant Glenn ascended the stairs to the wax room for his reading. Kath went first.

She was away for nearly an hour. It was only meant to take thirty minutes but then Kath was a believer. She came down clearly satisfied. 'He were great,' she said, 'really fantastic.' It was Pamela's turn next. She was still

worried about all those boats in her life and all those hidden harbours to be explored. She approached the wax room with some trepidation. Clairvoyant Glenn was sitting in the corner holding a pack of ordinary playing cards. All Pamela noticed was his filthy hands and dirty fingernails, and the stains on his trousers. The kind of man that would usually occasion flight rather than shared intimacy. His hair was still very wet. Pamela was impeccably groomed. She kept her legs tightly folded. When he started to speak you immediately noticed his speech impediment and a bronchial problem. He was also slightly spastic. She folded her arms as well, just for good measure. Glenn began:

'Could you split them into three? Do you know somebody called Tony, darling?'

'Tony, yes.'

'All right, love. Could you split them into three? Who is this Tony, darling? All right, sweetheart.'

'He's, he's just a friend that I know, that goes in our local.'

'Does he wear a uniform for a job?'

'No.'

'Are you sure?'

'Positive, yes.'

'Well, maybe somebody around this Tony that is going to start wearing a uniform within the next six months and they won't be very satisfied.'

'Mmm.'

'Are you with me? Could you pick one out, pet?'

'Right.'

'Do you know somebody in the spirit world, darling, called Gilbert?'

'No.'

'A long time since, when you was a child.'

'Gilbert, no.'

'He's taking me down a narrow road.'

'I can't think of anybody called Gilbert.'

'You can't?'

'No.'

'All right, sweetheart.'

'There's a Jack in spirit, duck. A Jack. I'm going back on your mother's side.'

'Uh, there's, there's a friend on my mother's side called Jack.'

'That's dead?'

'Eh, no, no he's not dead.'

'No, I mean a Jack that's dead.'

'Yes, yes, no, I don't think there's a Jack that's dead.'

Glenn was getting nowhere fast. Pamela started to squirm. Apart from being a well-groomed lady in her forties, Pamela was also very suntanned and obviously attractive to men. Glenn changed tack:

'Are you having marriage problems, sweetheart?'

'Yes.'

'It's all right and then all of a sudden it flares up?'

'Yes.'

'Darling, we've been talking about it splitting up before and make a final break.'

'Right.'

'But somehow we still seem to be hanging on.'

'Right.'

'Are you with me?'

'Right.'

'Darling, I feel that you are going to hang on for a bit longer. Are you with me?'

'Right.'

'But I feel that within the next two years there will be a final split-up.'

'Right.'

'Are you with me?'

Clairvoyant Glenn had just predicted the demise of her marriage. Pamela held her posture rigid but blinked noticeably. The false starts from Glenn that had preceded this were quickly forgotten as Pamela's mind raced through the implications of this verbal salvo. The salvo had clearly knocked her off guard.

'Who's Ken?'

'I don't know any Ken.'

'Are you sure?'

'Yeah, positive.'

'Again, could you watch out for a Ken because I feel as though there is a Ken that we have not got to trust within the next few weeks.'

'Right.'

Clairvoyant Glenn was having more problems so he returned to familiar and safer territory.

'Could you shuffle them again, please? Could you split them into two, please?'

'Right you are.' (Sigh.)

'Your marriage, is it on and off?'

'You could say that.'

'Is your husband with us?'

'What, what d'you mean, with us? Eh, yeah.'

'Your husband's living but I don't feel that he's . . . I feel that he's away from us.'

'No, no, he's not.'

'All right.'

'He . . . he's with you, your husband?'

'Yes, yes.'

'Does he keep floating?'

'No, no.'

''Cos I've got him going away and then keep coming back.'

'No, no, he never goes away.'

'Can you watch out for this in the next few months?'

'Yeah.'

He tried again.

'Who does a lot of paperwork, who studies?'

'I don't know – nobody at this present time.'

'Are you sure?'

'Yeah.'

'Because·they're telling me about somebody who's studying, love, or who's about to study if not now, and they're telling me that they will be very successful in what they're doing.'

Then he had a partial success.

'Have you got three children round you?'

'No, I've got –'

'Two.'

'Two.'

'Why have I got three then, I wonder – I've got three children round you. Is one, hang on, ah, why have I got three? You haven't lost one, have you, sweetheart?'

'No, I haven't lost one, no.'

'Why have I got three with you?'

'I don't know.'

'I've got three children with you, come on, sweetheart? I've got three with you, not two, you haven't lost one that's dead, have you?'

'No, no. I've had an abortion if that's . . .'

'Ah.'

'. . . anything to do.'

'Ah, ah, sad, that's why I had three with you . . .'

'Mmm.'

'. . . and then was stuck. I couldn't have gone no more but I knew there were three – I should have known that. That's why I said "Have you lost one?" Are you with me?'

'Yeah.'

In his moment of triumph he returned to Gilbert. He shouldn't have pushed his luck.

'Are you sure you don't know a Gilbert in spirit, duck? 'Cos I still got a Gilbert here, darling.'

'Not that I can think of.'

'Well, love, could you shuffle them again, please?'

Pamela squirmed some more. Most of the salvos had landed some miles off but Clairvoyant Glenn clearly noticed that attractive woman sometimes have marriage problems. Clairvoyant Glenn finished the reading by asking whether she was satisfied or not – she said she was. She was visibly relieved it was all over.

She returned to the others slightly shaken. It's not every day you're told your marriage is going to finish, for sure. It was her daughter's turn next. She put her cigarette out and had a last gulp of wine. But she needn't have worried. It was all wedding bells and two children. Clairvoyant Glenn picked up thirty quid for the evening's work. The women, as one of them put it, got something to think about for the next six months. 'It's better than going to the doctor,' said another one. 'All they tell you is what you want to hear, and give you some pills.'

I went to see Glenn at his house on the Manor Estate in Sheffield the next morning. Glenn was thirty and had been a professional clairvoyant for four years. Before that he was a labourer in an engineering firm for ten years. His former workmates, he said, thought it was all very funny. 'They always say things like "I bet your business is pathetic now that the price of tea bags has gone up". Some of them used to think that I was crackers.' For a year, Glenn had an office in Sheffield city centre, but the rates forced him to operate from his mother's house. It looked poor. Glenn preferred party bookings at other people's homes.

He said he'd had the gift since he was four. He could clearly see children that others couldn't see riding around with him on his bike. His father told him to get a grip, but became something of a believer when Glenn later predicted a winner in a horse race for him. The gift left Glenn until he was fourteen, when one weekend the family was planning a trip to a caravan outside Skegness. Glenn refused to go – he said he could see blue lights. He ripped his trousers and locked himself in the toilet. His parents forced him to go. At Worksop, their Reliant Robin collided with a coach. They were all detained in hospital but only the mother was seriously injured. His father was, however, converted.

His father had now been dead for seven years but Glenn said he regularly came back to him. Glenn had also got a girlfriend in the spirit world called Janet. She died three years earlier of pneumonia. Glenn didn't foresee it. Glenn clearly believed in his gift but it was another thing trying to make a living from it. As he himself said, 'It can be very draining, very tiring trying to get through to people. A day's work in an office doing clairvoyance takes more out of you than a day's labouring in a factory. Some people's aura you just can't get through but you have to try.' He said that he just used the cards 'to calm himself down' because if he didn't use them he often tended to shout a bit to make himself heard over his spirit guide.

He saw blue lights only the previous week when he was looking out of his front window. His mother had to tell him there wasn't anything there *yet*. A few minutes later a neighbour's son was knocked down and an ambulance, blue light flashing, arrived at the exact spot.

Ninety-five per cent of Glenn's clients were women. One went to see him every three weeks. Are women simply more gullible than men? Are they more superstitious? Are they more intuitive? Less rational? According to Glenn, men did believe as well but they were afraid to admit to their mates that they'd been to a clairvoyant in case they were laughed at. He said men were too worried about what other men thought of them. 'Perhaps they should organise party bookings,' he said.

As I left Manor Estate, with its skinheads with their tattoos, and its dogs mounting each other on the pavement, tongues lolling about, I came across harsh reality again. There was nothing extraordinary about that estate. I started to think about the readings I'd attended and couldn't suppress a laugh. Until, that is, I saw some blue lights flashing.

But then police and ambulances aren't alien to Manor Estate. Are they?

6 · The road to Mandalay

Alice laughed. 'There's no use trying,' she said: 'one *can't* believe impossible things.'
  'I dare say you haven't had much practice,' said the Queen.
Lewis Carroll, *Through the Looking-Glass*, 1872

Charismatic Christians

Like a large section of the population, I attended church when young but ceased this practice as soon as I could (i.e. as soon as parental control slackened). I had never seen the point of enduring all that tedium every Sunday. The only people who were obviously Christians I had encountered since I stopped going to church were those who stand in the central shopping precincts of towns, including Sheffield, every Saturday afternoon giving their testimony to assorted groups of bemused punks and skinheads who come for a laugh. Fashions may come and go, punks may wear frills and go romantic, mods may have their heads shaved, but the appearance of those Christians never seems to change – short back and sides, glasses, timeless, tasteless pullovers, unattractive, unappealing, depressing. Christianity as a pair of crutches and a sling. You walk past as they go on about hellfire, thinking, I'd rather have hellfire even with the skinheads than an eternity with them. I thought Christianity was having a hard time. Churches were being closed and turned into cinemas, rock venues, even carpet warehouses. A host of exotic Eastern religions had captivated the young. Ten years ago the average age of church congregations seemed about sixty. It must be seventy now, I thought.

And so, on a cold wet Sunday evening in Sheffield, I dragged myself away from the box, with its own multifarious spiritual messages and moral creeds, to St Thomas's church – an Anglican church, part of the Charismatic movement. The first shock was that the car park was full, indeed not just the car park but all the adjoining streets. There must be a pub opening early around here, I thought. Through the rain I went towards the old stone church. I went inside; it was bright, warm and surprisingly packed. I rubbed my eyes. There were old people, middle-aged people and hundreds of young people who did not conform to my stereotype of young Christians. Ordinary young people – punks, New Romantics in make-up (male and female both) and even the occasional heavy-metal fan (denims, leather jacket – JESUS LOVES YOU in bold letters on the back).

I sat on the balcony for a better view. The hymns seemed traditional enough in terms of their words but they were sung differently – with a new enthusiasm and force. About half the congregation lifted up their hands during the hymns. It was as if they were making it clear that the hymns weren't aimed at the others, they weren't meant to rebound in a horizontal frame but to go upwards. The service was certainly different. Members of the congregation offered spontaneous prayers. 'I'd like just to say, Lord, you're great.' There was humour and even laughter. Two people offered prayers at exactly the same time and consequently you couldn't make out what they were saying. The next person to pray said, 'Praise be to the Lord for he can hear more than one prayer at a time.' Loud laughter. The next said, 'Praise be to the Lord for he can take a joke.' The normal human responses of appreciation and joy had been invited into the church instead of being forced to wait outside in the rain. (When I used to go to church, one of the very worst things you could do was laugh.) The overall feeling in this church was one of people enjoying themselves and demonstrating that this was not incompatible with worshipping God. Dancing, clapping, laughing – the two hours passed quite quickly.

St Thomas's, Crookes, is part of the Charismatic movement, a movement which has had a dramatic impact on all of the major Christian churches. A neo-Pentecostal movement with the emphasis on the Holy Spirit and, most importantly, the experience of the Holy Spirit. The General Synod of the Church of England has published a report on the Charismatic movement within that church. They recognised at the outset that it is somewhat hard to define and indeed there is no immediately acceptable definition either to those who feel themselves part of it or to those from outside the movement. The central feature of the movement is an overwhelming sense of the presence and power of God, perhaps not seen in the Christian church for quite a while. The Charismatic movement represents the resurfacing of a strand of Christianity kept suppressed for a very long time. A supernatural, nonrational strand focusing on gifts, visions and miracles. A strand successfully suppressed before the Reformation and after the Reformation in all the main churches. (The Quakers, those who shook under the influence of the Spirit, being a notable exception.) These gifts, visions and miracles have been peripheral to church life certainly throughout the past three centuries

– decorum, formalism and clericalism have ruled OK. In the twentieth century, however, things have started to change with the birth and rise of the Pentecostal movement, and in the 1970s these suppressed roots of Christianity started to burrow their way into the major churches, including the Anglican and Roman Catholic churches.

In the Charismatic movement there is an emphasis on demonstrable gifts from the Holy Spirit. One such gift is that of 'tongues' in which Christians speak in a new, unknown language which may or may not be a language currently 'on the earth'. Many believe they speak in Hebrew (although few seemed inclined to check this). Tongues is a highly desirable and central gift. As the General Synod said, 'This gift has become almost the central recognition symbol for charismatics . . . And for the charismatic who is visiting a new church or fellowship, the sound of tongues will . . . make him feel instantly at home.' I talked to a number of people who had this gift. Most offered the same type of explanation for the phenomenon. 'It's difficult to praise God in English' or 'I had nothing more to say to him in English'. To Charismatics this gift represents baptism in the Holy Spirit and it is something which is sought keenly. Charismatics speak tongues in fellowship groups to praise God, and in addition they often interpret each other's tongues.

Sally, who had been a Charismatic for one year, acquired the gift of tongues while sitting alone watching *That's Life*. She said that God told her to pick up a Bible in the middle of the programme and she then spoke for an hour in a new language. She described the experience of the Spirit entering her as 'like drinking liquid through the top of her head'. Her conversion was quite sudden; her parents, she pointed out, greatly disapproved. Another gift, which Sally was now actively seeking, is that of prophecy. Prayer is an important channel for prophecy. Prayer to Charismatics is not a form of thinking aloud, but a form of dialogue – when Charismatics pray they expect a response, they wait for messages from God (prophetic or otherwise). The examples of prophecy I was offered were not, however, entirely convincing. One person received an image of an orange during prayer about a fellow student. When he told her about this, she said that she had been ill and the doctor had told her to eat more oranges. Fairly low-level stuff. Another gift which Charismatics hope to acquire is that of healing. As the General Synod noted: 'The mood which has swept in is one of expecting miracles. No longer does miraculous healing need explaining – now it is non-healing which has to be explained.' One Charismatic medical student I talked to, Julie, had witnessed evidence of this. A woman whose spine was twisted had her spine suddenly straightened during a special healing service. Her surgeon was in the congregation and he proclaimed it a miracle. The National Health Service, however, weren't interested in miracles and had given the woman little attention when she returned to hospital ('You don't need to come back then'). Julie, herself a keen squash player, had had a bruised bicep tendon healed during a healing service. She said she had been very sceptical to begin with but was convinced in the end by evidence such as this.

Along with this emphasis on the power of the Holy Spirit and the power of good and love came a parallel emphasis and recognition of the power of Satan and evil. The General Synod talked in terms of 'Spiritual warfare . . . with a renewed awareness of the demonic, and with it the exercising of "deliverance ministries".' All the Charismatics I talked to had strong views about the Devil and personal experience of his methods. Exorcism was becoming increasingly popular. Julie, the medical student, talked about schizophrenics in her congregation being exorcised. There had, however, been problems in this area. St John's College, Nottingham, reported to the General Synod that 'There were some odd or worrying goings-on. One or two of the Charismatic students were inclined to find demons under every bed and indulged in exorcistic activity in the neighbourhood.'

The impact of the Charismatic movement on the Christian church has been immense. A new enthusiasm and commitment is very evident. People and money have flooded in. St Thomas's in Sheffield had a congregation of 250 in 1971 and an annual income of £10,000. In 1985 the congregation was 750 and the annual income was £100,000. People were putting their money where their mouths were. (St Michael Le Belfry in York, for instance, had a congregation of six in 1966 and over one thousand in 1985.) The new style of service and the new message attracted young people. Young people liked the physical aspects of the movement – the body used for expression – in prayer, in song and in dance; the congregation touch in greeting and touch for healing. Inhibitions were left outside the church – speech flew out, in new and dramatic forms. No more Sunday morning Christians; the Holy Spirit is about all the time and must be consulted at all times. More members of the churches played important functional roles and the role of the vicar seemed to be much less central. Fellowship groups had grown up around the churches, each with a dozen or so members (St Thomas's had thirty such groups), to help Christianity be a week-long exercise. The groups were designed for Bible study but also to sort out personal problems. An emphasis on helping each other to help God.

Every Charismatic I talked to remarked that the Charismatic Christians they had encountered before their conversion were not how they had previously imagined Christians to be. 'They weren't spotty and insecure,' said Julie. 'They were quite normal but with a certain sparkle – I wanted some of that sparkle.' The normality and indeed attractiveness of the Christians seemed to be an important factor in the conversion process. Christianity could then be viewed not as a crutch but as a bonus for people who had a lot going for them already. Julie made this point about herself – she had lots of boyfriends, money, a happy family, good looks and she was happy; she certainly didn't need a crutch, she just (selfishly?) wanted to be even happier. She said she was, as well, she was now full of joy. 'But,' she said when she was leaving, 'to be full of joy all the time is terribly tiring.'

Finals

He sat staring into his coffee cup. There was perfect silence, even the clock had stopped. Then his lips started to tremble. He began reciting, inaudibly at first, but it grew louder. It turned into a chant – rhythmic, hypnotic, spellbinding.

> 'Eysenck developed the incubation theory of neurosis in 1979.
> Eysenck developed the incubation theory of neurosis in 1979.'

But why is it called the 'incubation theory'? He grabbed at his notes. 'Ah, here it is' – lecture three of the clinical psychology course – 'Theories of Neurosis'. But there was a big gap in the middle of his notes. (He had missed the lecture and had to copy the notes up from a friend, but part of his friend's notes were illegible. He had meant to ask him about it but, well, he must have forgotten.) The gap was immediately preceded by the words 'Eysenck's Incubation Theory'. Oh, great! It was 1 am.

He made his way back down to the kitchen. Finals started tomorrow and finals, he knew, were final. For the past month this student, Ben, had been working late. Lectures had finished and so he could afford to work late into the night, often finishing about 3 am. 'It's better if you revise before going to sleep,' he'd tell his friends, hoping thereby to convince himself. The nights were becoming extended. This night, the night before the first exam, bed seemed a very long way off.

Everyone else in Ben's house was asleep. He shared his rented house in Sheffield with ten others. Nine students (one other psychology student, two medics and six geologists) and one working a supermarket check-out (whom one of the geologists, Nick, had met on a field trip to the west coast of Scotland). There should only have been seven living in the house (because there was only one toilet and that is a council regulation – seven to a toilet) but there were three couples, and one pair of adjoining rooms meant as a single living space had been transformed into two separate, claustrophobic ' living spaces. It had all helped to keep the rent down. But now, with finals approaching, the overcrowded house was generating a certain amount of stress. The stress had been increased by a visit from the council three days previously. They wanted to know who lived in the house. They were extremely suspicious. Nick showed the man from the council around the house. 'And who lives here?' said the man from the council. 'Oh, Ben does,' said Nick, in a room strewn with bras and pants and dresses hung over the backs of chairs (Ben was half of a couple). 'Oh,' said the man from the council, unable to make up his mind whether Ben was a pervert or a womaniser. But Nick was believed (he was very believable) and a potential crisis – an eviction just before finals – was narrowly averted.

The kettle came to the boil and Ben could feel the pressure building up inside. His future was in the balance. He was a good student – good A levels, good second-year exams, but he wanted to do postgraduate research in psychology. In order to get a grant, he needed an upper second-class honours degree. His assessed work had been given first-class marks but this amounted to only 30 per cent of the final degree assessment and he had directed a disproportionate amount of time in his final year to this work. The bulk of the assessment, 70 per cent, depended on the examination – seven finals papers, six on consecutive days. If he messed them up, his research, his career prospects, his self-respect would fly out the window. He normally didn't get anxious about exams but finals had an ominous ring to them. *Finals*. He had worked into the morning for weeks now, reading, writing, thinking. He always did stay up late. That was why there were so many gaps in his lecture notes. Late parties meant that he missed the nine o'clock and many of the ten o'clock lectures. But staying up late then was for pleasure, now it was for earnest. The 2 am feeling of the partygoer is a bit different from the 2 am feeling of the student engaged in last-minute revision.

Wild associations flew through his head. I'll top myself, he thought. 'Student jumps off Arts Tower' – he could see the headlines. It was reckoned that the Arts Tower claimed about one student a year, usually a foreign student from Hong Kong or Malaysia. They're probably culturally conditioned to do it at the slightest hint of failure, he thought, and Eysenck's views on conditioning flooded his mind again.

He worked at an ordinary oak dining table which would comfortably seat six. But it would be sacrilege to use it for eating now. It was the revision table. Books piled high, Xeroxed articles piled even higher, lecture notes, scrap paper, doodles and pens covering every inch of the table. They hadn't been moved for a month. Ben knew the position of every article, every jotting, every doodle on the table. His girlfriend Kathy was forbidden to go within three feet of it. (Meals were eaten off their knees.) It was a ritual to sit at the table. The whole process had acquired enormous symbolic significance. He usually did it slowly – sitting on the chair, pulling it up under the table and casting his eyes over the pillars of Xeroxed articles (at 3p a page), over the edifices of books (long overdue from the library with fines mounting daily), over this great heap of knowledge and learning.

Ben knew that university was a rat race and he had studied propositional logic long enough to know that in a rat race, only a rat can win. But he couldn't do anything about the nature of universities; his choice was simple – winning rat or losing rat – and he didn't want the latter. Finals had made all his fellow students behave strangely. Books which could not be taken out of the library were hidden in the wrong section so that no one else could find them. There were more psychology textbooks in the Ancient History section, in the fortnight before finals, than in the psychology section. Occasionally, you would find the book you were looking for only to discover that the essential chapter had been razored out. Reference reading was a very frustrating experience.

'Stress produces major pathologies in rats,' Ben had read three hours previously, and he knew it to be true.

All the final year students were competing against each other with few rules or standards of conduct. Ben could imagine some of the keener students reading a reference and then swallowing it lest anyone else see it. Lest anyone else catch a glimpse of that gem of knowledge. The gems were hidden away and hoarded to be studied in perfect secrecy. Ben had competed with the best of them. The table with its mound of books and articles reflected the sum of his achievements. The books and articles had all been acquired against the odds. Now there was the minor matter of committing them to memory, of understanding them, of neuroxing (instead of just Xeroxing). The whole lot. It was now 2 am.

Ben was drowning in lecture notes. Still images, apparently unconnected, each one tied in with personal and extraneous detail, flashed before him. But now, for the first time, he could see that they might just fit together. As he read through the notes and the references, the frames flickered a bit but eventually he could see some form of motion. Incubation theory started to come to life and stagger through his consciousness. It wasn't an unpleasant experience. 'If only I'd done this earlier,' said Ben as he reflected on what he had been doing instead, and felt himself drowning again.

Ben and Kathy shared a room in an old terraced house in Crookes. The room was on the first floor. A tree grew up from the back garden and its branches reached towards their window. They once thought this enchanting, especially when the tree was in bloom. But this summer, some mysterious fungal growth covered the tree and no one in the house seemed to notice it or tried to do anything about it (pluralistic ignorance, thought Ben, Introductory Social Psychology, Lecture 3). So now long, diseased fingers stretched out towards the window, and when you opened the window for air, they came right inside. This particular night it was windy and the branches knocked loudly against the window. The fingers wanted in. But despite the noise, Kathy slept soundly – before, that is, breaking into a bout of snoring. At first, Ben was amused for it broke the monotony and he knew all there was to know about sleep and dreaming and, from physiology, about the functions of snoring. This new stimulus caused (or 'elicited', as he liked to put it) an unconditioned stream of lecture material to gush forth about rapid-eye-movement sleep and non-REM sleep, about spiky alpha waves and slow ponderous delta waves, about the evolutionary theory of dreaming. But enough was enough. The snoring continued. And not just from Kathy, he could hear Nick snoring from the room next door (Nick was also doing finals but wasn't worried, although, as it turned out, he should have been) and from somewhere else in the house. All Sheffield seemed to be snoring while he was stuck with incubation theory and rats with rapid eye movements. He made himself another cup of coffee. It was now 3 am.

The coffee was strong, sweet and black. Incubation theory was now properly neuroxed. Ben wanted to laugh. Here he was, wanting an academic career, and yet he was doing exactly those things that everyone from school teacher to university lecturer had warned him against – revising the night before an exam. But they didn't know. He had contemplated taking some speed (slimming tablets pinched two years earlier from his mother) but he had heard the story about the student who took speed for finals and had simply written his name over and over again. He doubted whether it was true, but he didn't want to risk it. Furthermore, he didn't know whether speed, like a bottle of wine that has been opened, went off with time. The coffee had made him feel cheerful, even a little manic (it's probably my neurotransmitters, he thought). Kathy stopped snoring. He paced the room. Dread, anxiety, fear were replaced by a sense of exhilaration. Incubation theory was clear. He'd cracked it. It was the others that would have yolk on their faces tomorrow, the lazy bastards who had gone to bed by 10 pm. He was looking forward to seeing their faces when they picked up the exam paper in the morning. He was looking forward to seeing some of them throwing up their half-digested facts and precious articles. At least I'll know who the culprits are. It was all incredibly funny.

It got light early. Dawn doesn't break, it creeps up on you. It crept up on Ben very quickly on this particular morning. It was ten to five. 'Time I was in bed,' he said loudly. It was the new day, the day he'd been dreading for a year. Finals had begun. He didn't wash his face or brush his teeth, he just climbed into bed like some little furry animal who has just managed to survive a major threat. Kathy stirred. 'What time is it?' she said. 'Never mind,' said Ben. (Kathy was a second-year student and her exams were not until later.) 'Did you work hard?' she said. 'No,' said Ben. And then a cock, possibly the only cock in all of Crookes, possibly indeed the only cock in all of Sheffield, crowed three times. And then it too retired.

Getting yourself noticed

As the recession tightened its grip, the whole country choked, but in the north the grip seemed to be that much tighter. One reaction by the young to the steely grip of the economic climate was a mad scramble for style. A mad scramble for an appearance that would make one an individual again. The north had seen nothing like it. In the 1930s there was just the flat-cap brigade. Fifty years on we have legions of Mohicans, New Romantics and Kraftwerk lookalikes (who wouldn't have shamed the Third Reich) all queuing up at the dole counter.

Days on the dole are long and boring. Drab wet streets, drab dry houses. But there's always the night. The lights gradually fade and suddenly the night is with us. The stage is set. A thousand pubs, a thousand clubs. Bright lights, people, laughter, a chance to stand in the spotlight and be – yourself, or someone else, more likely.

Being on the dole is about being one of the army of the unemployed. Like all armies – faceless and nameless. But style combats this, style lets you fight back. It makes you stand out. It gives you a face, it may even give you a name. A face to be seen, a face to be looked at, a face not to be ignored. Style gets you noticed. That can be very important.

Individuation is never complete. Style is never purely original. Style slips into patterns: skinhead, punk, heavy-metal fan, NF supporter, Rastafarian, rocker, ted, mod, post-mod, original mod, headbanger, torn-clothes aficionado, David Bowie lookalike, neo-Nazi, young socialist, hippy, ageing hippy, schoolboy hippy. The list is endless. As Peter York, associate editor of *Harpers & Queen* magazine, has pointed out, every youth culture over the last two decades is currently being recycled. Never has style been needed more. No one style will do. We need them all. Style versus the UB40 – the great equaliser.

Christine was twenty and unemployed. She had been unemployed for almost exactly one year, having dropped out of university. One of the first things she did with her new-found leisure time was to change her appearance. Not in any slow subtle way but quickly, suddenly and dramatically. Her hair was swept up into a spiky bob above the ears and down to the neck on each side. She had a ritual to keep her hair like this, a painful but necessary daily ritual:

'When I get up, I scrape out the remains of the previous day's can of hair spray. I do this in my room so there's usually bits of flaky white stuff all over the cassette recorder. It takes about five minutes, depending on my pain threshold that day, because combing out hair spray is incredibly painful. Then I stick a load of gel or setting lotion on it. I only wash my hair about once a fortnight, because the gungier it is, the better it sticks up. Sometimes it gets so gungy that there are little white flakes in my hair, but when this happens, I just stick my head under the tap to remove the bits – that way I can wash them out without getting rid of the gunge. Then I get a piece of hair and pull it up as hard and straight as I can and dry it so that it stands up stiff. When all the hair is standing up, I get a jumbo-sized can of hair spray and spray the roots, and then I pull the hair up at the roots while aiming a hot blast from the hair dryer at them. Then I spray the whole thing all over and blow it with the hair dryer so that it sets – like concrete! If I think it still needs a bit more support, I spray over the sides and roots again. Then another quick spray all over and a bit of gel on the back to smooth it down. It takes about one hour a day – I have to do it every day. And I get through about three jumbo cans of hair spray a week.

'I've had my hair like this for about six months, I thought it was really me. I hate the attention I get, though, because most of it is really abusive. People

'Style and manners maketh man'

come up to me in the street and say really nasty things. I never thought people could be like that. It's nearly always men – men that pass you in the street. One bloke came up to me and said, "I think you put it in the wrong socket, luv" – but he didn't say it in a jokey way, he was really threatening. Also, a bus conductor picked on me – tried to make out I'd paid the wrong fare, and started shouting at me – and I knew I hadn't. Then one time I was walking up the street and a bunch of policemen came out of a building. They started shouting at me across the street, saying things like, "Do you think we could fit a helmet on it? Can I have a feel?" I don't know why they do it, though, because I wear the same clothes as I've always worn, and it never happened to me then. I think men feel threatened by my hair. It's as if they think I'm trying to make some kind of statement, and they're saying, "Who the hell do you think you are, trying to be different?"'

Style maketh the person. You can look like a Mohican, you can be treated like a Mohican (i.e. uncivilised), you can even feel like a Mohican (threatened, virtually extinct). At least you are something. It may even get you noticed – and not just by the sneering public. UB40 (the band) have often been described as the voice of recession-bitten Britain – songs about the unemployed joining the army to escape the dole queue. Songs about hard reality. But one of the most popular bands of the 1980s so far has been the Human League. Songs about girls plucked from nowhere because of their looks to become a member of a successful rock band. Songs about soft fantasy.

Sheffield is the home of the Human League. Hard Steel City, home of soft plastic fantasy. The fact that one of the female members of the group really was plucked from nowhere just adds to the fantasy. You can see the girls with their distinctive, elegant, individually styled gowns and long black elegant gloves dancing and waiting. Dancing in that exaggerated practised style which that type of girl does to that type of Human League song. Dancing and waiting – to be picked out and turned into someone new. A life away from the rain and wet and drabness of Sheffield's streets. A life away from the dole. A life in the sun. Most of them will have a long wait.

Trevor, however, felt that it was imminent. When Trevor walked down the street, people stopped and stared. Tall and dark – but with a shower of ringlets and a peroxide kiss curl in the middle of his forehead. His outrageously effeminate hairstyle triggered the initial head-turn but my attention was drawn principally to the clothes. He made them himself – out of curtains.

He was swathed in a voluminous black cape with matching vest, boots and trousers. Without the ringlets and a strategically placed Dexy's hat he might have been mistaken for a sartorially elegant Hammer version of a vampire – except that no self-respecting mid-European nobleman (even a Hammer films one) would wear a cloak made out of blackout curtains.

When the weather was brighter, he would wear reversible outfits fashioned from strikingly patterned curtain material, enhancing the look with plenty of make-up. When we met he wore just a touch of mascara, because he was working for the Manpower Services Commission, which didn't leave much time in the mornings for getting his 'look' together. Before this job he was unemployed for a number of years.

'When I was on the dole I used to spend all my money on travelling around the country to different nightclubs, which meant I didn't have anything left to spend on clothes. I used to rifle my mum's drawers to see if I could find anything, and I came across all this curtain material, which I realised I could make into clothes really cheaply. I sometimes got the basic ideas in various clubs – but from clubs down in London – in London they've got all the resources, but they don't seem to know how to use them. It was in Manchester that I saw really different looks – I think they make more of an effort up north because they're kind of striving against ignorance. Once you start making the clothes, you sort of develop into making other things too. Like I've got a friend who's making his own shoes now – sort of ballet-type shoes; and I used to make hats – all you need is a bit of net and a few feathers. Oh, and then I found some toothpicks in one of the drawers when I was hunting for curtain material, so I painted them black and other colours and stuck diamanté and bits of broken glass onto them and made them into earrings. I'm making them for a lot of my friends now. I don't really notice other people's reactions until people start throwing things or spitting at me. Girls are too shocked to be abusive. The thing is, when I've got a lot of make-up on, I get less aggro, because people just assume I'm a woman.'

The creations sported by Trevor's friends were all originals – or so they liked to think. Rather than praising them for their individuality, however, Trevor bemoaned their anti-intellectualism.

'You see some in the street wearing something really striking and you think they must be really interesting – but when you get to meet them, all they want to talk about is the way they look. I had all my best discussions when I was still at school.'

And Trevor did make it – in the summer of 1984 he was famous – for a while. He was hailed as 'The Most Beautiful Man in the World' by all the tabloids. He was plucked from obscurity in 1984 from his native Sheffield by Mickie Most, record producer and entrepreneur, to become the next pop superstar. The gauntlet was thrown down to Boy George and Marilyn – they were warned, they had a new rival – six foot two inches, cavalier tresses, hairless chest, long fingernails, mascara, stubble – a real gender bender if ever there was one. He was hyped to the hilt. Spread out in the tabloids for public consumption, elevated to huge posters. A record was released but 'Cold As The Coldest Sea' got a rather icy reception from the record-buying public, despite all the hyperbole.

But one year later the tabloids had tired of him. Howcher was last year's big deal, last year's boy wonder. He's now back in Sheffield – his fame nevertheless guaranteed. There goes Trevor, they say, as he parades down the street, hair and cloak billowing. The most beautiful man in the world. Once.

He greets his friends – there they all sit, the style boys (and the occasional female hanger-on, usually very plump). The boys who are going to make it to the top using style, panache, individualism as their hand grips.

A boy with cropped blond hair bleached oh-so-white, harem pants and vest (on a cold summer's afternoon in Sheffield), a boy with baggy cotton pants (not quite harem pants these, but nearly), and cavalier tresses (again). A black boy with Grace Jones cut, dark suit; his modest sartorial style compensated by a camp manner so grossly overplayed that it needs a cigarette to get the performance right. All in a Sheffield coffee bar, for God's sake. But they have been validated and the huge validation stamp towers over them. Howcher showed it was possible. The Human League used to sing about it.

In Trevor's case, it was the Manpower Services Commission he was plucked from, but after a year he was put back down. But no matter. He was still a shining star that was far from extinguished, back in Sheffield at least. A group of teenagers passed by and gawped at Trevor and his mates. 'He made a quarter of a million,' said one star-struck teenage.

I did my cynical turn.

'He did, he really did, a quarter of a million quid.'

'For one record?'

'Well, he had to do a bit of posing as well, for photos and things. He's famous – there's a lot of money in modelling, you know.'

'So if he's famous, why hasn't my mum heard of him then? When she can tell you with some authority that Boy George hasn't been to bed with Marilyn yet and that he's in love with an American film star. She can even make a fair stab at Boy George's real name.'

'Who the fuck's your mum anyway?'

Well, quite. I went back to studying the group who'd shown that anything was possible. Trevor, who for years had been hounded around Sheffield as a queer and a fairy, had suddenly found himself not just famous but proclaimed as the most beautiful man in the world – note 'man'. That's why he acquired the stubble, to act as a sign vehicle of masculine gender, to compensate for the steady stream of sign vehicles hurtling in the opposite direction. So there they were – the style merchants with the world at their elegantly sandalled feet, discussing tonight's big event – the opening of the new club to be fronted by Trevor – Le Bon-Bon – 'a melting pot of style', as it said on the ticket.

Le Bon-Bon was to open in Turn-Ups – a club owned by Les Vickers, one of the biggest scrap dealers in Sheffield and famous (once) for scrapping the *Ark Royal*. To attract custom on every night of the week, it's necessary for most nightclubs to vary their theme a little bit. So on Monday nights at Turn-Ups they had drinks at half-price and denims allowed, on Tuesday nights it was reggae night for a mainly black clientele. On Wednesday nights it was, as one bouncer put it, 'weirdo night' for Trevor and his likes, and then it was back to the more ordinary clientele for Thursdays, Fridays and Saturdays. The precursor of the current club was the Sin-Bin but Le Bon-Bon was an attempt to attract the up-market weirdo and to deny access to the rougher element of the Sin-Bin – the punks and the skins.

Trevor was to select and play the records. 'It's going to be seventies funk' said one of the cognoscenti – '"Supernature", "I Lost My Heart To A Starship Trooper", that kind of thing.'

'Why?' I asked naively.

'Trevor likes it,' he replied.

'Oh,' I said, if it was good enough for him, and all that.

And play the records he did. And that's not all – he got dressed up and winked at some of the lucky boys. No speaking, mind, none of the usual DJ patter. Trev's singular style said it all, he thought. The cavalier tresses were gathered up inside a little sailor's hat, complemented with extremely large gold earrings and a little white sailor's top. He was smiling a lot and clearly enjoying playing his record collection to us. The cognoscenti had informed me that the Human League and ABC were sure to turn up to pay homage to Trev, but it was not to be. There were, however, lots of Boy George clones, invariably little plump blokes who had discovered (perhaps like Boy George himself) that they could disguise their mature puppy fat with a shapeless dress. And there were lots of Trevor clones – cavalier tresses, harem pants, bare midriff a must (now we know why Trevor went as a sailor). One female also sported the look – she wasn't going to let the boys have all the fun.

Now seventies funk does provide some problem for weirdo dancing because it is good, solid disco music. It's difficult not to do good, solid disco dancing to it. But the boys did their best. They expressed their individuality all right – they waved their arms about wildly (but, as it turned out, almost in unison) and they punctuated their dancing with the occasional roll on the dirty floor. But again, they nearly all did it – like orchestrated steps from a fixed routine. Not so much gay abandon as abandoned imagination. A desperate attempt to do something outrageous, to be original.

Now, if a new nightclub is to make it, the disc jockey has to have a host of skills. He must be able to get the punters on to the dance floor and keep them there, and I've even talked to club DJs who say they can lose an exact proportion of the punters back to the bar when the bar sales are flagging. But Trevor didn't seem to want to be bothered by these mundane skills, and eventually he paid the price – one unfortunate choice of record emptied the dance floor. Now this was original; the party people had stopped partying. One lone male fan-dancer then took the floor (I suspect he'd been held in reserve for just such a contingency) and started his routine. Trev's moment had come. The hat came off, the tresses were shaken out, and Trevor got down to it with the fan-dancer. For a moment the audience, for that is what the style merchants had become, gaped (in unison) and then they too got down to it. The record wasn't so bad after all. Just look at Trevor. Oh, how could we doubt you, Trevor? Isn't this just divine?

I sidled off to one of the bars. They weren't doing much business. The bouncer was standing there looking morose. So what did he make of Wednesday nights and the melting pot of style?

'Oh, I don't mind the weirdos,' he said. 'They never cause any trouble. They're always very quiet and leave right when you tell them.'

'But what about all the camping about?'

'Oh, I just ignore it and leave them to it as long as they don't try to touch me. They don't buy much drink though, they don't seem to need it.'

And another Trevor clone walked past, high on narcissism, intoxicated by his looks, drunk on the attention he was being paid by the Boy George clones – plump and passé.

'At least they've got their dreams, I suppose,' said the bouncer.

'And their egos intact,' I replied. 'And that's something.'

A tale of two drug users

They were sitting in the park where they'd played as children, watching the next generation fight for possession of the slide. A dog had done its pooh right in the middle of the swings. It was just like old times. They were best of friends separated by somewhat different fates, reunited by the summer holidays. Both had bloodshot eyes, a bit watery and a bit sore. It was definitely like old times. They were both happy, not euphoric, mind, not high, just happy, contented, pleased to see each other again. Colin giggled, then Frank giggled. Like the pox, giggling is highly contagious. One rather harassed young mother, two screaming brats in tow, threw them a filthy look. You could see the premature worry lines etched on her face; one brat had turned purple with the sheer effort of being heard above the cacophony of the swings. She dragged it along by the hood of its plastic kagoul. The kagoul had a rip in it – it obviously wasn't the first time she'd used the hood to lead the brat along this way. The child's purple face reminded Colin of one particular experience he'd had with acid, in which everyone he met had a purple face. He found it not frightening in the least but hilarious, and he spent the whole day at his university going round wide-eyed staring at people. They were used to it. 'I'm just a bit weird,' he kept saying. 'I'm OK.' They let him be.

He started giggling again, remembering this experience, enjoying his private joke. Frank giggled also. The mother with the lines was clearly annoyed. She thought they were laughing at her, 'immature little shits, nothing better to do than hang about the swings, laughing at people'. Colin stopped giggling for a moment – he suddenly realised what was happening and he didn't want to hurt her feelings – he didn't want to hurt anybody. But Frank was bent double in his fit of laughing and when the harassed mother stomped off and nearly trod in the pooh, well, that was it. He was off again. Private joke but public nuisance.

They went back to Frank's house. His parents were out. Frank rolled a joint. 'First of the day,' he said in a way that reminded Colin of what Frank's dad always said with his lunchtime pint. Colin and Frank grew up together on a working-class estate in Sheffield. Both were brighter than average. Colin was also conscientious. At school, he studied while Frank acted the clown. Colin got O levels and A levels. Frank didn't, but he got a lot of laughs. Colin got into a Midlands university – he had successfully completed two years. Frank got one temporary job working as a forecourt attendant – but he'd been sacked for bad time-keeping. 'I didn't want to work there anyway,' he said, 'I was intending to leave.' Frank had been on the dole for the past three months waiting for his best mate to get back from the 'uni'. 'Then it'll be like old times.' It was, a bit. They had been to the park, it had rained, someone had got annoyed at them, Frank had rolled a joint. They sat on the bed in Frank's room. The Smiths were producing the sounds. 'Did you see old Morrissey on *Top of the Pops* with the branch sticking out of his trousers? Weren't he fucking great?' said Frank.

'Absolutely brill, I watched it in the JCR. We all got up and had a bop to it,' said Colin.

'Oh, I watched it with my dad, he kept taking the piss and saying he knew where he'd like to stick the branch,' said Frank.

'It was a great night,' said Colin. 'We'd all had a lot of dope before it and one girl had dropped some acid. She was a bit of a silly cow though – she dropped a whole tab and started weeping and things – a bit of a neurotic bitch if you ask me. She kept looking for someone to comfort her. Do you remember the night you dropped two tabs and lay in my garden all night watching the stars, and your multicoloured piss when you were having a wee? Or the night we went camping and I was reading the message from God in the sky. I thought I was a frigging prophet. I tried writing some of it down. But it was all just a load of bollocks the next day.' He fished in his pocket and pulled out a crumpled piece of paper. ' "Turtles are lentils in my soup" – What the fuck was I going on about?'

Colin and Frank were both twenty. They had been taking some form of drugs for the past four years. The range of substances they'd both taken was very similar – some speed, a few barbiturates, dope and acid – the pattern had always been a bit different. Their initiation to drugs and the drug culture was identical. A friend had been to his local youth club to hear a talk on the dangers of drugs. The local police spokesman had shown them some slides of the offending substances and talked to them about the short-term and long-term effects. The friend had only listened to the short-term ones. He particularly liked the idea of speed (he even liked the name). 'It makes you feel really big and euphoric, you don't get tired.' The friend was convinced. The long-term effects – depression, apathy, suicide – sounded boring, so he didn't listen. He put the word out to his acquaintances, 'I wouldn't mind that there speed,' and, lo and behold, some pills came back. He paid through the nose for them but he didn't mind.

Now this character was a bit cautious and he reckoned that things wouldn't be quite so bad if Frank and Colin joined him for his initiation. Frank and Colin didn't know much about speed at the time but it sounded

OK – 'It makes you feel really big and gives you lots of energy, you could run all day' (Colin was a keen athlete) 'or shag all day' (Frank wasn't). They were convinced. Colin, even more cautious, went to his local library to read up about the effects before the appointed night and he calculated that, on balance, it was OK. 'No more dangerous than an Outward Bound school weekend, the book reckoned,' he reported back. Frank wasn't interested – he was more concerned with fixing up a partner to try its all-day effects on.

The big night came. Colin took one pill, the friend took one pill, Frank took one pill and then asked for another twenty minutes later because he didn't feel that different. The only noticeable effect was that he was getting a bit irritable. Two or three made him distinctly aggressive. The disco gave him the opportunity to vent it. 'I don't know about shagging all day, it just makes me take offence more easily,' he said later.

Colin had to agree but then they were hooked – not on amphetamine itself, because the tiny amount that they had taken probably meant that any noticeable effects were more attributable to their expectations and the social setting rather than any chemical changes in their brain, but hooked on the feeling of secrecy and cliquishness and danger. Colin liked to get on the bus with some in his pocket. He felt just that little bit different. Speed made him feel big all right, even when he hadn't taken any. Fridays became speed night.

But Colin didn't like Saturdays any longer. They were so miserable. It didn't seem to bother Frank so much. On Saturdays they would go to the pub and he'd be as cheerful as you like – after a few pints. Colin went back to his library book to read up about hash. He had started to feel that hash was more appropriate for his developing image – he was an A level student now.

'It's only mods and skinheads who take speed, you know. I want to try dope. It makes you more laid-back. It doesn't make you on edge all the time.'

Frank didn't mind being on edge – he thought Colin was just a little frightened of some of the rows they'd been getting into. He agreed to try dope but he kept Fridays free for speed. He even stopped mentioning to Colin that he was taking it. He liked talking to the customers at the filling station really fast on Friday afternoons (when he actually took it), skipping his tea, and then on to the disco. 'I don't mind a bit of aggro. I've got the bottle for it, you see. That's the difference between you and me.'

A school friend of Colin's came up with the grass – a tiny sample just to try. It had been in the school friend's pocket for weeks. He hadn't the bottle to try it himself. Colin and Frank were at a loss what to do with it. They knew you smoked it in a joint with tobacco, but they weren't quite sure how to go about constructing a joint. Frank's dad had smoked roll-ups when Frank was a child but had stopped years ago. It was Benson and Hedges now. 'I could have learned something useful from him for a change if he hadn't stopped rolling his own,' said Frank. Colin studied his library book with a good photo of a joint in it but with absolutely no guidance on how to go about constructing one. Neither of them smoked normally and they didn't really relish the idea of puffing away at something even if it was going to make them incredibly randy (according to Colin's library book). The grass was stored away.

They met acid at a party. 'A bit stronger then dope,' said Colin, 'and no messing about with Rizla papers.' Frank was all for it. Again it was a friend of a friend who gave them the tabs. They all sat around waiting for it to happen – and it did – some of the cognoscenti kept throwing records in the air. Colin didn't know why at first but when one came tumbling to earth with a thousand afterimages flickering behind it, he understood. There was snow on the ground and Frank and Colin both went to run their fingers through the new multicoloured phenomenon. They were giggling a lot. Everything was so different. When Colin went home that night and was introduced to his mother's new fancy man, he couldn't keep his face straight. The fancy man's bald pate was a bright sparkling red and it seemed to be flashing on and off like a traffic light. His mother's face was green. It was, by necessity, a very private joke.

So Colin eventually went off to university well prepared for many of his new experiences. Indeed, with about ten tabs of acid on his person, for his personal use. It'll be less risky than trying to score off people I don't know, he thought. He sold a few tabs to help pay for a new pair of boots. Frank stayed at home dropping speed, dropping acid, dropping anything that he could get his hands on. Even he didn't have the bottle for heroin.

It wasn't his boring work that led him to do it, thought Colin – he'd met some students at university who were just the same – keen experimenters, keen gamblers, big turtles. They'd take anything that was going. Not so Colin – just dope and acid now, with a respectable fortnight between each trip. And a constant monitoring of his experiences.

So Colin sat there, getting into the Smiths, trying to write some more poetry. It was still appalling. Frank just rocked his head and closed his eyes. 'I love getting smashed out of my fucking brain,' he said. The turtles had certainly come home to roost.

7 · Playing the part

By the time an actor knows how to act any sort of part he is often too old to act any but a few.
Somerset Maugham, *The Summing Up*, 1938

Social performance

I spent four years in the streets and nightclubs of Sheffield, tape recorder and pen in hand, talking to the characters, describing the scenes and trying (sometimes desperately) to follow the plot. So what kind of drama did unfold before my eyes? What was really going on?

It sometimes helps to look at real life in dramaturgical terms – at least we usually try to understand drama. And there may even be similarities between real life and the dramaturgical version. The sociologist Erving Goffman said: 'All the world is not, of course, a stage, but the crucial ways in which it isn't are not easy to specify' (1976, p. 75). It's not just that there are 'characters' in real-life settings, where 'scenes' sometimes occur and 'performances' are sometimes disrupted. It's not just that the odd 'prima donna' often failed to attend on cue and then demanded a large sum of money for his performance even when he had 'overacted'. No, it's something more than this.

Let us consider, for example, what might be some of the most basic aspects of social performance. Erving Goffman suggests we should first look at 'front' – which he defines as 'the expressive equipment of a standard kind intentionally or unwittingly employed by the individual during his performance' (loc. cit., p. 32). He suggests that there are three standard components of social 'front'. There is the 'setting' (including the furniture and the physical layout), 'appearance' and 'manner'. Front is crucial, he argues, in that it is that part of the individual's performance which acts to define the situation for those who observe it. The various parts of front may all act together to represent a consistent whole, but the components of front need not be consistent. An individual may be dressed in clothes of low status but his manner may suggest otherwise. Alternatively, an apparently high-status person in a high-status setting may act deferentially or apologetically.

An example of a front with consistent components which Goffman himself mentions is provided by MacGowan's (1908, p. 187) description of a Chinese mandarin:

Coming closely behind . . . the luxurious chair of the mandarin, carried by eight bearers, fills the vacant space in the street . . . He is an ideal-looking official, for he is large and massive in appearance, whilst he has that stern and forbidding aspect . . . This is the kind of air that the mandarins put on when they appear in public. In the course of many years' experience, I have never once seen any of them, from the highest to the lowest, with a smile on his face or a look of sympathy for the people while he was being carried officially through the streets.

But consider Andrew, the unemployed Oxford graduate (pp. 49–50) who had trouble reconciling the various aspects of his social front – he very much looked the part of the Oxford graduate, he had access to the right settings (or would have if he applied for certain jobs) but his manner was discrepant. As he put it: 'Oxford degrees stand you in good stead for the jobs I don't want or wouldn't be socially equipped to deal with – the City, the senior Civil Service, merchant banks and so on.' Andrew consequently found himself unemployed and considerably isolated because although education had provided him with an intellect equipped to deal with middle-class professional life it had not altered his basic social repertoire. Even if he had wanted to get on with upper middle-class gents from the City it is doubtful whether he ever really could have.

The components of front can be consciously changed and manipulated. The con man (pp. 102–8) may carefully choose the setting to negotiate his business deals. The VIP lounge of a nightclub does nicely – all chrome and velvet. This matches his appearance (Italian suit, Cartier watch) and manner (loud, confident, brash). The living room of his council flat would be less useful in this respect. There would be a clash – such a clash or contradiction might lead to confusion, anxiety and worry about the reliability of the deals being offered. Cars of course provide one important aspect of mobile setting and the care some individuals take in selecting cars, not as forms of transport but as manipulated microcosms to project their personality and social front, is startling. Alternatively, consider the self-employed painter (pp. 39–43) now desperate to show how he's gone up in the world. The settings in which he operates are somewhat restricted – his business deals are concluded in other people's homes, his work is confined to the outsides or insides of other people's houses, usually halfway up a ladder.

But he can change some aspects of the setting – he can get his name painted on the side of his daffodil-yellow Datsun for a start (for £40), and thereby redefine the situation – from odd-job man (probably 'dole-queue scrounger') with some work on the side to self-employed painter and decorator – a man at work and not ashamed to demonstrate it publicly. Masher Metham's appearance again may be restricted by the job he does – the painter's white overalls are after all ubiquitous but his manner definitely proclaims his new status. He whistles as he works even when orders are short, and even when he is acutely anxious about further work. He's his own boss and he needs to show it *constantly*.

The problem for Andrea, the midget (pp. 85–90), was somewhat different. A normal teenager with normal desires and interests but acutely aware of society's reaction to her physical disability. People generally thought that there was an associated mental retardation. So Andrea reacted (strategically) by going on the CB circuit as Smiley (with Big T, her fat friend) and divorcing her 'manner' and 'appearance'. Her manner was, as it always is, sociable, gregarious, highly normal – not socially or intellectually retarded – and was perceived as such, without the mantle of her distinctive appearance to hide it. She made many friends that way – by restricting access to aspects of her social front. She may have been thought 'a right teaser' but that's quite a lot better than being 'just a dwarf'.

Social front can of course be manipulated but while engaging in such manipulation, individuals may fail to change some small, insignificant features which can then act as telltale signs. Consider the 'big spender' (pp. 111–12, described by the minder) – out to meet a woman in his Rolls-Royce, with his chauffeur in a pinstriped suit whom he simply called 'driver', as if he was used to a life of ordering chauffeurs about. Mobile setting, appearance and manner quite consistent, but the car was not taxed. Rod Johnson on the door of a nightclub looks out for these small signs that most of us might miss. A punter may have donned a suit and tie but if he hasn't brushed his shoes, well, that's it – according to Rod. 'The wrong attitude – straight away you can tell,' he says. A social front that doesn't quite work. Cockney's survival depends on his ability to manipulate social front in a variety of settings and on the sheer adaptability of his manner.

Another important aspect of social performance is what Goffman calls the 'dramatic realization' of the performer. 'While in the presence of others, the individual typically infuses his activity with signs which dramatically highlight and portray confirmatory facts that might otherwise remain unapparent or obscure' (loc. cit., p. 40). Goffman uses the example of nursing to illustrate this. He argues that because successful medical diagnosis depends on careful observation of symptoms over time, nurses may check things like shallowness of breathing and colour and tone of the skin while they are chatting to patients. The problem with this, however, (according to Goffman) is that the patient and the patient's family and friends will think that the nurse is simply visiting and 'wasting time' unless, that is, she engages in some demonstrable activity such as administering a thermometer or hypodermic. Nurses have therefore to dramatise their work. So do unemployed steelworkers decorating their house, gamblers, clairvoyants and a host of others. Fred Smith, the unemployed steelworker (pp. 31–5), took his breaks out of doors when he was decorating his house. At the end of the day he sat, with the grime still on his face, on his front step, at the exact time the employed were returning from their work. His work was going on indoors and not visible to the naked eye – his work breaks were taken outside and highly visible. Punters in a casino watch the roulette wheel intently, often making notes at the same time to show that they have a system and that they're not just mug punters making random bets (pp. 95–101). The clairvoyant (pp. 149–56) may wave his arms in a dramatic fashion and talk in a loud voice so that he can be seen to be dealing with forces not immediately apparent to the likes of you and me (and the paying customer); simple silences while he consulted these 'forces' would not do.

There may be a price to pay for all of this, however. As Sartre suggested, 'The attentive pupil who wishes to *be* attentive, his eyes riveted on the teacher, his ears open wide, so exhausts himself in playing the attentive role that he ends up by no longer hearing anything' (1957). Bouncers may indeed pay this price – in continually having to demonstrate their attentiveness to detail while they stand at the doors of nightclubs, they may miss quite obvious things and trouble may therefore ensue. The clairvoyant's dramatic realisation may lead to trouble in a different way, his communication with 'the other side' – dramatically enacted – may lead him to miss entirely many of the subtle and not so subtle cues telling him whether he's on the right track or not. Consequently, some readings of clairvoyants have more cul-de-sacs than the average middle-class estate.

Another important aspect of social performance is what Goffman calls 'idealization' – 'the tendency for performers to offer their observers an impression that is idealized in different ways' (loc. cit., p. 44). Both positive and negative idealisation may occur. Examples of positive idealisation are the use of status symbols to express material wealth and the use of very correct or hypercorrect language by the lower middle class to indicate higher social status (see Ellis and Beattie, 1986). The debt collector wearing a suit to portray the professional role and not to go as a 'heavy' is an example of positive idealisation (see p. 111). Or consider the 63-year-old massage-parlour customer – John, now retired, who spent £44 a week in this particular pursuit (pp. 122–5). His performance role at the massage parlour was that of an ordinary, decent, respectable member of society requiring a professional service; he was (demonstrably) not like 'some who frequented such places'. To this end his performance showed considerable signs of positive idealisation. He didn't just chat to the masseuse and tell her a little about himself. He didn't just 'try to understand her'. He sent her postcards with little notes on them when he was away, and wrote a letter to her every week and told her (often) that he'd like her to marry his son (although, of course, he would never introduce them). He was always polite and pleasant. Some customers went to the massage parlour dirty and refused to have a shower, but not John. Not just scrupulously clean, but with all the respectable mores of society shining through, highly visible, for this most limited form of social interaction.

In the case of negative idealisation, the performer again idealises the performance but in the opposite direction. An example of this is provided by Ralph's (1950) work on 'the junk peddler . . . vitally interested in keeping information as to the true financial value of "junk" from the general public. He wishes to perpetuate the myth that junk is valueless and that the individuals who deal in it are "down and out" and should be pitied.' (p. 26.)

I found many different types of idealisation in Sheffield. Cockney's manner and appearance had to be exactly right in every detail – together they had to spell success. People may have known he was a bit dodgy but the clothes, the Cartier watch (later exchanged for a Piaget 'because Cartiers are becoming too common') and the confident manner had to indicate that he was first and foremost 'a success' and not one of the unqualified, untalented bums trying to make it at the bottom of the ladder, 'bobbing and weaving', 'ducking and diving', 'wheeling and dealing'.

Similarly, some of the black pimps I met had devoted a large proportion of their time and money (perhaps, on most criteria, too great a part) to idealising their chunky gold-bracelet image and cool performance. But not so the white pimp discussed in detail (pp. 117–20). He dressed down, presumably to corroborate his 'just one of the lads' image and his view of his service as just that of 'a bloke to a bloke'. Idealisation of appearance and performance is also clearly something which performers look out for.

Consider again Joy's comments when the well-recommended clairvoyant Glenn turned up at the beauty parlour both scruffy and wet, obviously having walked from the bus (p. 150). 'It doesn't pay to look too prosperous, that's what Albert always says,' said Joy. (Albert, her husband and frequently cited source of information, was a successful businessman who clearly practised negative idealisation.) Glenn's appearance was, however, in reality consonant with his home situation and his real economic position. Joy's belief in a core aspect of social performance, which wasn't in fact operating in this particular case, probably led Glenn to be perceived in a more favourable light than he might otherwise have been. (His dirty fingernails, however, led others to have their doubts. There are clearly limits to what performers think other performers should stoop in the process of negative idealisation.)

In the social world, the performer can rely on his audience to accept small, even apparently insignificant cues as a sign of something greater and more important. But as Goffman points out, this convenient fact has one very inconvenient implication. 'By virtue of the same sign-accepting tendency, the audience may misunderstand the meaning that a cue was designed to convey, or may read an embarrassing meaning into gestures or events that were accidental, inadvertent, or incidental and not meant by the performer to carry any meaning whatsoever.' (Loc. cit., p. 59.) Masseuses must not yawn or laugh – if they did they would be unprofessional, they would convey impropriety, disrespect, disdain. Bouncers may yawn or laugh but they should not trip, stumble or fall, stutter or appear nervous. Masseuses may stutter or appear nervous, however. It's not that broad meanings are not being read into accidental, inadvertent or incidental acts in each and every case; rather that certain broad readings are perfectly compatible and appropriate for certain social performances but not others. Bouncers can be bored or derisive, masseuses cannot. Both groups must exert what Goffman calls 'synecdochic responsibility' for their actions 'making sure that as many as possible of the minor events in the performance, however instrumentally inconsequential these events may be, will occur in such a way as to convey either no impression or an impression that is compatible and consistent with the overall definition of the situation that is being fostered' (loc. cit., p. 59). The good punter or the big spender reaching into his wallet or back pocket for another tenner must take great care to demonstrate that he is not in the least concerned with the number of tenners that are left there. His momentary focus of regard on the wad must not be sufficiently long to suggest that any quick counting or checking is taking place. To do so would have very serious consequences indeed. Ask any croupier or nightclub manager.

What has been said thus far about the characteristics of social performances leads one inevitably to the issue of misrepresentation. As Goffman puts it:

If this tendency of the audience to accept signs places the performer in a position to be misunderstood and makes it necessary for him to exercise expressive care regarding everything he does when before the audience, so also this sign-accepting tendency puts the audience in a position to be duped and misled; for there are few signs that cannot be used to attest to the presence of something that is not really there. And it is plain that many performers have ample capacity and motive to misrepresent the factors; only shame, guilt or fear prevent them doing so. (Loc. cit., p. 65.)

In life, misrepresentation is rife and can be extremely threatening. As Goffman again notes:

the more closely the impostor's performance approximates to the real thing, the more intensely we may be threatened, for a competent performance by someone who proves to be an impostor may weaken in our minds the moral connection between legitimate authorization to play a part and the capacity to play it. (Skilled mimics, who admit all along that their intentions are unserious, seem to provide one way in which we can 'work through' some of these anxieties.) (Loc. cit., p. 67.)

Consider John, the van driver with the Silver Shadow and the tan (pp. 76–81), performing nightly in the restricted social setting of the nightclub, his appearance and manner shaped to perfection. He has a VIP pass, he knows the staff, he gets drinks served quickly at the bars (even if his finances dictate that he does not get served too often). He's a rich man, to all intents and purposes. Put him beside a genuine millionaire and ask a hundred bored housewives on their night out, or a hundred girls in their late teens on their hen night, to select the impostor, and watch them fail as their stereotypes, their heuristics, their intuitions fall tumbling around them.

But this may not, at first, seem too serious. After all, nightclubs are manufactured 'safe' environments for people to let themselves go, to come out of themselves, to live crazy (in Michael Jackson's words). One nightclub manager said to me, 'We don't care how people act once they're inside, as long as it doesn't encroach on our operation. The married women remove their wedding rings for the night and for one night they're single. So what?' But what if it happens night after night – the same front presented, the same appearance, the same manner, the same basic story? Everyone's prepared to accept some degree of illusion in a nightclub, everyone's prepared to allow some degree of misrepresentation – but only some. When it is internally coherent and longitudinally consistent, then perhaps it is a different matter. And when the individuals go to great lengths to conceal their other identity during the day, then things become more serious.

Of course, some types of misrepresentation are worse then others. Again Goffman notes:

While it is felt to be an inexcusable crime against communication to impersonate someone of sacred status, such as a doctor or a priest, we are often less concerned when someone impersonates a member of a disesteemed, non-crucial, profane status, such as that of a hobo or unskilled worker . . . Also, we distinguish between impersonation of a specific, concrete individual, which we usually feel is quite inexcusable, and impersonations of category membership which we may feel less strongly about. (Loc. cit., p. 67.)

The majority of misrepresentation I came across was of the less serious 'category-membership' kind – rich man (by a van driver), playboy (bus driver), jetsetter (West Indian road sweeper), woman of considerable independent means (masseuse), but executed in a serious and consistent way and not simply put on temporarily or for a laugh. However, other, slightly more specific kinds of misrepresentation did occur. Thus I found a number of bogus doctors (for example, by a surprising number of foreign students), a bogus Sheffield Wednesday footballer (a fitter who once got a schoolboy trial for the team) and many bogus sauna receptionists (the masseuses themselves). On the streets of Sheffield there were many men who said that they had opted for early retirement when in fact they had been made redundant with quite a few years of work ahead of them. They became retired in terms of their social performances and they cultivated a retired image. One year an active 49-year-old, the next a retired fifty-year-old 'slowing down', taking things easily. Performance and image consistent with the new reality. In the clubs few people impersonated Tony Knowles but a surprising number impersonated Tony Knowles's manager. A perennial form of misrepresentation was the bogus nightclub owner, sometimes named (a selection of 'nearly men' who at some time in their careers had attempted to acquire the capital to open a nightclub).

The list is endless – identities often engendered by the night and foisted onto the day. Identities realised through appearance and manner and backed by the usual props – clothes, cars, even acquaintances. Identities plausible in terms of accounts, explanations and stories to every and any attentive audience. Such is the reality of Steel City today.

Teams and the secrets of the home game

Acquaintances are crucial in the social world for stability and for credibility. One's performance as a big spender, a competent bouncer, a good punter, a playboy or whatever, may fall considerably short without the presence of others to corroborate the stories and, perhaps most importantly, the act. Goffman coined the term 'team' to refer to 'any set of individuals who co-operate in staging a single routine' (loc. cit., p. 85). Team mates are bound together by a bond of 'reciprocal dependence'; they 'co-operate to maintain a given definition of the situation before their audience' (loc. cit., p. 85) but while doing so cannot maintain that particular impression before one another. Team mates are 'in the know' and the team must display 'dramaturgical discipline' – public disagreement between team members should be avoided because, as Goffman notes, it 'not only incapacitates them for united action but also embarrasses the reality sponsored by the team' (loc. cit., p. 91). An example comes from Howard Becker on the teaching profession – if teachers together are to sustain an air of professional competence then they must make sure that when angry parents come to the school with complaints, the headmaster will back up the staff at least until the parents have departed. They must present a united front to project the desired impression.

Teams may choose to operate on home ground because 'control of the setting may give the controlling team a sense of security' (loc. cit., p. 99). Trevor Howcher and his friends took over a nightclub one evening a week for a theme night – to establish a home ground (pp. 173–4). The theme being that of style merchant, the striking individual, the weirdo. Their new home setting guaranteed them security with bouncers of their very own to protect this and keep out offending nonmembers and normals. And yet the whole concept of being 'an individual' is by their definition to be in contrast, to be a bit different. Difficult when the club is founded on that principle. Difference becomes stylised individuality – set weirdness, routinised abnormality. For Cockney and his friends the home ground was the VIP lounge of numerous nightclubs where the ordinary punter was made to feel uncomfortable.

In Sheffield, I discovered many performance teams operating on a variety of home grounds – bouncers in a nightclub, for example, cooperating to maintain a given definition of the nightclub situation as 'safe' and 'a good environment to enjoy oneself in' (pp. 90–95). They must sustain a common front; they may argue and criticise punters but never each other, when on the job. The apparent and perceived efficiency of the team depends on this cooperation. The apparent and projected efficiency of the team can prevent trouble arising.

Teams also share secrets. Goffman distinguishes 'dark secrets' – 'facts about a team which it knows and conceals and which are incompatible with the image of self that the team attempts to maintain before its audiences' (loc. cit., p. 141) – 'strategic' secrets relating to the 'intentions and capacities of a team which it conceals from its audience in order to prevent them from adapting effectively to the state of affairs the team is planning to bring about' (loc. cit., p. 141), and 'inside' secrets – 'ones whose possession marks an individual as being a member of a group and helps the group feel separate and different from those individuals who are not "in the know"' (loc. cit., p. 142). In the case of the bouncers I studied, one dark secret was the fact that one of their members was awaiting trial on a charge of grievous bodily harm – in an affray he had used a baseball bat hidden in reception. This constitutes a dark secret because it is incompatible with the image that bouncers wish to convey. They wish to be seen as professionals who can 'handle trouble' and 'sort it' without recourse to offensive weapons and without turning wild in tense situations. This particular individual's behaviour was not compatible with this image. He was subsequently fired. Masher Metham's losing his job for a clocking offence was a dark secret incompatible with the highly motivated, self-employed painter and decorator image. So dark, in fact, that Masher Metham felt he had to avoid the previous members of his work team. His attitude to work had changed and he greatly regretted his past. He had to make it, but completely alone, so that his dark secret would be secure.

A strategic secret for bouncers is the way they use the DJ in clubs to coordinate their activities – to call them to an incident in the first place and subsequently guide them in an indirect and subtle fashion so as not to alarm the other customers. Troublemakers who really wanted to be left alone to do real violence could incapacitate the DJ – if they were aware of this strategic secret concerning his real role. A series of strategic secrets for nurses revolved around the handling of death and dying (pp. 133–4). For example, moving dying patients onto a side ward 'so as not to disturb the other patients' or relying upon doctors to break the news of death, even when this meant telling relatives that the patient was still doing 'poorly' when he or she was long gone. Side wards, of course, have an additional benefit in that their comparative privacy means that the 'dramatic realization' of the nursing role becomes less important and nurses can concentrate more on actual care of the sick regardless of how it may appear.

Bouncers have many 'inside' secrets because of the very special nature of their job – the hard interface between management and customer – constantly watching, constantly displaying their attentiveness. Being 'in the know' is one way of demonstrating how attentive you've been. They pick up secrets about clients, which they share, and secrets about staff. In one club, the bouncers shared eagerly the secret of how a nightclub owner with a reputation for being hard had lost nearly all his teeth in a fight with a particular customer. It was important for them to know about this because they felt it demonstrated the owner's real capacity and his limitations. A bouncer's prior history of violence, including the use of offensive weapons outside the context of a nightclub, would be an inside secret and, possibly depending on its nature, a strategic secret. Mick's head-butting, for example, which had got him into trouble with the police in the past, could clearly be used strategically. He was very useful for close encounters of the toe-to-toe aggro kind. Such secrets were not, however, dark in the way that the use of the baseball bat in the context of the nightclub was.

The two drug users (pp. 175–8) shared many strategic and inside secrets – they discovered how to get the substances and how to take them. They knew about their effects and could tell (with some reliability) what others had taken. They enjoyed the feeling of secrecy and – because they were breaking the law, and because some of the drugs were potentially harmful – the danger. Being part of this team gave them an identity and a role. The fact that one member of the team belonged to another team as well, and had an additional identity – as student – probably will turn out to be crucial. The whole life of the remaining member, Frank, revolved around this restricted team, his social being was played out on a very narrow stage indeed.

Or consider Cockney out with a famous footballer – a formidable team indeed, two amiable playboys, two big spenders out for a night on the old 'shampoo'. Cockney's six custodial sentences are certainly a dark secret here. An important strategic secret with this team is that he can only really sustain the playboy image because he possesses a VIP pass and, like most moderate spenders but highly visible personages, receives some complimentary drinks from the management. In the case of inside secrets, Cockney's whole life revolves around them – they are his stock in trade, his currency. The footballer may make use of some of this inside knowledge for get-rich-quick deals. The secrets of this team must be kept for the situation, as defined by the members, to continue to exist. Cockney and the footballer are linked together in a bond of 'reciprocal dependence'.

Goffman makes the following interesting points about the nature and interconnection of these different types of secret:

Inside secrets may have little strategic importance and may not be very dark. When this is the case, such secrets may be discovered or accidentally disclosed without radically disrupting the team performance; the performers need only shift their secret delight to another matter. Of course, secrets that are strategic and/or dark serve extremely well as inside secrets, and we find, in fact, that the strategic and dark character of secrets is often exaggerated for this reason. Interestingly enough, the leaders of a social group are sometimes faced with a dilemma regarding important strategic secrets. Those in the group who are not brought in on the secret will feel excluded and affronted when the secret finally comes to light; on the other hand, the greater the number of persons who are brought in on the secret, the greater the likelihood of intentional or unintentional disclosure. (Loc. cit., p. 143.)

Inside secrets may be traded in a way that dark or strategic secrets cannot be. The story about the nightclub owner and the missing teeth was traded by bouncers in a way that the story of the baseball bat could not be. And it's not just that inside secrets are generally less serious. Thus, I met one 'playboy' whose wife worked in a massage parlour, he worked during the day as a decorator. He liked Dom Pérignon and had many famous friends. His finances were the result of deals he could pull off, using his famous friends and other contacts. His real work (i.e. the decorating) couldn't entirely finance his life style. Now, in this particular person's case, the occupation of his wife was an 'inside' secret, certainly not bandied about but carefully traded to those in the know. His real work, however, was a dark secret. Being a decorator by day was not compatible with the image he and his friends (his team) were trying to project. His wife's work, however, did not clash with the image, especially since he maintained that she did not need to support him. On most criteria, however, the wife's occupation is the more serious secret but it was never 'dark' in the way that his own occupation was.

Or consider the unemployed middle-class graduates with their jumble-sale clothes, their new 'individuality' and their host of radical activities (pp. 51–3). The major dark secret underpinning this group was surely their family background – because they were all to the last woman comfortably middle-class. There were no working-class conscripts in this group. Peace-shop volunteers with fathers of senior rank in the army. Not as desperate for a job as some of the graduates from working-class backgrounds because their dole could be supplemented, on request, by parents. Their background was also a strategic secret – it enabled them to engage in such activities without endangering their chances of a job at the end of it. Together they formed a very cohesive team.

Of course, in the case of institutions like casinos, strategic secrets may also be somewhat 'dark'. Card counting, that is, trying to work out the relative probability of a high or low card being dealt in blackjack by memorising all the cards from the four packs used, is not illegal but it is not desirable from the casinos' point of view. Good card counters win. Croupiers, inspectors, pit bosses and gaming managers must be constantly on the look-out for card counters and must intervene delicately but firmly when they come across it (pp. 95–7). Card counters can usually be detected from their pattern of betting (and their pattern of winning). Now presumably such interventions are not entirely compatible with the image that casinos wish to convey – an image of a place where everyone has a free hand (provided it's legal) to beat the system, to overcome the casino's edge. A casino presumably would not wish to have attention drawn to its interventions with card counters because its image would be affected. Thus the secret is dark.

The way that casinos find the names of guests who have won a lot of money to make sure that they sign up as members before they leave in order to get them back to the casino (and thereby look on the winnings as 'borrowed money') is strategic but not very dark (pp. 96–7). Casinos want to make money by giving punters a chance to beat them. That is all that is happening here. Who's who in the casino is perhaps the most common inside secret to the employees – the staff know all the good punters and all the mug punters. The knowledge operates effectively as an inside secret and all the 25p chips in the world, and all the studied nonchalance in the world of the mug punters, cannot override this.

Secrets, by their very nature, are dangerous, since it is possible for others to learn the secrets of any team and thereby threaten its privileged position. An 'informer' is someone who pretends to be a member of a team but then subsequently 'sells' its secrets to the audience. The burglar I interviewed had to cope with informers at a number of levels. Professionally, qua burglar, he's been grassed on a number of times by members of his own team but he has also had to cope with informers in his social world – in his world of sunbed tans and expensive leather jackets, in his guise as aspiring rock star. Here he was a member of a different team but here too his performance could be (and was frequently) disrupted by informers telling interested parties the real source of his income. This burglar's life was an insecure one, and he continually had to monitor his team's composition and performance lest he be grassed on in more ways than one.

Goffman distinguishes an informer from a 'shill' – 'someone who acts as though he were an ordinary member of the audience but is, in fact, in league with the performers' (loc. cit. p. 145). 'Typically, the shill either provides a visible model for the audience of the kind of response the performers are seeking, or provides the kind of audience response that is necessary at the moment for the development of the performance.' (Loc. cit., p. 146.) An example of this is the 'find-the-lady' con, where a dealer holds up three cards for the audience's inspection, one being a queen (or other picture card). After some chat, he places the cards face down and invites anyone from the audience to pick the queen. The shill is the confederate in the crowd who gets the betting going by placing the first bet. Laurie Taylor discovered, when he looked into the find-the-lady con, that there were often as many as six confederates in the audience – more shills than real audience sometimes (see Taylor, 1984, p. 60). A more respectable example of this phenomenon is the wife at the dinner party listening to her husband's anecdote – hanging on every word as if she's hearing it for the first time (see Goffman, 1976, p. 146). The nightclub owner encouraging Cockney's colourful anecdotes in the presence of punters is acting as a shill in a temporary team alignment with Cockney, as the people of the night entertain the less frequent habitués of the nightclub scene. Cockney may at times be banned from the nightclub as his performance becomes more odious, but at times he needs the owner in cooperation as shill just as the con man in find-the-lady needs the eager (confederate) gambler and the husband needs the eager wife. The composition of Cockney's team is crucial to his successful performance.

A different type of role to that of the informer and the shill is the 'go-between', defined by Goffman as someone who 'learns the secret of each side and gives each side the true impression that he will keep its secrets; but he tends to give each side the false impression that he is more loyal to it than to the other' (loc. cit., p. 148). In nightclubs again, owners and managers may act as go-betweens between the police and the underworld who often frequent such places (although the presence of each side at times seems to act as an affront to the other side). The go-between can of course turn informer.

Lest it be thought that only nightclub owners have the capacity to play the different roles of informer, shill and go-between at different times, consider Mrs Hill from Brick Street (pp. 26–31). Mrs Hill is noted as a sympathetic listener, she is always ready to lend her ear to the stories and the complaints of the newly redundant classes. She forms with them the team of individuals with lots of time on their hands. But she can then act as informer to the team of retired individuals – those who never had to suffer the degradation and disgrace of involuntary redundancy, and those busy in various pensioners' clubs. She can tell her retired friends about the sleeping on the job that went on and how really there's no one else to blame for unemployment but the people themselves. She can become a shill and act as rapt audience, encouraging the stories told by the unemployed (and told by them a thousand times because there's not much else to do). And she can even serve as a go-between between those made redundant with the stigma of shame clearly on them and the genuinely retired – those who 'have done their bit'. A go-between for those who deserve their respite from work and those who do not. There is genuine power in such a capacity and Mrs Hill shares this power with nightclub owners and other privileged members of a town of decay.

Maintaining character

Teams cooperate together and maintain their secrets, lest the reality they foist on their audience be discovered. As Goffman says, 'the members of each team tend to maintain the line that they are what they claim to be: they tend to stay in character.' (Loc. cit., p. 166.) In order to stay in character, backstage familiarity is avoided, in Goffman's terms 'lest the interplay of poses collapses and all the participants find themselves on the same team, with no-one left to play to' (loc. cit., p. 116).

Consider, for example, the setting of a university with its two opposing teams of players – lecturers and students. Lecturers teach, students learn; lecturers transmit the information, students receive the wisdom. Of course, for the purposes of learning a more interactional perspective might at times be beneficial, but lectures, seminars and even tutorials (see Beattie, 1983, chapter 6) display the transmitter–receiver pattern with the role of transmitter firmly established on the lecturers' side. The pattern is justified, explained and reinforced by the rather narrow concept many lecturers have of students whom they often only encounter in the academic context – on the academic stage, so to speak, of lecture and tutorial. Ben, the final-year student, didn't get the opportunity to meet lecturers socially and discuss broader issues until after he had graduated (see pp. 161–5). It might perhaps be disquieting for some academics to encounter students in contexts other than the academic one because the delicate interplay of poses

Over page: Two opposing teams – Professor and students

might indeed collapse and dramatic team realignment have to occur. No more intellectual and wise teacher locked in a performance with nonintellectual and dull students, but pupils one and all, striving for answers (in desperation, some of the time). But all performances involving both teams would then suddenly have to change character. Lack of backstage familiarity probably helps in allowing this particular show to run and run.

Or consider the masseuse and the particular forms of social interaction she engages in with her clients (pp. 120–24). The massage parlour provides the stage – the only stage on which these performers can get together. She has the role of sex kitten, but not so much a playful kitten as a disciplined one with the normal human (or even feline) displays of boredom, mirth or self-centred playfulness kept firmly under control. She is also surrogate wife – a ready listener and a good talker ('for the quiet ones'). Her best client, John, is a pillar of society albeit a pillar with a distinct cant (as he frequents massage parlours and devotes much of his finances to the maintenance of this activity). A hard-working man, now retired but active and enjoying his retirement, his respectable side highly idealised – for the benefit of the masseuse, the audience in this one-man show. Here, backstage familiarity must be avoided at all costs, not just because if they met in a different context their mutual acknowledgement would give the game away. No, much more than that – if they met they might just discover that they both worry about varicose veins and they both tell lies much of the time. And that the kitten and the pillar have a good deal more in common than their narrow performance might allow them to believe.

Backstage familiarity is risky because it may result in secrets, including dark secrets, being exchanged (for the masseuse, the fact that she is obsessed with the emergence of varicose veins may be one such dark secret) and the whole performance collapsing. But even if such secrets are not exchanged, it may still have to be avoided, because the appearance of such familiarity alone may be enough to discredit the show. Boxers in the weigh-in should act like opponents and not like the friends they often are, otherwise it is hard for the audience to take the bout seriously as a real clash of opponents. A boxer of course does have a good deal in common with his opposite number and they do share a code and language which can act to align them as a single team. So do the police and the underworld when out in nightclubs or casinos, collecting information for the furtherance of their discrepant careers. Apparent fraternisation, however, can discredit their avowed opposition and, on occasion, each side will complain to the management about the presence of the other side. It's not so much that strategic secrets will be passed in such encounters but rather that they have a lot in common and can be seen to have a lot in common. This is clearly dangerous for the ordinary punter to witness.

The working consensus does generally prevail and backstage familiarity is suppressed but, as Goffman notes, 'at moments of great crisis, a new set of motives may suddenly become effective and the social distance between the teams may sharply increase or decrease' (loc. cit., p. 166). The masseuse's client is 'rolled' while he is at the massage parlour (this apparently is not such a rare phenomenon because clothes are hung up, sometimes with money in them, and on occasion employees of the massage parlour will tip off characters from outside that a well-heeled punter is on the premises). Furthermore, it is embarrassing for some punters to report a loss from such a place. In anger the character portrayal drops – the highly idealised pillar-of-society front dissolves as he mouths his retributions. Anger is the undoing of many fine and coherent performances. Or consider the lecturer, donnish, wise, in command, turning up to deliver a lecture to the second-year honours group only to discover that the lecture he has prepared is not what was expected or timetabled (again not an unknown phenomenon). The lecture nevertheless goes ahead but is peppered with more anecdotes and jokes than usual – many self-reflexive – perhaps approximating more clearly students' own performances when they are required to give a lecture (on project work, for example). But again, as Goffman notes, 'when the crisis is past, the previous working consensus is likely to be re-established albeit bashfully' (loc. cit., p. 166).

The working consensus is the rule, but in order to keep it going it is necessary to have a number of less apparent channels and currents of communications underpinning it. Channels and currents which have to remain hidden because if they suddenly did spring above the surface they would contradict the definition of the situation so carefully constructed. Consider how the members of a team talk about the audience in their absence, when the team members are 'backstage' where the audience cannot see or hear them. In the massage parlour, the masseuses make jokes about clients' bodies and manner. Students criticise and ridicule lecturers' performances, but usually only when backstage in the coffee room or library. They remain perfectly polite and attentive while in the lecture theatre itself.

Team performance and the working consensus between teams are also dependent on some degree of collusion between the members of the team. Performers may surreptitiously send or receive important information, often through subtle nonverbal signals, without directly impinging upon the delicate 'situation'. Bouncers cast glances at each other to indicate that they should temporarily display meanness and look threatening when certain difficult customers are about to be refused entry, but this communication is executed in such a way that it does not affect or disrupt the main activity of allowing other customers to enter. The masseuse throws a look to her massage-team partner to tell her to get on with it. The student throws his neighbour a look which says 'Do you have any idea what this lecturer is talking about?' A nightclub owner, who has to play the role of genial host to all his customers, touches his ear with his finger as an assistant manager passes to indicate that he wants a way out of his current conversation and that the manager should tell him that there's a telephone call for him. Team members must collude to maintain an effective performance.

Goffman also identified a related phenomenon which he called 'derisive collusion', a type of communication which functions 'to confirm for the performer the fact that he does not really hold with the working consensus, that the show he puts on is only a show, thereby providing himself with at least a private defence against the claims made by the audience' (loc. cit. p. 183). An example Goffman provides is that of jazz musicians forced to play 'corny' music. They will make it even more corny to amuse their team mates and to signify their contempt for the audience. The masseuse can overdo the sexy behaviour in exactly the same way and for the same ends – to amuse her fellow masseuse (see p. 123) and to signify contempt for the customer. The bouncer may exaggerate his door technique by stepping physically in front of some punters (who are acquaintances), not to signify contempt, but rather to challenge the consensus of the thick heavy employed at the door of clubs. Many bouncers I talked to did have real concerns about their image (I found this quite surprising at first) – one way of trying to challenge the image is to talk to the punters and demonstrate that they are indeed articulate mammals and not something else. Another way is to exaggerate the behaviour expected of them – not so much a display of contempt for the audience as a subtle ridicule challenging their preconceptions.

Teams collude in a number of different ways to keep the performances going. The various shows continue with teams keeping their secrets, presenting different fronts and avoiding backstage familiarity. And if the secrets are that much darker in Steel City today, the fronts that much more planned and manipulated, and the teams bonded that much more tightly, then that gives some hint of the ultimate reality of life there in the 1980s.

I started this chapter with a quote from Goffman in which he said: 'All the world is not, of course, a stage, but the crucial ways in which it isn't are not easy to specify.' I have tried to show that this dramaturgical perspective developed by Goffman provides a useful way of ordering some of the observations I made about a variety of social performances in Sheffield. It is useful to think about social fronts and performance teams maintaining different types of secret. It is useful to think about the lengths to which some people go to avoid backstage familiarity. It is useful to think about team collusion and the various roles that individuals can and do play.

The dramaturgical perspective can ultimately link up with other perspectives, including a political one. As Goffman says about these two perspectives, they

intersect clearly in regard to the capacities of one individual to direct the activity of another. For one thing, if an individual is to direct others, he will often find it useful to keep strategic secrets from them. Further, if one individual attempts to direct the activity of others by means of example, enlightenment, persuasion, punishment or coercion it will be necessary, regardless of his power position, to convey effectively what he wants done, what he is prepared to do to get it done and what he will do if it is not done. Power of any kind must be clothed in effective means of displaying it and will have different effects, depending upon how it is dramatized. (Loc. cit., p. 234.)

The performance team of the Conservative government found it useful indeed to keep many strategic secrets from those written about in these pages. In the end the inhabitants of Steel City, faced with numerous factory closures and constant cutbacks in the steel and coal industries, weren't sure about the determinants of their own fate. They weren't even sure whether they were surviving a major clinical operation or an economic holocaust. They weren't clear whether Mrs Thatcher was the top consultant surgeon ('curing' unemployment and 'operating' to save industry) or the battlefield commander ('fighting' inflation and 'winning the battle of the economy'). But survive it they did – more or less. They even started to claw their way back up the slippery slope, renegotiating their new levels of power and status and their new identities on the way. I have tried to shed a little light on how this power (or powerlessness) and these identities were dramatised and displayed. Indeed dramatised by sometimes desperate performers in front of a variety of willing audiences (myself included) in Steel City today. I have tried to give a glimpse of life in an industrial town in the 1980s. A town which was at the centre of the first industrial revolution and a town unfortunately in the front line of the devastation caused by the second. A town in which many of the social performances were indeed precarious.

8 · Postscript

We cannot remain consistent with the world save by growing inconsistent with our past selves.
Havelock Ellis, *The Dance of Life*, 1923

Changes

I made the observations reported in this book over a four-year period from 1981 to 1985. In 1981, the major redundancies in the steel industry were just starting to bite. By 1985, the recession's teeth had closed on the bone. Steel City suffered badly during this period and there is no sign of any end to the decline. But some things have changed. The pawns in this giant economic game have sometimes switched positions. Some have advanced a few places, some retreated a few. There is no checkmate in this economic game, but there is stalemate, and we seem to be approaching it. Industries trimmed back, and cut back to be competitive and fighting fit, with no sign of diversification or expansion. Stalemate. But what of the pawns?

Brick Street is still there. There's still no graffiti and no vandalism. Mrs Hill and Mrs What's-her-name still live side by side, they still don't like each other and Mrs Hill still doesn't know Mrs What's-her-name's real name, or says she doesn't. Fred Smith eventually finished decorating his house and got a job with a builder. He's a happy man now. He still leaves the grime on when he gets home from work. His daughter went to college to postpone another crisis. Mr Forrest and Suki the dog sold their house in Crookes and moved downmarket to Handsworth to save money, but they aren't happy there and want to move back. Brian, whom we last saw making the day last, got a job as an attendant in a museum. He's happy too – the work is very steady. He still runs and the asthma has mysteriously disappeared. He tells me that he recently met a woman on one of his fell runs whose husband died last year, she too had developed asthma. 'It's a funny thing, the mind,' he says, for once recognising the connection between his redundancy and his physical disorder. Masher Metham is still painting and still whistling. He's got a few weeks' orders in hand. Bobby, the striking miner, went back to the pit after the strike finished. He said it was a bit rough at first but it's settling down now. He found the work hard after a year's lay-off. John, the unemployed working-class graduate from Clay Cross, is still working in the iron foundry. Andrew, the unemployed Oxford graduate, has left Sheffield. Jane, Sue and Melanie, the three unemployed middle-class graduates, went their separate ways in the end. Sue now works for a voluntary organisation in Northern Ireland, Melanie works as a clerk in the dole office, Jane is unemployed in London. Sheffield is still full of homeless people. Lee and Carol still live in the same house, they haven't managed to move yet. Lee has had some more outbursts in the meantime, some with a hammer. Kevin has still got his dog Sash, but hasn't managed to find a job. Neither has Lee.

Josephine's, 'Sheffield's ultimate nitespot', is still packed and the business A & S Entertainments is continuing to expand. Dave Allen is opening a new casino in Reading and hoping to open a new nightclub in London. John with the Silver Shadow and Debbie have split up. Debbie said she got fed up with all the bullshit in the end; she married someone else – 'somebody with real money for a change'. The new husband is a businessman of dubious persuasion and the police have called several times. John lost his job and his Silver Shadow, he now drives an Austin Cambridge. Tony Habershon, the star-struck DJ, didn't retire in the end – he said he couldn't give up the nightclub scene and the glamour. He still does a bit of DJing and still gets propositioned. Andrea, the dwarf, still works for the detective agency and still hasn't got a full-time job. Charlie, her Prince Charming, never returned. Rod Johnson still stands at the door of Josephine's and still looks for those small telltale signs, particularly the scuffed shoes. Naploeon's, the casino, is still making lots of money.

There's still a lot of 'bobbing and weaving' going on in Sheffield. Cockney is still on the scene, getting by somehow, although his wife has left him. She just got fed up in the end. Patrick is still doing different jobs but concentrating more and more on store-detecting and being a bouncer. Vinny, the boxer, has hung up his gloves. His friend, Bomber Graham, became nationally known; nobody even remembers Vinny's last fight. Vinny is doing a bit more bouncing now and feels that his future lies in 'property'. Bill, the pimp, is still fixing men up with women and still says he isn't really a pimp. Anita gave up her other jobs to concentrate on the sauna work because it was the most lucrative and then she left Sheffield to do the same work elsewhere.

Danny, the burglar, did a few more jobs and got arrested again. He's currently on the run in France, or Manchester, depending on whom you believe. Cockney says he saw him in a pub last week in Sheffield making an heroic escape from the police before returning to France (or Manchester). The nurse is still nursing, sometimes still in the face of blatant racism. The demand for store detectives is increasing, and Syljen are expanding. The prize store detective, Ron Teskowski, left to form his own agency. Tony, the car salesman, is still very anxious about his future and still not selling many cars. The dancer, Gary Jones, is still going strong and getting many bookings. He now manages SMAC 19 and another 'raunchy' white group. He says you can always find bookings for raunchy dancers. The clairvoyant is still desperately trying to foresee the future.

Some people are still on the road to Mandalay. St Thomas's is still full of Charismatic Christians and there are many people on the streets of Sheffield still waiting for gifts from the Holy Spirit. Miracles are expected, but some of them are a long time coming. Ben, despite his last-minute revision, got a first and went on to do postgraduate work. He says that some parts of the psychology course now make sense to him for the first time. Trevor, as we have seen, made it for a while. He was famous; once. This is still a good deal better than nothing. He's at least got his cuttings. Colin has gone back to university with some acid bought in Sheffield. His friend Frank has been left behind, again. The construction of his joints has improved enormously, though, and he is smoking more and more. He is selling some hash to make ends meet. Frank now feels that he isn't probably going anywhere, after all, but he doesn't mind any longer.

References

Alison, A., *The Principles of Population*. Vol. 2. Edinburgh, 1840.

Banks, M. H. and Jackson, P. R., 'Unemployment and risk of minor psychiatric disorder in young people: Cross-sectional and longitudinal evidence.' *Psychological Medicine*, **12**, 789–98, 1982.

Barry, D., Factories Enquiry Commission, Second Report, 1840.

Beattie, G., *Talk: An Analysis of Speech and Non-Verbal Behaviour in Conversation*. Open University Press, Milton Keynes, 1983.

Chadwick, E., Report from the Poor Law Commissioners on an Inquiry into the Sanitary Condition of the Labouring Population of Great Britain, 1842.

Eisenberg, P. and Lazarsfeld, P. F., 'The psychological effects of unemployment'. *Psychological Bulletin*, **35**, 358–90, 1938.

Ellis, A. and Beattie, G., *The Psychology of Language and Communication*. Weidenfeld & Nicolson, London, 1986.

Engels, F., *The Condition of the Working Class in England*. Basil Blackwell, Oxford, 1958.

Gaskell, P., *The Manufacturing Population of England*. London, 1833.

Goffman, E., *The Presentation of Self in Everyday Life*. Penguin, Harmondsworth, 1976.

Griffiths, F., The First Annual Report of the Medical Officer of Health for the Borough of Sheffield for the year 1873. Sanitary Department, Council Hall, Sheffield, 1873.

Hepworth, S. J., 'Moderating factors of the psychological impact of unemployment'. *Journal of Occupational Psychology*, **53**, 139–45, 1980.

Jackson, P. R. and Warr, P. B., 'Age, length of unemployment, and other variables associated with men's ill-health during unemployment.' MRC/SSRC SAPU Memo 585, 1983.

MacGowan, J., *Sidelights on Chinese Life*. Lippinatt, Philadelphia, 1908.

Maguire, M. and Bennett, T., *Burglary in a Dwelling*. Heinemann, London, 1982.

Pollard, S., Introduction. In S. Pollard and C. Holmes (eds.), *Essays in the*

Economic and Social History of South Yorkshire. South Yorkshire County Council, Sheffield, 1976.

Puzo, M., *Inside Las Vegas*. Grosset & Dunlap, New York, 1977.

Ralph, J. B., 'The junk business and the junk peddler.' Unpublished MA report, Department of Sociology, University of Chicago, 1950.

Sartre, J. P., *Being and Nothingness*. Methuen, London, 1957.

Taylor, L., *In the Underworld*. Allen & Unwin, London, 1984.

Thunhurst, C., *Poverty and Health in the City of Sheffield*. Sheffield City Council, 1985.

Townsend, P. and Davidson, N. (eds.), *Inequalities in Health – the Black Report*. Penguin, Harmondsworth, 1983.

Warr, P., 'Work, jobs and unemployment.' *Bulletin of the British Psychological Society*, **36**, 305–11.